BUDDHIST FORMAL LOGIC

DR. B. C. LAW TRUST FUND
Volume 1

BUDDHIST FORMAL LOGIC

PART I

A Study of Dignāga's Hetucakra
and
K'uei-chi's Great Commentary on the Nyāyapraveśa

by

R. S. Y. CHI
B.Sc., M.A., D.Phil. (*Oxon*), Ph.D. (*Cantab*)
Indiana University, U.S.A.

MOTILAL BANARSIDASS
Delhi Varanasi Patna Madras

Head Office: Bungalow Road, Delhi 110 007
Branches: Chowk, Varanasi 221 001
Ashok Rajpath, Patna 800 004
6 Appar Swamy Koil Sreet, Mylapore,
Madras 600 004

First Published : The Royal Asiatic Society of Great Britain, 1969
Reprint : Delhi, 1984

ISBN: 0–89581–763–2

Printed in India by Shantilal Jain at Shri Jainendra Press, A-45, Phase I, Naraina, New Delhi 110 028 and published by Narendra Prakash Jain for Motilal Banarsidass, Delhi 110 007.

佛家之形式論理學

第一輯 陳那因輪論及窺基因明大疏淺則

一九六三年秋 齊思貽題於劍橋英王學院

FOREWORD (1968)

Revisions of works in any discipline invariably change the character of the original, but none so radically as revisions of books on logic. As in dramas with intricate plotting, the slightest adjustment results in drastic changes. The revision of a book on logic is, even more than most, a complete rewriting. The writer's various attempts to set down a coherent system will inevitably lead him to repudiate some points in earlier efforts, but this should not seem disturbing if one remembered that he is actually publishing a continuing, self-critical, self-revising "work-in-progress".

The strictures on revisions may at first seem out of place in a foreword to a book which has never been published in any form whatsoever. A brief account of the publishing history of this work may help to clarify this anomaly. The first draft of this work was written in 1961-63. A year later, it was accepted for publication by the Royal Asiatic Society. In 1965, Messrs. Luzac & Co., the Society's printers, requested a fair copy of the manuscript which could then be photographically reproduced. I agreed, but with the secret notion that the retyping of the manuscript would subtly incorporate a rewriting as well. However, revision proved to be, as I perhaps should have known, far more involved than I had expected. In the face of these difficulties, I procrastinated. Two years passed.

While I was thus beset with my self-inflicted complications, the printers proceeded on their own to reproduce the very copy which they had hoped to replace with a "fair copy" from me. It was with a mixture of dismay and pleasure that I received the news in April 1968 from the Society that the galley proofs were now ready, and that, incidentally, I would have to bear the costs of any alterations exceeding 15% of the text. I was "hoist by my own petard".

I am now constrained to present to the public a work whose inadequacies are all too clear to me. Its value may be, after all, in setting forth a construct, without and beyond which I could not have advanced my thoughts on the subject. The contretemps between the printers and myself may have turned out for the better after all, for it is probable that, were it not for their enterprise, no part of my "work-in-progress" would have seen the light of day.

The question may be fairly asked: why encumber the literature with a work which one wishes beforehand to repudiate? The answer is that the mistakes embodied in the earlier enterprise might be instructive. The coherent exposition of certain ill-formulated concepts, as well as their subsequent correction, seems a most effective way of developing my thesis. Further, the publication of this work in this form, gives me an opportunity -- perhaps to be cherished -- of anticipating the critics, by correcting myself.

To mention but a few examples: my lengthy derivation of the Hetucakra can be greatly reduced by resort to a short cut; my theory of "narrow functions" is faulty and unmanageable; my interpretation of several topics, such as Nāgārjuna's reductio ad absurdum method and the catuşkoţi, is far from correct.

Under the present circumstances, though it is not possible to abandon the old exposition in favour of a new, I have, nevertheless, been provided with a chapter in which some of my grosser mistakes can be corrected -- a provision for which I am deeply grateful to the Society.

In May 1967, I was invited to speak before the opening Symposium of the Joint Meeting of the Association for Symbolic Logic and the American Philosophical Association at Chicago. My paper, "Buddhist Formal Logic and Its Consequences" represents my views at that time. At the symposium, Professor Karl Potter of Minnesota and Dr. Douglas Daye of Wisconsin, who commented on my paper, contributed valuable suggestions and posed a number of pertinent questions which I had not dealt with adequately in the body of the paper. I have since incorporated my answers into my paper, which in its expanded form is included in this book as "Introduction, 1967".

The catuşkoţi has been considered an insoluble problem for centuries. In December of 1967 I read a paper ("A Tentative solution of the Problem of Four-Corner Negation") at the University of Chicago, which I believe solves the problem. The solution depends on applying Bertrand Russell's vicious-circle principle and my explanation of "unavoidable mistakes"; namely, "under cultural circumstances x, a mistaken theory y is inevitable". The paper is unmanageable in length and needs further revision: it will appear as an article. For the moment, I can only say that it corrects my earlier explanation of the catuṣkoṭi which is erroneous.

One last word as to style: my Chinese-styled English, so faulty in grammar and awkward in manner, is at least genuine, without being polished by my western friends. I hope its awkwardness will not annoy the readers too much, and its foreign-ness amuse them a little.

Indiana, 1968 R. S. Y. C.

INTRODUCTION 1966 - 67

(i) DIGNĀGA'S HETUCAKRA AND TRAIRŪPYA

Logically speaking, a discipline can be roughly divided into three stages: its fundamental concepts at the bottom level, its major theory at the middle level and the elaboration of its theory at the top level, somewhat like the root, the trunk and the branches of a tree. In the actual process of development, when a new discipline is introduced, either historically by thinkers, or pedagogically by teachers, the middle part usually comes first; it is the least sophisticated portion of the entire task and it can be easily formalized mathematically. Fundamental concepts are taken for granted at this level without being thoroughly investigated. The bottom part usually comes last; it is normally the philosophy of that discipline.

The reason why I have made this almost tautological statement is that the introduction of Indian logic to the West, mainly by philologists such as Th. Stcherbatsky, followed a quite different path. Topics of all three levels appear to be unfathomably profound; the elementary topics are no less obscure and puzzling. It seems that a work solely devoted to its elementary theory such as Dignāga's Hetucakra, without touching either the 'top' or the 'bottom', expressed in a more understandable language at its appropriate level, is still lacking. This is the humble aim of the present work.

Information about historical, textual and bibliographical matters is rich in most of the books by philologists; it will not be repeated in this work. The text of the Hetucakraḍamaru is very brief; I might as well paraphrase it in full.

THE WHEEL OF REASONS

Homage to Mañjuśrīkumārabhūta.

Homage to the Omniscient One, who is
The destroyer of the snare of ignorance.
I am expounding the determination of
The probans with three-fold characteristics. (1)

Among the three possible cases of 'presence', 'absence' and 'both'
Of the probans in the probandum,
Only the case of its 'presence' is valid,
While its 'absence' is not. (2)

The case of 'both presence and absence' is inconclusive,
It is therefore not valid either.

The 'presence', 'absence' and 'both',
Of the probans in similar instances, (3)
Combined with those in dissimilar instances,
There are three combinations in each of three.

The top and the bottom are valid,
The two sides are contradictory. (4)
The four corners are inconclusive because they are 'too broad',
The centre is inconclusive because it is 'too narrow'.

Knowable, produced, impermanent, (5)
Produced, audible, effort-made,
Impermanent, effort-made and incorporeal,
Are used to prove the properties of being:
Permanent, impermanent, effort-made,
Permanent, permanent, permanent,
Non-effort-made, impermanent, and permanent. (6)

When two tops or two bottoms meet,
The probans is valid.
When two corresponding sides meet,
It is contradictory. (7)

When corresponding corners meet,
It is inconclusive because it is 'too broad'
When the centres of two crosses meet,
It is inconclusive because it is 'too narrow'. (8)

Since there are nine classes of probans,
Accordingly we have nine sets of examples:

Space-pot, pot-space, (9)
Pot-lightning-space,
Space-pot, (space-pot), space-pot-lightning,
Lightning-space-pot,
Pot-lightning-space,
Space-atom-action-pot. (10)

The above concerns the 'determined probans' only;
As regards the 'doubtful' ones,
There are also nine combinations of
'Presence', 'absence' and 'both'. (11)

The treatise on the Wheel of Reasons by Ācārya Dignāga.

Abstract language in Indian logic during the fifth centry must have been very inadequate, otherwise the explication of the Hetucakra would not have been so primitive. It was written in such a strange way that it takes us quite some time and effort to re-phrase it into an understandable language. It is easy to visualize that it must have perplexed ancient students to a considerable extent before they could grasp what was all about. It is not unlikely that some of them might just recite the text like a dāraṇī without understanding a thing; this can be proved by the multitude of mistakes in the segmentation of the text in a Tibetan version. When logic was transmitted to Japan, the words 'top secret' have been used in the sense of secret formulae of alchemists. Even in our own century, the Hetucakra has been described by St. Stasiak as 'mysterious'.[1]

In modern logic we have the operation 'class inclusion', symbolized by the formula '$a \subset b$', where the classes 'a' and 'b' are variables and the operators '$\subset$' ('is included in') is a constant. Suppose we do not have such abstract device, how can we express the concept of class inclusion?

One way to solve the problem is to borrow two particular concret classes 'a_1' and 'b_1', which are constants, such that the relation $C(a_1, b_1)$ can represent such a concept. In other words,

$$(a \subset b) = (a\ C(a_1, b_1)\ b) \quad \text{Df.}$$

For instance, if we use a familiar example a_1 = human beings, b_1 = mortal beings, class inclusion may be represented by C (human beings, mortal beings).

Such a way is, of course, primitive and arbitrary, but using a particular symbol '$\subset$' is no less arbitrary; it is merely more convenient in writing.

This is precisely what Dignāga did when he had no adequate abstract terminology. He chose the following classes:

a_1 = things being produced by effort; b_1 = things transient.

In such a way he employed two sets of concrete words to represent one set of abstract class relationships.

1. St. Stasiak: Fallacies and their Classification According to the Early Hindu Logicians (Rocznik Orientalistyczny VI, 1929, pp. 191-8).

The frequent occurrence of synonymy and polysemy in Indian works, such as '*sādhya*' and '*pakṣa*', '*tattulya*' and '*tajjātīya*' and '*sapakṣa*', '*vipakṣa*' and '*asapakṣa*', has made the terminology of Indian logic desperately confusing. In this work I shall not list these terms and give a comparative study of them, (such a task could be better handled by philologists) but merely apply those terms which are comparatively familiar to scholars today, regardless of the priority of their origin. For this reason I use the terms introduced by Uddyotakara and Dharmakīrti, although the concepts had been introduced by Dignāga at an earlier period.

Two sets of technical terms are fundamental in Dignāga's logic, namely, the set of operators in propositions, and the set of classes in syllogisms. Dignāga introduced three operators: *-vyāpaka*, *-avṛtti* and *-ekadeśavṛtti*; Uddyotakara added one more: *avidyamāna-*. The set of classes in syllogisms will be discussed later.

It is usually desirable to introduce something unfamiliar by means of comparing it with something familiar. Before I interpret the operators introduced by Dignāga, I should like to discuss the socalled 'categorical propositions' in traditional logic, i.e., the forms A, E, I and O. The propositions such as 'All a's are b's', or more precisely, 'Every member of class a is a member of class b', obviously convey some information about two classes a and b; the information involves the condition of four sub-classes ab, $a\bar{b}$, $\bar{a}b$ and $\bar{a}\bar{b}$, and such condition could be nothing but whether they are empty or not.

It is therefore quite natural and convenient to choose 'being non-empty' ($a \neq 0$) and 'being empty' ($a = 0$) as 'primitive ideas'. In the language of predicate calculus, one may choose $(Ex)\phi x$ and its negation as primitive ideas, instead of choosing $(x)\phi x$ and $(Ex)\phi x$ as shown in many modern works such as *Principia Mathematica* (2nd edition, 1927, p. 127). The expression $(x)\phi x$ may be defined in terms of $(Ex)\phi x$ and $\sim(Ex)\phi x$. In other words, the pair 'always' and 'sometimes' are replaced by the pair 'sometimes' and 'never'. Such an alteration is suitable for the purpose of the present work.

We are not told in traditional logic, however, to what extent the information is necessary and sufficient; in other words, how many and which one of the four sub-classes should be specified. Because of the ambiguity in defining the four categorical propositions, a variety of interpretation is possible. P. F. Strawson has explicitly described the ambiguity by means of formulating the four types in three different ways.[1] Some traditional laws collapse in the first interpretation, and some other laws collapse in the second. All the laws can be satisifed in the third, but the formulated interpretation becomes remote from the meaning of the words 'all' and 'some' in ordinary speech.

If we consider the four possible conjunctions fx. gx, fx. - gx, - fx. gx and - fx. - gx and use (Ex) and - (Ex) as primitive ideas, the three ways of interpretation can be re-written as follows:

Interpretation 1:

A - (Ex)(fx. - gx)
E - (Ex)(fx. gx)
I (Ex)(fx. gx)
O (Ex)(fx. - gx)

Interpretation 2:

A (Ex)(fx. gx) . - (Ex)(fx. - gx)
E - (Ex)(fx. gx) . (Ex)(fx. - gx)
I (Ex)(fx. gx)
O (Ex)(fx. - gx)

Interpretation 3:

A (Ex)(fx. gx) . - (Ex)(fx. - gx) . (Ex)(- fx. - gx)
E - (Ex)(fx. gx) . (Ex)(fx. - gx) . (Ex)(- fx. gx)

The operators I and O cannot be expressed by conjunctions for interpretation 3.

In the present discussion there is only one individual variable x, and the so-called 'apparent variable' is apparently redundant; it would be more convenient to use class form such that $a = \hat{z}(fz)$ and $b = \hat{z}(gz)$:

	Interpretation 1	Interpretation 2	Interpretation 3
A	$(a\bar{b}=0)$	$(ab\neq 0)\,(a\bar{b}=0)$	$(ab\neq 0)\,(a\bar{b}=0)\,(\bar{a}\bar{b}\neq 0)$
E	$(ab=0)$	$(ab=0)\,(a\bar{b}\neq 0)$	$(ab=0)\,(a\bar{b}\neq 0)\,(\bar{a}b\neq 0)$
I	$(ab\neq 0)$	$(ab\neq 0)$	
O	$(a\bar{b}\neq 0)$	$(a\bar{b}\neq 0)$	

1. P. F. Strawson: Introduction to Logical Theory (1952) pp. 167-73.

This can be further simplified by the following device. Let us fix the sequence of the four sub-classes in a convenient way, say ab, a$\bar{b}$, $\bar{a}$b, $\bar{a}\bar{b}$. Then let us use symbols to denote the condition of the four sub-classes according to the above-mentioned sequence. Since the sequence is fixed, the names of the sub-classes may be omitted without causing any ambiguity. Let the symbols '0', '1' and '-' represent respectively 'being empty', 'being non-empty' and 'being unspecified'. The result is reduced as follows:

	Interpretation 1	Interpretation 2	Interpretation 3
A	(-0--)	(10--)	(10-1)
E	(0---)	(01--)	(011-)
I	(1---)	(1---)	
O	(-1--)	(-1--)	

The extent of information is clearly shown in this notation: In the first interpretation, the information of one sub-class is given. In the second, the information of two sub-classes is given for A and E, but that of only one sub-class is given for I and O. The third interpretation is indefinite at the present stage, but it will be clear when it is completely formulated later.

Logicians in the 18th and 19th centuries were less tolerant than our contemporaries. Quite a few of them abandoned the traditional system but established their own. Among them the French logician J.D. Gergonne remarked: "Aristotelian logic had fallen into general discredit during the 18th century, although still taught in some Gothic academies".[1] In his own system Gergonne suggested five operators as following:

a C b	<u>est contenu dans</u>	inclusion
a I b	<u>est identique á</u>	equivalence
a H b	<u>est hors de</u>	exclusion
a X b	<u>s'entre-croise avec</u>	intersecting
a Ɔ c	<u>contiens</u>	inverse inclusion

1. According to the English version rendered by Prof. W.C. Kneale in the <u>Development of Logic</u>.

They can be symbolized as following:

a C b	$(ab\neq0)(a\bar{b}=0)(\bar{a}b\neq0)$	(101-)
a I b	$(ab\neq0)(a\bar{b}=0)(\bar{a}b=0)$	(100-)
a H b	$(ab=0)(a\bar{b}\neq0)(\bar{a}b\neq0)$	(011-)
a X b	$(ab\neq0)(a\bar{b}\neq0)(\bar{a}b\neq0)$	(111-)
a Ɔ c	$(ab\neq0)(a\bar{b}\neq0)(\bar{a}b=0)$	(110-)

From the above it is obvious that Gergonne's system gives the information of three sub-classes, namely, ab, a$\bar{b}$ and $\bar{a}$b.

Let us now return to Dignāga. The operators -vyāpaka, -avṛtti and -ekadeśavṛtti represent respectively inclusion, exclusion and intersecting. The first two are equivalent to Strawson's second interpretation of A and E. The third is a new one, which is the conjunction of Aristotle's I and O, and the disjunction of Gergonne's X (intersecting) and Ɔ (inverse inclusion). Let us call it the operator 'U'.

The operator U is closer to everyday language than the operator I. When one says "There are sensible people in the world", it actually implies "There are even more people who are not sensible". Such propositions belong to the type U and not type I.

a A b	$(ab\neq0)(a\bar{b}=0)$	(10--)
a E b	$(ab=0)(a\bar{b}\neq0$	(01--)
a U b	$(ab\neq0)(a\bar{b}\neq0)$	(11--)

Dignāga's system gives the information of two sub-classes ab and a$\bar{b}$. Both Dignāga and Gergonne's systems are unambiguous, and they are mutually definable:

1. (a E b) = (a H b)
   (a A b) = (a I b) v (c C b)
   (a U b) = (a Ɔ b) v (a X b)

2. (a H b) = (a E b)
   (a X b) = (a U b) . (b U a)
   (a I b) = (a A b) . (b A a)
   (a C b) = (a A b) . (b U a)
   (a Ɔ b) = (a U b) . (b A a)

We may say Dignāga's system is 'narrower' than Aristotle's, and 'broader' than Gergonne's; it is midway between the two.

With a new system of operators, Dignāga could establish a set of theorems comparable to those of Aristotle. He was, however, interested in nothing but one particular property of transitivity, i.e., the AAA form of syllogism. The reason is that in his time, logic was essentially an instrument for doctrinal debate.

Dignāga obviously excluded a fourth possibility: that both sub-classes ab and $a\bar{b}$ are empty; Uddyotakara added it two centuries later. Let us call this case the operator 'Y'. His system can exhaust all possible cases when two sub-classes are specified:

a A b	$(ab \neq 0)(a\bar{b}=0)$	(10--)
a E b	$(ab=0)(a\bar{b} \neq 0)$	(01--)
a U b	$(ab \neq 0)(a\bar{b} \neq 0)$	(11--)
a Y b	$(ab=0)(a\bar{b}=0)$	(00--)

The four sub-classes are of equal status; the reason why in all the above-mentioned systems two sub-classes, ab and $a\bar{b}$, seem to be more important than others is as follows:

1. In natural language and convention in logic, positive statements are more 'primitive' than negative ones; therefore the sub-class $\bar{a}\bar{b}$ is left unspecified.
2. The property of transitivity of formal implication $(x)(fx \supset gx)$ or class inclusion $(a \subset b)$ plays an important role in logical inference, particularly in formulae called 'syllogisms'. The sub-class $a\bar{b}$ is relevant to such cases, it is therefore specified.
3. The reverse of formal implication or of class inclusion is less familiar in natural language, therefore the sub-class $\bar{a}b$ is not specified.
4. The sub-class ab is specified because of existential import.

Let us assume that the content of Indian syllogism is the same as that of our familiar syllogism of 'barbara mood', i.e. either

$(x)(fx \supset gx).(x)(gx \supset hx) \supset (x)(fx \supset hx)$, or

$(a \subset b).(b \subset c) \supset (a \subset c)$, despite the fact that both the Indian five-membered and three-membered syllogisms differ from our familiar three-membered syllogisms in form.

Before I explain the Hetucakra, or the 'Wheel of Reasons', I should interpret the second set of technical terms, i.e. the terms for four classes:

'hetu', 'sādhya' (sometimes called 'pakṣa'), 'sapakṣa' and 'vipakṣa', which are abbreviated as 'h', 'p', 's' and 'v' respectively.

The Hetucakra was intended to be an extensional study of various kinds of major premises about whether they can yield valid syllogisms. Since all major premises are propositions, the Hetucakra can also be considered as an extensional study of propositions.

The criterion for non-triviality varies greatly with time; what is non-trivial today might be trivial in Dignāga's time, and vice versa. Despite Dignāga's original intention, we are more interested in propositions. I should therefore interpret the Hetucakra in two different ways in the following sequence: (1) as a study of propositions, (2) as a study of major premises of syllogisms.

Interpretation 1 of the Hetucakra

The first interpretation concerns propositions instead of syllogisms. Let us consider two classes a and b in the formula $(a \subset b)$, or two properties f and g in the formula $(x)(fx \supset gx)$. The classes h, s and v can be defined as follows:

$h = a$ Df. $\qquad$ $h = \hat{z}(fz)$ Df.

$s = b$ Df. $\qquad$ or $\qquad$ $s = \hat{z}(gz)$ Df.

$v = \bar{b}$ Df. $\qquad$ $v = \hat{z}(-gz)$ Df.

In the text of the Hetucakra, Dignāga applied the three operators A, E and U to the relation between two classes b and a, and also between $\bar{b}$ and a. By putting three pairs in the form of row and column vectors and taking their product, he formed a matrix as shown in the following. Such a matrix was called by him 'The Wheel of Reasons'.

$$\begin{bmatrix} b\,A\,a \\ b\,E\,a \\ b\,U\,a \end{bmatrix} . \; [\,\bar{b}\,A\,a \quad \bar{b}\,E\,a \quad \bar{b}\,U\,a\,]$$

$$= \begin{bmatrix} (ab{\neq}0)(\bar{a}b{=}0) \\ (ab{=}0)(\bar{a}b{\neq}0) \\ (ab{\neq}0)(\bar{a}b{\neq}0) \end{bmatrix} . \; [(a\bar{b}{\neq}0)(\bar{a}\bar{b}{=}0) \quad (a\bar{b}{=}0)(\bar{a}\bar{b}{\neq}0) \quad (a\bar{b}{\neq}0)(\bar{a}\bar{b}{\neq}0)]$$

$$= \begin{bmatrix} (1\,\text{-}0\,\text{-}) \\ (0\,\text{-}1\,\text{-}) \\ (1\,\text{-}1\,\text{-}) \end{bmatrix} . \; [(\text{-}1\,\text{-}0) \quad (\text{-}0\,\text{-}1) \quad (\text{-}1\,\text{-}1)]$$

$$= \begin{bmatrix} (1100) & (1001) & (1101) \\ (0110) & (0011) & (0111) \\ (1110) & (1011) & (1111) \end{bmatrix}$$

In the above process he took b and $\bar{b}$ to operate against a. The rəason for his manipulation in such an arbitrary way is that by this method he could derive more possible ways of combination which are distinct from one another. The elements of the column vector are of the form (x-x-), and those of the row vector are of the form (-x-x); therefore, when the product is taken, all elements become fully specified.

The nine types given in the matrix are nothing but operators, except that the new operators are free from 'unspecified condition' of sub-classes. All the nine are uniquely defined in terms of existential condition of the four sub-classes and they are distinct from one another. In order to make a distinction, let us call the three operators 'primary' and the nine operators 'secondary', or alternatively, 'partially specified' and 'fully specified' respectively.

Dignāga's set of primary operators does not include the operator Y (00--), yet in the centre of the matrix of secondary operators, the operator (0011) turns out unexpectedly through the back door. Obviously the three-operator system is not exhaustive. Uddyotakara's four-operator matrix can easily be derived by a similar process.

$$\begin{bmatrix} b\,A\,a \\ b\,E\,a \\ b\,U\,a \\ b\,Y\,a \end{bmatrix} \cdot [\bar{b}\,A\,a \quad \bar{b}\,E\,a \quad \bar{b}\,U\,a \quad \bar{b}\,Y\,a]$$

$$= \begin{bmatrix} (ab \neq 0)(\bar{a}b = 0) \\ (ab = 0)(\bar{a}b \neq 0) \\ (ab \neq 0)(\bar{a}b \neq 0) \\ (ab = 0)(\bar{a}b = 0) \end{bmatrix} \cdot [(a\bar{b} \neq 0)(\bar{a}\bar{b} = 0) \quad (a\bar{b} = 0)(\bar{a}\bar{b} \neq 0) \quad (a\bar{b} \neq 0)(\bar{a}\bar{b} \neq 0) \quad (a\bar{b} = 0)(\bar{a}\bar{b} = 0)]$$

$$= \begin{bmatrix} (1\text{-}0\text{-}) \\ (0\text{-}1\text{-}) \\ (1\text{-}1\text{-}) \\ (0\text{-}0\text{-}) \end{bmatrix} \cdot [(\text{-}1\text{-}0) \quad (\text{-}0\text{-}1) \quad (\text{-}1\text{-}1) \quad (\text{-}0\text{-}0)]$$

$$= \begin{bmatrix} (1100) & (1001) & (1101) & (1000) \\ (0110) & (0011) & (0111) & (0010) \\ (1110) & (1011) & (1111) & (1010) \\ (0100) & (0001) & (0101) & (0000) \end{bmatrix}$$

The result of sixteen secondary operators is so handy that it seems to be incredible that the ancient Indian logicians should follow a roundabout path by first introducing the concepts of sapakṣa and vipakṣa. Such case is not unusual; the progress of human thought sometimes travel along a zigzag path, and sometimes truths are hidden undiscovered not because they are too profound but because they are too obvious. For instance, several truth functions were introduced higgledy-piggledy since ancient Greeks, but the total of sixteen truth functions were not introduced until our own century. (They were introduced almost simultaneously by E. L. Post and L. Wittgenstein in 1921).

Dignāga's original intention of formulating the Hetucakra was to have an extensional study of various ways of major premise regarding whether it can yield a valid syllogism. An even more fundamental problem is whether all the sixteen ways are possible; in other words, whether the condition of one sub-class can be independent of the condition of other sub-classes. There are various answers to this question.

Most logicians assume a non-empty universe. The condition that a class is empty implies the condition that its complement is non-empty, i.e.,

$(a=0) \supset (\bar{a}\neq 0)$, or $\sim(Ex)\phi x \supset (Ex)(\sim\phi x)$.

Among the four possible combinations, i.e., $(a\neq 0).(\bar{a}\neq 0)$, $(a\neq 0).(\bar{a}=0)$, $(a=0).(\bar{a}\neq 0)$, and $(a=0).(\bar{a}=0)$, or, in simplified notation, (11), (10), (01) and (00), the last one is excluded.

When there are two classes, if three sub-classes are known to be empty, the remaining one should be non-empty. J. Venn mentioned this point explicitly in the Symbolic Logic, pp. 142-9. If a non-empty universe is assumed, among the sixteen cases, the case (0000) is excluded.

The convention of Aristotelian non-empty universe is even narrower. It is assumed that $(a\neq 0), (\bar{a}\neq 0), (b\neq 0), (\bar{b}\neq 0)$. From this assumption the following relations hold:

$(ab=0) \supset (a\bar{b}\neq 0).(\bar{a}b\neq 0)$

$(\bar{a}b=0) \supset (\bar{a}\bar{b}\neq 0).(ab\neq 0)$

$(a\bar{b}=0) \supset (ab\neq 0).(\bar{a}\bar{b}\neq 0)$

$(\bar{a}\bar{b}=0) \supset (\bar{a}b\neq 0).(a\bar{b}\neq 0)$

or,

(0---) ⊃ (011-)
(-0--) ⊃ (10-1)
(--0-) ⊃ (1-01)
(---0) ⊃ (-110)

In other words,

(0---) ⊃ ((0111) v (0110))
(-0--) ⊃ ((1011) v (1001))
(--0-) ⊃ ((1101) v (1001))
(---0) ⊃ ((1110) v (0110))

From the above there are eight possible cases. We have to add the case in which no sub-class is empty, i.e. (1111), and also have to subtract two cases (0110) and (1001) which appear twice in the list; finally there are seven cases left: (1111), (1110), (1101), (1011), (1001), (0111) and (0110).

Let us return to Strawson's interpretation of Aristotelian operators: The first two can easily be expressed by the following table, while the third one is not so ready:

Interpretation 1

A	E	I	O
		1111	1111
		1110	1110
		1101	1101
		1100	1100
1011		1011	
1010		1010	
1001		1001	
1000		1000	
	0111		0111
	0110		0110
	0101		0101
	0100		0100
0011	0011		
0010	0010		
0001	0001		
0000	0000		

Interpretation 2

A	E	I	O
		1111	1111
		1110	1110
		1101	1101
		1100	1100
1011		1011	
1010		1010	
1001		1001	
1000		1000	
	0111		0111
	0110		0110
	0101		0101
	0100		0100

When the condition $(a \neq 0).(\bar{a} \neq 0).(b \neq 0).(\bar{b} \neq 0)$ is imposed, Strawson's first interpretation becomes a new one, which is close to, if not completely identical with, his third interpretation. The second interpretation, which has been an intermediate stage, becomes unnecessary. This can easily be illustrated by the following table:

Condition not imposed

A	E	I	O
		1111	1111
		1110	1110
		1101	1101
		1100	1100
1011		1011	
1010		1010	
1001		1001	
1000		1000	
	0111		0111
	0110		0110
	0101		0101
	0100		0100
0011	0011		
0010	0010		
0001	0001		
0000	0000		

Condition imposed

A	E	I	O
		1111	1111
		1110	1110
		1101	1101
1011		1011	
1001		1001	
	0111		0111
	0110		0110

Now Aristotelian operators can be uniquely formulated as follows:

Assume $(Ex)\, fx.\ (Ex){\sim} fx.\ (Ex)gx.\ (Ex){\sim} gx.$

A $\quad \sim (Ex)(fx. \sim gx)$

E $\quad \sim (Ex)(fx. gx)$

I $\quad (Ex)(fx. gx)$

O $\quad (Ex)(fx. \sim gx)$

or

Assume that $(a \neq 0). (\bar{a} \neq 0). (b \neq 0). (\bar{b} \neq 0)$

A $\quad (a\bar{b}=0)$

E $\quad (ab=0)$

I $\quad (ab \neq 0)$

O $\quad (a\bar{b} \neq 0)$

Dignāga's operators are also existential, but he did not assume a non-empty universe. He gave the existential condition explicitly each time as an independent premise. Each of his operators is a conjunction of two distinct premises.

A $\quad (Ex)(fx. gx). \sim (Ex)(fx. \sim gx)$

E $\quad \sim (Ex)(fx. gx). (Ex)(fx. \sim gx)$

U $\quad (Ex)(fx. gx). (Ex)(fx. \sim gx)$

or

A $\quad (ab \neq 0). (a\bar{b}=0)$

E $\quad (ab=0). (a\bar{b} \neq 0)$

U $\quad (ab \neq 0). (a\bar{b} \neq 0)$

Because of the diversity in assumption, theorems true in Aristotelian logic may be false in Dignāgean logic, and vice versa. One of the major differences is the relation $\sim (Ex)(fx. \sim gx) \supset (Ex)(fx. gx)$. This is true in Aristotelian logic, because $(x)(fx \supset gx) \equiv \sim (Ex)(fx. \sim gx)$, and

$$(x)(fx \supset gx) \supset (Ex)(fx. gx).$$

It is false in Dignāgean logic, because $(fx. gx)$ and $(fx. \sim gx)$ are independent of each other.

There are two different kinds of information: relative and absolute. The formula '$a \subset b$' gives the information about the comparison of the extension of two classes; whether these two classes themselves are empty or non-empty is a different kind of information.

A null class is included in any class, and can be included in any other null class. Therefore the information '$a \subset b$' is not relevant to the information '$a \neq 0$'. Consequently the formulae $(a \subset b) \supset (a \neq o)$ and $(x)(fx \supset gx) \supset (Ex)(fx . gx)$ are false in Dignāgean logic.

Instead of making a general assumption in the very beginning in order to cover all cases, Dignāga, like most other Indian logicians, employed in every individual case an additional premise in order to make the major premise existential. The following comparison will make this point clear:

Aristotelian:	Dignāgean:
Assume that	
$(Ex)\, fx . (Ex) gx . (Ex) - fx . (Ex) - gx.$	No such assumption.
$(x)(fx \supset gx) = -(Ex)(fx . - gx)$ Df.	$(x)(fx \supset gx) = -(Ex)(fx - gx).$ $(Ex)\,(fx . gx)$ Df.

The two systems are identical except that Dignāgean system is more versatile. An old Indian metaphor can be applied here: "If you want to cover the entire earth with cow-hide just to protect your own feet, why not wear a pair of shoes?"

A few logicians, including Uddyotakara, J. N. Keynes and G. H. von Wright, allow for the possibility of an empty universe. Uddyotakara and Keynes tried to find out factual realization in order to justify their claim that an empty universe is possible.

For the sake of convenience, let us re-phrase Uddyotakara's example in the form of traditional three-membered syllogism:

Major premise: All knowable things are nameable;

Minor premise: All things are knowable;

Conclusion: All things are nameable.

He treated this syllogism like all the other types of the barbara mood. This one is, in fact, no longer of the form $(x)(fx \supset gx) . (x)(gx \supset hx) \supset (x)(fx \supset hx)$, but the form $(x)gx \;.\; (x)(gx \supset hx) \supset (x)hx$, because the word 'all' is not a subject but a quantifier. His fatal mistake, however, is that the major premise of this syllogism is not a case for empty universe (0000), but a case for the type (1000), in which $(a=b)$, $(\bar{a}=0)$ and $(\bar{b}=0)$.

The reason why he chose a wrong example will be explained in the next chapter.

The example of Keynes is erroneous too:

"No Trinity men are in the first class;
No Trinity men are in any other class than the first;
No non-Trinity men are in the first class;
No non-Trinity men are in any other class than the first."[1]

His mistake is too obvious to be pointed out; no wonder he had abandoned it himself in the third edition of his book.

Despite the failure in establishing an example, the case (0000) is typologically indispensable; a scheme without it is incomplete, whether one takes an existential or non-existential line. It is wrong to deny its typological necessity because it is not realized; it is equally wrong to assert its factual realizability because it is typologically necessary.

In mathematics it is not infrequent that a system remains uninterpreted or a limiting case remains undefined. There is no reason why logicians should not tolerate the empty seat of a limiting case.

A Comparison of Primary Operators

Aristotle	Ⓐ	~(Ex)(fx. ~gx)	$(a\bar{b}=0)$	(-0--)
(Strawson	Ⓔ	~(Ex)(fx. gx)	$(ab=0)$	(0---)
Table 1)	Ⓘ	(Ex)(fx. gx)	$(ab\neq0)$	(1---)
	Ⓞ	(Ex)(fx. ~gx)	$(a\bar{b}\neq0)$	(-1--)
Aristotle	Ⓐ	(Ex)(fx. gx). ~(Ex)(fx. ~gx)	$(ab\neq0)(a\bar{b}=0)$	(10--)
(Strawson	Ⓔ	~(Ex)(fx. gx). (Ex)(fx. ~gx)	$(ab=0)(a\bar{b}\neq0)$	(01---)
Table 2)	Ⓘ	(Ex)(fx. gx)	$(ab\neq0)$	(1---)
	Ⓞ	(Ex)(fx. ~gx)	$(a\bar{b}\neq0)$	(-1--)
Gergonne	Ⓒ	(Ex)(fx. gx). ~(Ex)(fx. ~gx). (Ex)(~fx. gx)	$(ab\neq0)(a\bar{b}=0)(\bar{a}b\neq0)$	(101-)
	Ⓘ	(Ex)(fx. gx). ~(Ex)(fx. ~gx). ~(Ex)(~fx. gx)	$(ab\neq0)(a\bar{b}=0)(\bar{a}b=0)$	(100-)
	Ⓗ	~(Ex)(fx. gx). (Ex)(fx. ~gx). (Ex)(~fx. gx)	$(ab=0)(a\bar{b}\neq0)(\bar{a}b\neq0)$	(011-)
	Ⓧ	(Ex)(fx. gx). (Ex)(fx. ~gx). (Ex)(~fx. gx)	$(ab\neq0)(a\bar{b}\neq0)(\bar{a}b\neq0)$	(111-)
	Ↄ	(Ex)(fx. gx). (Ex)(fx. ~gx). ~(Ex)(~fx. gx)	$(ab\neq0)(a\bar{b}\neq0)(\bar{a}b=0)$	(110-)

1. J. N. Keynes: Formal Logic, 2nd edition (1887) p. 145, n. 1.
3rd edition p. 191, n. 4.

Dignāga	(A)	$(Ex)(fx.gx).-(Ex)(fx.-gx)$	$(ab\neq0)(a\bar{b}=0)$	(10--)
	(E)	$-(Ex)(fx.gx).(Ex)(fx.-gx)$	$(ab=0)(a\bar{b}\neq0)$	(01--)
	(U)	$(Ex)(fx.gx).(Ex)(fx.-gx)$	$(ab\neq0)(a\bar{b}\neq0)$	(11--)
Uddyotakara	(A)	$(Ex)(fx.gx).-(Ex)(fx.-gx)$	$(ab\neq0)(a\bar{b}=0)$	(10--)
	(E)	$-(Ex)(fx.gx).(Ex)(fx.-gx)$	$(ab=0)(a\bar{b}\neq0)$	(01--)
	(U)	$(Ex)(fx.gx).(Ex)(fx.-gx)$	$(ab\neq0)(ab\neq0)$	(11--)
	(Y)	$-(Ex)(fx.gx).-(Ex)(fx.-gx)$	$(ab=0)(a\bar{b}=0)$	(00--)

A Comparison of Secondary Operators

Aristotle

$$\text{(I)}\ 11{-}{-}\begin{cases}1111\\1110\\1101\end{cases}\qquad \text{(O)}\ 11{-}{-}\begin{cases}1111\\1110\\1101\end{cases}$$

$$\text{(A)}\ 10{-}1\begin{cases}1011\\1001\end{cases}\qquad \text{(I)}\ 10{-}1\begin{cases}1011\\1001\end{cases}$$

$$\text{(E)}\ 011{-}\begin{cases}0111\\0110\end{cases}\qquad \text{(O)}\ 011{-}\begin{cases}0111\\0110\end{cases}$$

Gergonne

$$\text{(X)}\ 111{-}\begin{cases}1111\\1110\end{cases}$$

$$\text{(Ͻ)}\ 110{-}\begin{cases}1101\\1100\end{cases}$$

$$\text{(C)}\ 101{-}\begin{cases}1011\\1010\end{cases}$$

$$\text{(I)}\ 100{-}\begin{cases}1001\\1000\end{cases}$$

$$\text{(H)}\ 011{-}\begin{cases}0111\\0110\end{cases}$$

Dignaga

$$\text{(U)}\ 11{-}{-}\begin{cases}1111\\1110\\1101\\1100\end{cases}$$

$$\text{(A)}\ 10{-}{-}\begin{cases}1011\\1001\end{cases}$$

$$\text{(E)}\ 01{-}{-}\begin{cases}0111\\0110\end{cases}$$

00-- 0011

Uddyotakara

$$\text{(U)}\ 11{-}{-}\begin{cases}1111\\1110\\1101\\1100\end{cases}$$

$$\text{(A)}\ 10{-}{-}\begin{cases}1011\\1010\\1001\\1000\end{cases}$$

$$\text{(E)}\ 01{-}{-}\begin{cases}0111\\0110\\0101\\0100\end{cases}$$

$$\text{(Y)}\ 00{-}{-}\begin{cases}0011\\0010\\0001\\0000\end{cases}$$

It is now possible that all the systems, ancient and modern, eastern and western, can be arrayed in a single spectrum by means of comparing them with reference to the extent of information about the four sub-classes. From the above diagrams we can see that the schemes are arbitrary and irregular, like various species of animals in a zoo. The traditional system is the least regular; it may have closer association with natural language, thus it is somewhat descriptive in nature.

The total number of sub-classes in dyadic relationship is four. The number of sub-classes specified in primary operators is rather irregular; it ranges from one to three.

In fact, the 'unspecified' also plays an important role in logic; it gives the function of flexibility. It could be regarded as a 'third value', in addition to the two values 'being empty' and 'being non-empty'. This is analogous to an interpretation of three-valued propositional logic by certain logicians in which the value 'undecided' was regarded as the third truth value in addition to truth and falsity.

The operators indicating dyadic class relationships are now defined by 'existential tables', which indicate the 'existential values' of four sub-classes, i.e. 'being non-empty' and 'being empty'; the system is analogous to E.L. Post's theory of elementary propositions, in which truth functions of propositions are defined by 'truth tables', which indicate the 'truth values' of four conjunctions of premises, i.e. 'truth' and 'falsity'. There obviously exists an isomorphism between various systems in logic; a general theory of operators will be given later.

Let us now consider the syllogism. Here the Hetucakra, in accordance with Dignāga's original intention, is not merely a study of various kinds of propositions, but one of various kinds of major premises of syllogisms.

If we formulate a syllogism of the barbara mood, there may be the following steps:

1. To prove that $(x)(fx \supset hx)$.
2. $(x)(fx \supset gx) . (x)(gx \supset hx) \supset (x)(fx \supset hx)$.
3. $(x)(gx \supset hx)$.
4. $(x)(fx \supset gx)$.
5. Therefore $(x)(fx \supset hx)$.

There are five 'members' in ancient Indian system; they are close to, if not completely identical with, the five steps mentioned above.

1. To prove that "Sound is transient"
2. It is so because it is produced.
3. Whatever is produced is transient, such as a pot.
4. Sound is produced.
5. It is therefore transient.

The third member is an 'exemplified major premise', therefore it is an 'existential major premise'. Dignāga suppressed the last two members and Aristotle suppressed the first two. The difference between the five-membered syllogism and the three-membered is a matter of formality and it is not material.

The word 'because' is the inverse of the word 'therefore'. It can be called an 'inverse material implication' and can be symbolized by the sign '$\subset$'. The second step can be symbolized as:

$(x)(fx \supset hx) \subset (x)(fx \supset gx) . (x)(gx \supset hx)$.

Here, again, I disagree with Stcherbatsky. He said: "This seems to be exactly the syllogism which Aristotle had in view in establishing his syllogism from example. He refers it to the class of inferences for one self, notiora quoad nos." (Buddhist Logic, Vol. I, p. 298). Whether the inference is for oneself or for others is not relevant to the problem whether the major premise is existential or not.

This particular point leads to the solution of the problem of the so-called 'exemplification', which is the third member of both the 'five-membered' and the 'three-membered' syllogisms; e.g. "Whatever is produced is transcient, such as a pot". Some authors consider this member as an example, while some others consider it as the major premise. Are an example and a major premise the same thing, or two different things?

If they are equivalent, then the Indian logicians would have committed the crudest fallacy in logic. In view of the general standard reached in Dignāga's time, such a fallacy is most unlikely. Moreover, according to Indian convention, only one example is necessary; a second one would be considered redundant. Proving by example should not have restricted the number of examples so strictly.

If these two are not equivalent, why should they be put together as one single member of syllogism? This can only be explained as follows:

This member is a major premise with existential import explicitly stated; it may be called a 'non-empty major premise'. It is in fact a conjunction of two distinct premises - a universal proposition and an existential proposition:

$-(Ex)(fx.-gx) \quad . \quad (fa.ga) \supset -(Ex)(fx.-gx) \quad . \quad (Ex)(fx.gx).$

In other words:

An example + A major premise = An exemplified major premise;

An exemplified major premise ⊃ An existential major premise.

The two propositions "All men are mortal" and "All unicorns are mortal" are similar in form. The difference between them is that in the first case there is an implied proposition "There are men", while in the second case there is no such implied proposition, because "There are unicorns" is false.

Usually an example plays only a minor role, such as the one in the following syllogism:

"Socrates is mortal,

Because he is human;

Whatever is human is mortal, such as Tom and Harry".

The importance of its role is not a logical problem but an empirical one. Its importance varies inversely with the obviousness of non-emptiness of the class of (gx.hx), or the readiness in finding an example.

In philosophical investigation, finding an example is not necessarily easy. Sometimes it is difficult to find an example because it is not familiar enough, but sometimes it is so because it is too familiar. People are used to ignore familiar things because they have taken those things for granted. To make a close analogy, one could not see one's own eyes. Under such circumstances, example becomes a decisive factor and therefore plays a major role. The Buddhists had a particularly trained technique in giving examples.

Interpretation 2 of the Hetucakra

The second interpretation is, in fact, in accordance with Dignāga's original intention. All four classes appear in this interpretation, namely: 'h', 'p', 's' and 'v'. The class 'sapakṣa' should be defined now in a way different from the way mentioned previously.

$$\begin{cases} h = \hat{z}(gz) \ \text{Df.} \\ p = \hat{z}(fz) \ \text{Df.} \\ s = \hat{z}(-fz.hz) \ \text{Df.} \\ v = \hat{z}(-hz) \ \text{Df.} \end{cases} \quad \text{or} \quad \begin{cases} h = b \ \text{Df.} \\ p = a \ \text{Df.} \\ s = \bar{a}c \ \text{Df.} \\ v = \bar{c} \ \text{Df.} \end{cases}$$

for the syllogism

$(x)(fx \supset gx).(x)(gx \supset hx) \supset (x)(fx \supset hx)$ or $(a \subset b).(b \subset c) \supset (a \subset c)$

The term 'sapakṣa' is so defined because (1) it refers to a class of things which are 'similar' to the class of things denoted by the minor term in its possessing the property denoted by the major term, and (2) these things are only similar to, but not identical with, the class of things denoted by the minor term. Therefore the class denoted by the minor term itself should be excluded from sapakṣa.

Concerning the term vipaksa, Dharmakīrti mentioned: "A case which is not similar is dissimilar - it can be different from it, contrary to it, or its absence". (Nyāyabindu, p. 104) Since its 'difference' and 'contrariety' are included in its 'absence', the last one gives the proper definition. We may say: "Vipakṣa is dissimilar to the class denoted by the minor term in not possessing the property denoted by the major term".

For the sake of convenience, let us drop the 'apparent variable' x's and use U and E to denote the universal and existential quantifiers respectively, e.g.

$U(\Phi \supset \Psi) = (x)(\Phi x \supset \Psi x)$Df.

$E(\Phi . \Psi) = (Ex)(\Phi x . \Psi x)$Df.

There are now three operatores, A, E and U, and four classes, h, p, s and v. If we take three classes p, s and v to operate against the class h, there should be nine possible combinations:

1. sādhyavyāpaka: $(p\ A\ h) = -E(f.-g).E(f.g)$
2. sādhyāvṛtti: $(p\ E\ h) = E(f.-g).-E(f.g)$
3. sādhyaikadeśavṛtti: $(p\ U\ h) = E(f.-g).E(f.g)$

4. sapakṣavyāpaka: $(s\ A\ h) = -E(-f.h.-g).E(-f.h.g)$
5. sapakṣāvṛtti: $(s\ E\ h) = E(-f.h.-g).-E(-f.h.g)$
6. sapakṣaikadeśavṛtti: $(s\ U\ h) = E(-f.h.-g).E(-f.h.g)$

7. vipakṣavyāpaka: $(v\ A\ h) = -E(-h.-g).E(-h.g)$
8. vipakṣāvṛtti: $(v\ E\ h) = E(-h.-g).-E(-h.g)$
9. vipakṣaikadeśavṛtti: $(v\ U\ h) = E(-h.-g).E(-h.g)$

For the sake of convenience, let us use the numerals from 1 to 9 to denote the nine operations sādhyavyāpaka, sādhyāvṛtti, etc.

The combinations of these numerals, i.e., 1.4.7, 1.4.8, etc. will denote various possible types in the Hetucakra.

The formulae 1 to 3 are obviously the minor premises. What are the formulae 4 to 9? Are they the major premises? The answer is negative. They are not themselves the major premises, but are implied information concerning the extension of various kinds of major premises.

If we classify the nine formulae into three groups, namely:
1, 2 and 3, which show the relation between the hetu and the pakṣa,
4, 5 and 6, which show the relation between the hetu and the sapakṣa,
7, 8 and 9, which show the relation between the hetu and the vipakṣa,
and take one from each group and combine them; then we shall have 3^3 or twenty-seven possible combinations.

The type 1 means that the minor premise is a universal affirmative proposition; the type 2, a negative proposition; the type 3, a particular proposition.

By the first special rule of the 'first figure' in the traditional logic, the minor premise must be affirmative; therefore the type 2, which denotes negative proposition, is excluded. In Indian logic, a particular conclusion such as the mood 'Darii' is not desired; therefore the type 3, which denotes particular proposition, is excluded.

When the types 2 and 3 are discarded from the list of possible combinations, the twenty-seven combinations are reduced to nine, namely: 1.4.7, 1.4.8, 1.4.9, 1.5.7, 1.5.8, 1.5.9, 1.6.7, 1.6.8, and 1.6.9.

If we take the conjunction of three factors, we can expand the products into lengthy formulae, e.g.

1.4.7 = sādhyavyāpaka-sapakṣavyāpaka-vipakṣavyāpaka
= (p A h) . (s A h) . (v A h)
= -E(f. -g). E(f. g). -E(-f. h. -g). E(-f. h. g). -E(-h. -g). E(-h. g)

In this way we shall have altogether nine such formulae. The process is cumbersome. Among the six factors not all of them are significant; we may well eliminate irrelevant factors without effecting the essential properties of the nine types.

First, the factor sādhyavyāpaka or (p A h) is redundant, because it is common to all nine types; we can therefore eliminate (f. -g) and (f. g).

Secondly, the factors (-f. h. -g) and (-h. -g) have no effect on formal implication. Now we have only two factors left: (-f. h. g) and (-h. g). We may re-write six operations from 4 to 6 as follows:

4. (s A h) ⊃ E(-f. g. h)
5. (s E h) ⊃ -E(-f. g. h)
6. (s U h) ⊃ E(-f. g. h)

7. (v A h) ⊃ E(g. -h)
8. (v E h) ⊃ -E(g. -h)
9. (v U h) ⊃ E(g. -h)·

Let us take the three pairs and put them in the form of row and column vectors and then take their product, we may obtain a matrix as in the following

$$\begin{bmatrix}4\\5\\6\end{bmatrix} . \begin{bmatrix}7 & 8 & 9\end{bmatrix}$$

$$= \begin{bmatrix}(s\ A\ h)\\(s\ E\ h)\\(s\ U\ h)\end{bmatrix} . \begin{bmatrix}(v\ A\ h) & (v\ E\ h) & (v\ U\ h)\end{bmatrix}$$

$$\supset \begin{bmatrix}E(-f.g.h)\\-E(-f.g.h)\\E(-f.g.h)\end{bmatrix} . \begin{bmatrix}E(g.-h) & -E(g.-h) & E(g.-h)\end{bmatrix}$$

$$= \begin{bmatrix}E(-f\ g\ h).E(g.-h) & E(-f.g.h).-E(g.-h) & E(-f.g.h).E(g.-h)\\ -E(-f.g.h).E(g.-h) & -E(-f.g.h).-E(g.-h) & -E(-f.g.h).E(g.-h)\\ E(-f.g.h).E(g,-h) & E(-f.g.h).-E(g.\cdot h) & E(-f.g.h).E(g.-h)\end{bmatrix}$$

In the above matrix of nine types, there are only four types which are distinct from one another:

A. E(-f. g. h). E(g. -h)
B. E(-f. g. h). -E(g. -h)
C. -E(-f. g. h). E(g. -h)
D. -E(-f. g. h). -E(g. -h)

The above can be further reduced to the following:

A. E(g. h). E(g. -h)
B. E(g. h.). -E(g. -h)
C. -E(-f. g. h). E(g. -h)
D. -E(-f. g. h). -E(g. -h)

They are corresponding to the following types respectively:

A. 4.7, 4.9, 6.7, 6.9,
B. 4.8, 6.8,
C. 5.7, 5.9,
D. 5.8,

Let us discuss the four groups in detail.

A. The four types 4.7, 4.9, 6.7 and 6.9 contain two factors in common: E(g.h) and E(g.~h).

$E(g.h) \supset \sim U(g \supset \sim h)$;

$E(g.\sim h) \supset \sim U(g \supset h)$.

The conjunction $U(f \supset g).\sim U(g \supset h).\sim U(g \supset \sim h)$ yields nothing, therefore these four types are 'inconclusive'. In this group the class g is 'too broad', as described by Dignāga.

B. The two types 4.8 and 6.8 contain two factors in common: E(g.h) and ~E(g.~h).

$E(g.h).\sim E(g.\sim h) \equiv U(g \supset h)$;

$U(f \supset g).U(g \supset h) \supset U(f \supset h)$.

These types are the so-called 'Barbara mood'; they are valid for a universal affirmative conclusion.

The difference between 4.8 and 6.8 is as following:

In type 4.8, there is a factor $\sim E(\sim f.\sim g.h)$.

Since $\sim E(f.\sim g) \supset \sim E(f.\sim g.h)$;

$\sim E(f.\sim g.h).\sim E(\sim f.\sim g.h) \equiv \sim E(\sim g.h)$;

$\sim E(g.\sim h).\sim E(\sim g.h) \equiv U(g \equiv h)$;

$U(f \supset g).U(g \equiv h) \supset U(f \supset h)$.

This is a special case of the Barbara mood.

C. The two types 5.7 and 5.9 contain two factors in common: ~E(~f.g.h) and E(g.~h).

Whether (f.g.h) is empty is unknown, therefore:

$(E(f.g.h) \vee \sim E(f.g.h))\ .\ (\sim E(\sim f.g.h).E(g.\sim h)$; or,

$(E(g.h).E(g.\sim h)) \vee (\sim E(g.h).E(g.\sim h))$; or,

$(\sim U(g \supset h).\sim U(g \supset \sim h)) \vee U(g \supset \sim h)$.

The last formula shows that if (f.g.h) is non-empty, the syllogism would be inconclusive like the type A; if it is empty, the conclusion would be $U(f \supset -h)$, which is 'contrary' to the original thesis to be proved $U(f \supset h)$, and the syllogism would be in the form of the so-called 'Celarent' mood.

Whether $(f.g.h)$ is empty is unknown, the conclusion may well be, but not necessarily, 'contrary'. Since the common factor $E(g.-h)$ implies $-U(g \supset h)$, the syllogism is called 'contradictory'.

Two points should be clarified at this stage.

(1) The aim of establishing a syllogism in Dignāga's time was to prove a thesis favourable to one's own doctrine in a debate. Since both disputing parties were committed to their own doctrines, the motive could hardly be objective. Therefore a syllogism involved not only the problem of validity, but also that of desirability. The situation is analogous to the debate in a modern court of law. A defence counsel is not supposed to give a reason, however objective and tenable it may be, which can lead to the conclusion that his client is guilty. This involves not only the question whether the reason is tenable, but also the question of who should raise it.

(2) Whether a syllogism is 'valid' or 'contradictory' is not identical with whether its conclusion is an affirmative or a negative proposition. The former is a matter of whether the conclusion confirms or negates the thesis, while the latter is a matter of linguistic form of proposition. In order to avoid confusion, all theses should be phrased in the form of affirmative propositions; e.g. we should say "Sound is impermanent" instead of "Sound is not permanent".

D. The type 5.8 contains factors $-E(-f.g.h)$ and $-E(g.-h)$. If we consider the major premise alone, $(f.g.h)$ is unknown, therefore:

$(E(f.g.h) \lor -E(f.g.h))\ .\ (-E(-f.g.h).-E(g.-h)$;

$((E(g.h).-E(g.-h)) \lor (-E(g.h).-E(g.-h))$;

$((E(g.h).-E(g.-h)) \lor -E(g)$;

$U(g \supset h) \lor U(-g)$.

The above yields either a universal affirmative conclusion, or a universal negative conclusion; it is, after all, inconclusive. The class g may be null, or at most equivalent to the class f; it is therefore called by Dignāga "too narrow".

If we consider both the minor and the major premises, there is the factor E(f. g) in the minor premise, which shows that the class of g is non-empty. The syllogism becomes a special case of the Barbara mood:

$U(f \equiv g).\ U(g \supset h) \supset U(f \supset h).$

So far in the consideration of validity of nine types of syllogisms we have chosen two factors (~f. g. h) and (g. ~h) from six factors. These two are essential for the condition of formal implication or class inclusion, which was called '<u>vyāpti</u>' by ancient Indian logicians. This term denotes not only formal implication but also material implication, which will be explained later.

The two factors can be symbolized in our simplified notation by (xx--). The same two factors had been chosen by Dignāga, and constituted the second and the third clauses of his celebrated law of the <u>Trairūpya</u>.

What is the point of establishing the concept of <u>sapakṣa</u>? Let us first compare the following syllogisms:

1. All men are animals;
   All animals are mortal;
   Therefore all men are mortal.

2. All men are featherless bipeds;
   All featherless bipeds are mortal;
   Therefore all men are mortal.

3. All men are 'tripeds';
   All tripeds are mortal;
   Therefore all men are mortal.

There are two possible interpretations for the first syllogism:

(a) All men are animals;
    All animals, including men, are mortal;
    Therefore all men are mortal.

(b) All men are animals;
    All animals, excluding men, are mortal;
    Therefore all men are mortal.

An old criticism, repeated by J. S. Mill, charged the Aristotelian syllogistic with being faulty on account of <u>petitio principii</u>. Such criticism obviously applies to interpretation (a).

Interpretation (b) is wrong too. The major premise becomes 'Some animals are mortal' and the syllogism is no longer AAA; there can be no inference from the two premises.

Dignāga managed to avoid the difficulty of both interpretations (a) and (b) by splitting the major premise "All animals are mortal" into two premises:

(i) There is no animal which is not mortal. (in so far as the opponent fails to provide with a counter-example)

(ii) There are non-human animals which are mortal. (therefore there are animals which are mortal)

The example is imaginary and not his own. The significance of the second premise is not particularly obvious in this case. It will become obvious in the next syllogism.

Many logicians, including Dignāga's critic Uddyotakara and several best interpretors of Dignāgean logic, made the mistake in considering Dignāga's major premise 'exclusive'; in other words, his major premise belongs to the type (b). This view is originated by the fact that his *sapakṣa* excludes the class of the minor term.

$(a \subset b) . (\bar{a} b \subset c) \supset (a \subset c)$, or
$(x)(fx \supset gx) . (x)(-fx . gx \supset hx) \supset (x)(fx \supset hx)$.

The above certainly has avoided the fallacy of *petitio principii*, yet it has committed a mistake far greater; it is a completely wrong formula. This is a dreadful misunderstanding of Dignāgean system, and it has turned its merits into defects.

The ingenuity in Dignāgean system lies in the fact that his *sapakṣa* is confined to the second clause of the *Trairūpya*, and has nothing to do with the third clause.

Sapakṣa:	$s = \hat{z}(-fz . hz)$ Df.
Vipakṣa:	$v = \hat{z}(-hz)$ Df.
2nd clause:	$(Ex)((-fx . hx) . (gx))$
or	$(Ex)(-fx . gx . hx)$
or	$(Ex)(gx . hx)$ because $(Ex)(-fx . gx . hx) \supset (Ex)(gx . hx)$
3rd clause:	$-(Ex)((-hx) . (gx))$
or	$-(Ex)(gx . -hx)$

The conjunction of the two clauses: $(Ex)(gx . hx) . -(Ex)(gx . -hx)$

The factor $(-fx)$ automatically disappears in the second clause, and it has never appeared in the third clause. The conjunction of the two gives the condition for non-empty formal implication $(x)(gx \supset hx)$ or non-empty class inclusion: $(b \subset c)$. In other words, the exclusion of the class of the minor term from sapakṣa does not imply the exclusion of the class of the minor term from the class of the middle term. That is to say, though the class of sapakṣa excludes the class of the minor term; yet the minor, middle and major terms of Dignāgean system are not different from those of Aristotelian system in extension.

There are two possible interpretations for the second syllogism:

(a) All men are featherless bipeds;
All featherless bipeds, including men, are mortal;
Therefore all men are mortal.

(b) All men are featherless bipeds;
All featherless bipeds, excluding men, are mortal;
Therefore all men are mortal.

The interpretation (a) has the same difficulty as that of the last syllogism. The major premise of the interpretation (b) becomes 'No non-human featherless bipeds is mortal', because there is no 'non-human featherless biped'. It becomes an 'E' proposition and the syllogism is no longer AAA.

The fault of the second syllogism becomes obvious according to Dignāga's way:

(i) There is no featherless biped which is not mortal.

(ii) There are non-human featherless bipeds which are mortal.

The premise (i) can be true, but the premise (ii) is obviously false, because there is no non-human featherless biped.

Syllogism 2 can be considered as valid in traditional logic, but not valid in Dignāgean logic. The next syllogism can make the position clearer.

The major premise of the third syllogism can be split into two:

(i) There is no triped which is not mortal.

(ii) There are non-human tripeds which are mortal.

The premise (i) is still true in Dignāgean logic, although it sounds somewhat misleading. The premise (ii) is false.

Apart from the difference that the minor premise of syllogism 2 is true and that of syllogism 3 is false, the premise (ii) of them are both false, and one cannot say that one is 'more false' than the other.

Dignāga's not being able to distinguish syllogisms 2 and 3 seems to be a defect of his system; it is in fact its merit. If we have already known the difference between "Nothing else has such a property" and "Nothing has such a property", we would also have known whether the thing in question has or has not such a property, this is precisely the factor which is to be proved by the syllogism.

This is a limiting case of J. S. Mill's objection to Aristotelian system regarding its defect in petitio principii.

I mentioned that certain logicians, including Dignāga's critic Uddyotakara, wrongly considered Dignāga's major premise 'exclusive'. Even some best interpretors of Dignāgean logic made such a mistake. Since their interpretation is explicit and their mistake is obvious, it is not necessary to quote their words or even mention their names. It is, however, interesting to see how Uddyotakara made his mistake.

Uddyotakara's misunderstanding of this point is revealed in his example of the case (0000). This is a limiting case, giving an example is like creating a perpetual machine, an absolut zero in temperature, a perfect black body, or evaluating the fraction 1/0. His method of working out the unworkable is as follows:

"All things are nameable, because all things are knowable."

No matter what the middle terms is, when it excludes the class of 'all things', which happens to be the minor term in this case, its class become empty. By the manipulating of excluding the class of the minor term from that of the middle term, he gave an artificial example for the empty universe.

In this single example, he has committed several different mistakes. The mistake relevant to the present topic is that he excluded the class of the minor term not only from sapakṣa, but also from the class of the middle term.

The Trairūpya

Almost all books on Indian logic have mentioned something about the Trairūpya, as a result the information about it in English language alone is surprisingly rich. Consequently I shall not repeat its original wording in this work; readers who are not familiar with it are advised to refer to any book on Indian logic, e.g. Buddhist Logic Vol. I, pp. 242-5, before reading this chapter.

The first clause of the Trairūpya concerns the minor premise; it was formulated by Dignāga somewhat implicitly. The second and the third concern the major premise, and they were formulated more explicitly. As a matter of fact, the last two have puzzled more people than the first.

Th. Stcherbatsky was one among many scholars who have misinterpreted the two clauses. His explication of the <u>Trairūpya</u> is both indefinite and misleading; his wording 'just', 'only', 'necessary' and 'in their totality' (p. 244, <u>Buddhist Logic</u>) are merely literally emphatic but vague in meaning.

Dignāga was not the only one who formulated the three clauses; logicians both before and after him had formulated three clauses vaguely similar but not equivalent to his. Professor Karl Potter has stated three stages in detail and raised the important question which stage Dignāga was at.[1] I hope I may give my tentative answer as follows:

The three stages may be formulated as follows:

Stage	Clause	Predicate calculus	Class logic	Simplified notation
I: Pre-Dignāgean	2	E(-f. g. h)	$\bar{a}bc \neq 0$	(1--1)
	3	E(-g. -h)	$\bar{b}\bar{c} \neq 0$	
II: Dignāgean	2	E(-f. g. h)	$\bar{a}bc \neq 0$	(10--)
	3	-E(g. -h)	$b\bar{c} = 0$	
III: Post-Dignāgean	2	-E(g. -h)	$b\bar{c} = 0$	(-0--)
	3	-E(g. -h)	$b\bar{c} = 0$	

In some Indian works on logic both positive and negative examples appear in syllogisms, while in some other works the negative examples do not appear. Whether a negative example should necessarily be present, or could be optional, or should never be present at all, was a matter in dispute. It happens that in two types of valid syllogism (1011) and (1001), the last figure indicates E(-g. -h). This does not mean, however, that E(-g. -h) should be a necessary condition for formal implication. At least we can say that it is peripheral to such a condition, if we do not discard it as completely irrelevant.

The mistake in the Stage I lies, therefore, in that the negation was put in a wrong place. Instead of the existence of something non-g without the

---

1. In his comments on my paper "Buddhist Logic and its Consequences" presented at the Joint Meeting of American Philosophical Association and Association for Symbolic Logic on 4-6 May, 1967 in Chicago.

property h, the condition should be the non-existence of something g without the property h. This can be clearly expressed in symbols:

incorrect:	$E(-g. -h)$	$b\bar{c} \neq 0$
correct:	$-E(g. -h)$	$b\bar{c} = 0$

Until Dignāga, the concepts of <u>sapakṣa</u>, <u>vipakṣa</u>, positive example, negative example and counter-example had not been well distinguished. This is the reason why in Stage I the third clause was wrongly formulated. The five concepts are completely distinct from one another; in particular, a negative example is not <u>vipakṣa</u>, and the presence of a negative example is not equivalent to the absence of a counter-example.

<u>sapakṣa</u>:	$s = \hat{z}(-fz. hz)$ Df.
<u>vipakṣa</u>:	$v = \hat{z}(-hz)$ Df.
positive example:	$(-fa. ga. ha) \supset (Ex)(-fx. gx. hx) \supset (Ex)(gx. hx)$
negative example:	$(-ga. -ha) \supset (Ex)(-gx. -hx)$
counter-example:	$(ga. -ha) \supset (Ex)(gx. -hx) \supset -(x)(gx \supset hx)$

The distinction becomes crystal clear when symbols are used; it is therefore perfectly understandable that ancient logicians could make mistake easily because they did not possess the same kind of tool which we possess today. What was regarded as profound subtlety in ancient times becomes plain talk now, and conversely, today's high school mathematics could become equally 'mysterious' if it were written in ancient non-symbolic language.

When all three stages are analyzed, we may conclude that the clause 3 of Stage I is superfluous, and Stage III is inadequate. This becomes a matter of correctness, and no longer a matter of opinion. This can answer the question why Dignāga, and not anybody else, was credited with the formulation of the <u>Trairūpya</u>, although some pre-Dignāgean logicians had done something vaguely similar.

There exists a difficult problem in the third clause. The presence of a counter-example can be symbolized by

$(ga. -ha) \supset (Ex)(gx. -hx) \supset -(x)(gx \supset hx)$.

It says that $(ga. -ha)$ implies $(Ex)(gx. -hx)$. But what would imply the absence of a counter-example, i.e. $-(Ex)(gx. -hx)$?

We can find nothing which plays such a role.

Logical inference has its obvious limitations; expecting too much is a cause of fallacies. One can prove that a class is non-empty in order to satisfy the second condition of the Trairūpya by providing with a concrete positive example, but how can one prove that a class is empty in order to satisfy the third condition by showing the absence of a counter example?

'Being non empty' and 'being empty' are not symmetric; the former is provable while the latter is not. If this is the case, no syllogism can strictly prove anything. In actual practice, however, some result has to be achieved. If it is not conclusive once and for all, it should be conclusive either up to the present moment, or for the duration of a debate.

The final result of a debate can be determined by the presence or absence of a single counter-example, $(ga. \sim ha) \supset (Ex)(gx. \sim hx)$. The failure in producing a counter-example by the opponent does not entail that a counter-example does not exist. It is sufficient, however, to put the debate to an end, in which the disputant has defeated the opponent. It is not a proof in its strict sense; it can only convince a third party that a counter-example cannot be produced by the party to whom the presence of it is desirable, despite whether such an example does or does not exist by itself. The position of the disputant is in fact strengthened by the weakening of the position of the opponent, who plays a positive role in concluding the debate.

If the function of a syllogism is so much limited, would it be too weak to prove the truth of any proposition at all?

The above seems to be invalidating the function of logical reasoning as a whole. If we examine the entire history of human thought, which proposition has been universally 'proved' to be true, once and for all?

DIGNĀGA AND THE DEVELOPMENT OF INDIAN LOGIC

I have nothing but admiration for Professor Chi's interesting comparative study of Indian and modern Western systems of logic, and I do not have any points to make in disagreement with what he has said. I do feel, though, that some of the references he makes to Indian logic require more understanding of the history of Indian thought than many of those here may command. Within the brief span of time allotted me I shall try to clarify certain aspects of Indian logic whose proper understanding is necessary if we are to appreciate Dignāga's contribution.

In particular, I wish to pose two questions: (1) why do historians of Indian logic credit Dignāga with "discovering pervasion (vyāpti)", and (2) was it a salutary thing for Buddhism that he did so?

A stock Indian inference is the following: "that mountain possesses fire, because it possesses smoke; like kitchen and unlike lake." As Dr. Chi suggests, we may interpret the terms of arguments such as this as ranging over classes. Thus there are five classes to be distinguished in the above inference: (1) the unit class that mountain, which is the pakṣa (abbreviated p); (2) the class of fire-possessing things, which is the sādhya (s); (3) the class of smoke-possessing things, which is the hetu (h); (4) the class of kitchens, which is the sapakṣa (a); and (5) the class of lakes, which is the vipakṣa (v).

Using these abbreviations in the fashion Dr. Chi indicates, and assuming that p, s and h are not empty classes (which was Dignāga's assumption), we may characterize the conclusion which a person offering an inference wants to prove as $p\bar{s}=0$.

In order to make the readers clear about the points which Professor Karl H. Potter has made, and to let them be familiar with background information, I have asked his permission to reproduce his paper, and he has very kindly given his consent, for which I am deeply grateful. The paper quoted here is from his first draft; its final version is expected to be included in his forthcoming book on Indian Philosophy.

The paper was read at the Joint Meeting of American Philosophical Association and the Association for Symbolic Logic held at Chicago on 4-6 May, 1967.

Next, let us consider the *trairūpya* or threefold mark, which Dr. Chi says has puzzled so many famous scholars. This formula of the threefold mark surely goes back well before Dignāga, although it is frequently associated with his name.

The reason for this association, as we shall see, is that *Dignāga* has reinterpreted the formula. The three rules which constitute this "threefold mark" are as follows:

(1) the *pakṣa* must fall completely within the *hetu*;

(2) the *sapakṣa* must occur partially or completely within the *hetu*;

(3) the *vipakṣa* must occur completely outside of the *hetu*.

Unfortunately, this formulation is not at all unambiguous, and the history of the development of the notion of pervasion is a history of the successive reconstruing of the second and third rules in the above formula. I shall consider three stages of this history.

Stage One. Everything here hinges on how the terms "*sapakṣa*" and "*vipakṣa*" are interpreted in the second and third rules, and symbolism helps in exposing the subtleties. As Vidyabhusana asserts, "an example before the time of Dignāga served as a mere familiar case which was cited to help the understanding of the listener" (S. C. Vidyabhusana, *Indian Logic in the Medieval School*, p. 95). In this earliest stage rule (2) was taken to mean that the *sapakṣa* constituted some class or other all of whose members share the property designated by the *sādhya* - call it the *s*-property - and the rule then stated that at least one of the members of that class also possesses smoke. That is, the rule required that $ash \neq 0$. Rule (3), likewise, was construed to mean that the *vipakṣa* consists of some class or other whose members all share the property of not possessing fire, and that none of those members have the property of possessing smoke. Thus rule (3) may be formulated, at this stage, as $v\overline{sh} \neq 0$. Rule (1) is relatively unambiguous; it states that $p\bar{h}=0$.

I especially call your attention to the definitions of the classes *a* and *v* as understood in this stage, as well as to two features about an inference as conceived of here. The first feature is this: that satisfaction of the three rules conjointly does not suffice to entail the conclusion. The situation is rather that one giving an argument is conceived to be citing examples in order to suggest that plausibility of his hypothesis; we are taken to be in a discussion during which one side claims something to be the case and in order to illustrate what he means, as well as to show that his claim is not altogether unreasonable, he provides examples. The second feature to note is this· rules (2) and (3) are independent of each other. It is possible to satisfy one without satisfying the other.

Stage Two. In this stage the understanding of rule (3) undergoes a distinct transformation, while the other two rules remain interpreted as before. In Stage One the *vipakṣa* was taken to be some particular class (e.g., the class of lakes). On the understanding of this second stage, the *vipakṣa* is to be construed as the class of all things which lack the *s*-property - in our stock inference, it will be the class of all fireless things. Rule (3) now is taken to state that $h\bar{s}=0$, that is, that the *hetu* class is completely within the *sādhya*.

This is a radical change, for it is now the case, where it was not before, that if all three rules are satisfied the conclusion is entailed. One may see this by consulting the diagram for Stage Two in the handout. (This diagram, though odd, may be accepted on the assumption that our *pakṣa* is properly qualified, which is to say that it falls outside the *sapakṣa*.) It will be seen from the diagram that the *pakṣa* falls completely within the *sādhya*, and that was the conclusion which was to be proved. However, the stock example, *lakes*, will no longer serve. For *lakes* is not the class of everything which lacks the *s*-property fieriness. In Stage Two, then, interest has swung from the giving of evidence suggestive of lawfulness to the actual assertion of lawful connection between smokiness and fieriness. This lawful connection is technically known as "pervasion" (*vyāpti*).

At this stage, while the *sapakṣa* still serves as positive evidence of concomitance between *h* and *s*, the *vipakṣa* is no longer an example but rather the complement of *s* itself. Rules (2) and (3) on this reading have completely different roles: whereas rule (2) involves giving evidence for concomitance by citing a particular instance instantiating both properties, rule (3) requires assent to a universal proposition "all *h* things are *s* things" (e.g., "all smoky things are fiery things") but does not require the production of specific evidence.

The two rules are still strictly speaking independent. One can find an instance satisfying rule (2) without feeling able to assert pervasion of h by s, and likewise one might feel inclined to assert pervasion without being able to come up with an actual instance of a thing which shared the two properties. It is evident, though, that Stage Two is a halfway house, since if one sincerely believes that rule (3) is satisfied, that pervasion does indeed hold, then he will have no doubt that an instance of concomitance can be found, even though he may not be imaginative to come up with one immediately upon request. Thus we are led to the third stage.

Stage Three. Here rules (1) and (3) are understood as in Stage Two; the change is in rule (2). In fact, in this stage rules (2) and (3) come to the same thing. For the sapakṣa is now construed as consisting of the class of all things which have the sādhya-property except the pakṣa itself. Rule (2) now says that the members of h, smoky things, must occur only in the sapakṣa, which means now the class of fiery things. Thus Rule (2) must be stated thus: $h\bar{s}=0$, which was precisely the way we found Rule (3) to read as well.

At this stage not only are rules (2) and (3) equivalent, but it follows that one of them is unnecessary. Rule (1) together with either one or the other of the other two rules is sufficient to entail the conclusion. The situation is as in the Diagram in the handout at the bottom, which is recognizable as the Venn diagram for BARBARA together with the assumed existence of a pakṣa.

The three stages I have identified can, I think, be associated with actual philosophers. The first stage antedates Dignāga; it was the view of the authors of the original expositions of the doctrines of the Nyāya school of Hindu thought. Just who was responsible for the second stage is not entirely clear. (Vidyabhusana seems to have thought that it came in with Asanga.) In any case it is likely that it was Dignāga's position, though this is extremely hard to ascertain, mainly because of the difficulty of maintaining the position of the second stage without perforce moving on to the third stage. The third stage is explicitly and unmistakably formulated by Dharmakīrti in his Nyāyabindu; Stcherbatsky's puzzlement over the trairūpya stemmed from his difficulty in explaining adequately why Dharmakīrti should promulgate a threefold mark in which one of the three rules is redundant and unnecessary.

It is worth commenting that examination of Dignāga's Hetucakra does not suffice to decide which stage Dignāga was at. It is likely that he had left the first stage, since he implies (though he does not actually assert) that all fallacies of inference can be somehow linked with the nine cases of the "wheel". But it is quite unclear whether he occupies the second or third stage, if we confine ourselves to what can be gleaned from this text alone.

Whoever discovered pervasion, whether Dignāga or someone else, was it a good thing that he did so? Most scholars of Indian logic have said that it was. They regularly praise Dignāga for making a remarkable breakthrough to a deductive, syllogistic logic. They apparently assume that recognition of the BARBARA-like relations in argument meant that Dignāga was somehow now on the right track. But the right track to what? Remember that the Buddhists were atomists in ontology, associationists in psychology, empiricists in methodology. In the history of Western philosophy concentration on deduction and the celebration of the syllogism as the paradigm of reasoning tended to spawn absolutism in ontology, innate ideas in psychology, rationalism in methodology. What happened in Buddhism as a result of its discovery of deductive logic was, I believe, a schizoid tendency which led to Dignāga's school's accepting the mysticism of the Mādhyamika. The realm of universals, where deduction holds sway, is unreal for these Buddhist logicians; the world of particular things, beyond the scope of reasoning considered as essentially deductive and general, though admittedly real became uninvestigatable. It was rather the Nyāya logicians, who held on to the inductive method characteristic of the earliest of our three stages, who maintained an interest in nature and suppose it possible for human beings to study nature's ways successfully. In the West as well, scientific progress was impeded by the ancients' passion for formal logic, and only spurted ahead when the value of providing concrete evidence for one's claims was clearly recognized and accepted. In the light of these historical tendencies perhaps we should rather admire the Naiyāyika, who despite the seductive attractions of the syllogism persisted in requiring the provision of concrete examples as at least making initially credible a person's claim that a proposition embodied a law of nature.

Karl M. Potter
University of Minnesota

p = pakṣa, e.g., that mountain s = sādhya, e.g., fiery things h = hetu, e.g., smoky things a = sapakṣa, e.g., kitchens v = vipakṣa, e.g., lakes	To prove: $p\bar{s}=0$ Assume: $p \neq 0$ $s \neq 0$ $h \neq 0$

trairūpya or threefold mark:

Rule (1): p must fall completely with h;
Rule (2): a must overlap h;
Rule (3): v must exclude h.

Stage One:

Definitions:

a = df. some class such that all its members have the s-property (e.g., fieriness)
v = df. some class such that all its members lack the s-property.

Interpretation of Rules:

(1): $p\bar{h}=0$;
(2): $ash\neq0$;
(3): $v\bar{s}\bar{h}\neq0$.

Stage Two:

Definitions:

a's definition as in Stage One.
v = df. $\bar{s}$.

Interpretation of Rules:

(1) $p\bar{h}=0$;
(2) $ash\neq0$;
(3) $h\bar{s}=0$. (=vyāpti)

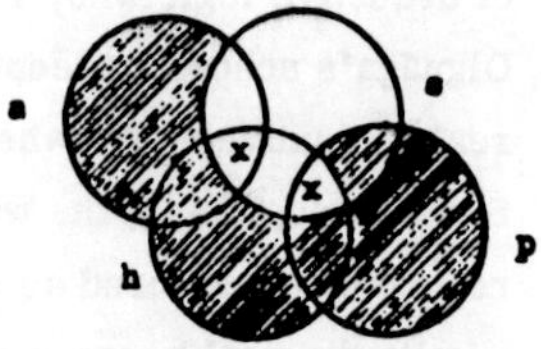

Stage Three:

Definitions:

a = df. $s\bar{p}$.
v = df. $\bar{s}$.

Interpretation of Rules:

(1) $p\bar{h}=0$;
(2) $h\bar{s}=0$; (=vyāpti)
(3) $h\bar{s}=0$.

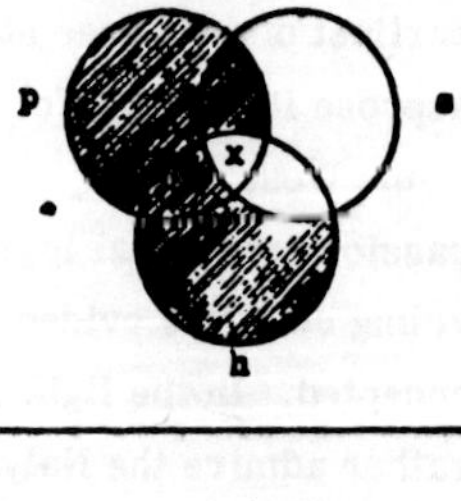

(ii) A GENERAL THEORY OF OPERATORS

1. Dyadic Operators of Order Two

Consider a set $\mathcal{L}$ of three sets A, U and V of two elements each:

$\mathcal{L} = \{A, U, V\}$

$A = \{a_1, a_2\}$

$U = \{u_1, u_2\}$

$V = \{v_1, v_2\}$

where $A \neq U$ and $A \neq V$; $U = V$ or $U \neq V$.

Take the product of A and U:

$A \times U = \{(a_1, u_1), (a_1, u_2), (a_2, u_1), (a_2, u_2)\}$

Specify a partition π_1 of the product set A X U such that every subset contains in their ordered pairs one element of A and both elements of U:

$\pi_1 = \{\{(a_1, u_1), (a_1, u_2)\}, \{(a_2, u_1), (a_2, u_2)\}\}$

For the sake of simplicity, use capital letters B and C to denote the two subsets, and use lower case letters b and c to denote the ordered pairs. Choose the subscripts for b and c in such a way that the corresponding subscripts of u are preserved in them.

$B = \{b_1, b_2\}$; where $b_1 = (a_1, u_1)$ and $b_2 = (a_1, u_2)$;

$C = \{c_1, c_2\}$; where $c_1 = (a_2, u_1)$ and $c_2 = (a_2, u_2)$.

Take the product of the two subsets B and C:

$B \times C = \{(b_1, c_1), (b_1, c_2), (b_2, c_1), (b_2, c_2)\}$

Use the capital letter D to denote the product set and use the lower case letter d to denote the ordered pairs:

$D = \{d_1, d_2, d_3, d_4\}$; where

$d_1 = (b_1, c_1)$, $d_2 = (b_1, c_2)$, $d_3 = (b_2, c_1)$, $d_4 = (b_2, c_2)$.

Repeat the process of product-partition-product. First, take the product of D and V:

$$D \times V = \{(d_1, v_1), (d_1, v_2), (d_2, v_1), (d_2, v_2), (d_3, v_1), (d_3, v_2), (d_4, v_1), (d_4, v_2)\}$$

Specify a partition π_2 of the product set D X V such that every subset contains in their ordered pairs one element of D and both elements of V.

In this case there are four such subsets:

$$\pi_2 = \Big\{ \{(d_1, v_1), (d_1, v_2)\}, \{(d_2, v_1), (d_2, v_2)\}, \{(d_3, v_1), (d_3, v_2)\}, \{(d_4, v_1), (d_4, v_2)\} \Big\}$$

Use capital letters E, F, G and H to denote respectively the four subsets, and use lower case letters e, f, g and h to denote the corresponding ordered pairs. Choose the subscripts of e, f, g and h in such a way that the corresponding subscrips of v are preserved in them.

$E = \{e_1, e_2\}$; where $e_1 = (d_1, v_1)$, $e_2 = (d_1, v_2)$;

$F = \{f_1, f_2\}$; where $f_1 = (d_2, v_1)$, $f_2 = (d_2, v_2)$;

$G = \{g_1, g_2\}$; where $g_1 = (d_3, v_1)$, $g_2 = (d_3, v_2)$;

$H = \{h_1, h_2\}$; where $h_1 = (d_4, v_1)$, $h_2 = (d_4, v_2)$.

Take the product of the subsets E, F, G and H:

E X F X G X H

$$= \{(e_1, f_1, g_1, h_1), (e_1, f_1, g_1, h_2), (e_1, f_1, g_2, h_1), (e_1, f_1, g_2, h_2), (e_1, f_2, g_1, h_1), (e_1, f_2, g_1, h_2), (e_1, f_2, g_2, h_1), (e_1, f_2, g_2, h_2), (e_2, f_1, g_1, h_1), (e_2, f_1, g_1, h_2), (e_2, f_1, g_2, h_1), (e_2, f_1, g_2, h_2), (e_2, f_2, g_1, h_1), (e_2, f_2, g_1, h_2), (e_2, f_2, g_2, h_1), (e_2, f_2, g_2, h_2)\}.$$

Since the quadruplets are ordered, the letters e, f, g and h may be omitted. The quadruplets can be represented by the subscripts alone, which have been so chosen that they correspond to those of the v's: Let P be the product set E X F X G X H,

$$P = \{(1,1,1,1), (1,1,1,2), (1,1,2,1), (1,1,2,2), (1,2,1,1), (1,2,1,2), (1,2,2,1), (1,2,2,2), (2,1,1,1), (2,1,1,2), (2,1,2,1), (2,1,2,2), (2,2,1,1), (2,2,1,2), (2,2,2,1), (2,2,2,2)\}.$$

2. Operators in General

Consider a set $\mathcal{L}$ of three sets A, U and V of i, j and k elements respectively:

$\mathcal{L} = \{A, U, V\}$.

$A = \{a_1, a_2, \dots a_i\}$

$U = \{u_1, u_2, \dots u_j\}$

$V = \{v_1, v_2, \dots v_k\}$

where $A \neq U$ and $A \neq V$; $U = V$ or $U \neq V$.

Take the product of A and U,

$A \times U = \{(a_1, u_1), (a_1, u_2), \dots (a_i, u_j)\}$

Specify a partition π_1 of the product set A X U such that every subset contains in their ordered pairs one element of A and all elements of U:

$$\pi_1 = \{\{(a_1, u_1), (a_1, u_2), \ldots (a_1, u_j)\}$$
$$\ldots$$
$$\{(a_i, u_1), (a_i, u_2), \ldots (a_i, u_j)\}\}$$

In the partition there are i subsets of j ordered pairs each.

Take the product of the i subsets. Let $A_1, A_2, \ldots. A_i$ denote these subsets, and let D denote their product set:

$$D = A_1 \times A_2 \times \ldots \times A_i$$

It is obvious that the product set D will contain j^i n-tuplets:

$$D = \{d_1, d_2, \ldots d_{j^i}\}.$$

Repeat the process of product-partition-product. First, take the product of D and V:

$$D \times V = \{(d_1, v_1), (d_1, v_2), \ldots (d_{j^i}, v_k)\}$$

Specify a partition π_2 of the product set D X V such that every subset contains in its ordered pairs one element of D and all elements of V:

$$\pi_2 = \{\{(d_1, v_1), (d_1, v_2), \ldots (d_1, v_k)\},$$
$$\ldots\ldots\ldots$$
$$\{(d_{j^i}, v_1), (d_{j^i}, v_2), \ldots (d_{j^i}, v_k)\}\}$$

In this partition there are j^i subsets of k ordered pairs each.

Then take the product of the j^i subsets. Let $D_1, D_2, \ldots D_{j^i}$ denote these subsets, and let P denote their product set:

$$P = D_1 \times D_2 \times \ldots \times D_{j^i}.$$

It is obvious that the product set P will contain ${}_kj^i$ n-tuplets:

$$P = \{p_1, p_2, \ldots p_{{}_kj^i}\}.$$

3. The General Interpretation

Let the sets ℓ, A, U, V and P mentioned above be called 'system', 'argument', 'primary value', 'secondary value' and 'operation' respectively.

<u>THEOREM</u>: For a system of i arguments, j primary values and k secondary values, it is possible to find ${}_kj^i$ operations such that no two of them are equivalent and such that every other operation in the same system of i arguments, j primary values and k secondary values is equivalent to one of them.

The above is a generalization of a theorem by E. L. Post. (E. L. Post: Introduction to a General Theory of Elementary Propositions. American Journal of Mathematics 43 (1921), p172).

4. Particular ways of Interpretation

The above mentioned system can be interpreted differently in various branches of logic and mathematics. It is hard to tell exhaustively how many possible ways of interpretation there can be, but it can be interpreted at least in the following topics:

a. truth functions of propositional logic,

b. quantificational logic,

c. class logic,

d. the logic of relations.

In each branch of logic, there are two types of interpretation: atomic and molecular. Such a distinction is particularly obvious in class logic.

a. The atomic interpretation: e.g. $a \cup b$ "The sum of class a and class b" is not a proposition.

b. The molecular interpretation: e.g. $a \subset b$ "The class a is included in the class b" is a proposition.

The molecular interpretation of $a \cup b$, and the atomic interpretation of $a \subset b$ are complicated and rarely used, although they do exist. In most cases, only one of the two interpretations are practically used.

5. Two-valued truth functions of order two

Consider a commonest example of the dyadic truth functions in propositional logic, where

Arguments = propositions;

Primary values = supposed truth values of individual propositions;

Secondary values = resultant truth values of aggregates of propositions.

$A = \{p, q\}$

$U = \{t, f\}$

$V = \{t, f\}$

Take the product of A and U:

$A \times U = \{(p, t), (p, f), (q, t), (q, f)\}$

Specify a partition π_1 of the product set A X U in the following way:

$\pi_1 = \{\{(p, t), (p, f)\}, \{(q, t), (q, f)\}\}$

Let B and C denote the two subsets:

$B = \{(p, t), (p, f)\}$; $C = \{(q, t), (q, f)\}$

Take the product of the subsets B and C:

B X C = {((p, t), (q, t)), ((p, t), (q, f)), ((p, f), (q, t)), ((p, f), (q, f))}

Let D denote the product set:

D = B X C.

Repeat the process of product-partition-product. First, take the product of D and V:

D X V = {(((p, t), (q, t)), t), (((p, t), (q, t)), f),
(((p, t), (q, f)), t), (((p, t), (q, f)), f),
(((p, f), (q, t)), t), (((p, f), (q, t)), f),
(((p, f), (q, f)), t), (((p, f), (q, f)), f)}.

Specify a partition, and let E, F, G and H be the subsets of that partition:

E = {(((p, t), (q, t)), t), (((p, t), (q, t)), f)};
F = {(((p, t), (q, f)), t), (((p, t), (q, f)), f)};
G = {(((p, f), (q, t)), t), (((p, f), (q, t)), f)};
H = {(((p, f), (q, f)), t), (((p, f), (q, f)), f)}.

Take the product of the subsets E, F, G and H:

E X F X G X H
= {((((p, t), (q, t)), t), (((p, t), (q, f)), t), (((p, f), (q, t)), t), (((p. f), (q, f)), t)),
.........}

Let P denote the product set:

P = E X F X G X H.

Since all the pairs are ordered, the extremely lengthy formula can be reduced to a matrix as following:

P = {(t, t, t, t), (t, t, t, f), (t, t, f, t), (t, t, f, f),
(t, f, t, t), (t, f, t, f), (t, f, f, t), (t, f, f, f),
(f, t, t, t), (f, t, t, f), (f, t, f, t), (f, t, f, f),
(f, f, t, t), (f, f, t, f), (f, f, f, t), (f, f, f, f)}.

The above corresponds to the systems of Lukasiewicz and Carnap as follows:

P = { Vpq Apq Bpq Ipq
Cpq Hpq Epq Kpq
Dpq Jpq Gpq Lpq
Fpq Mpq Xpq Opq }

P = { cC1 cC2 cC3 cC4
cC5 cC6 cC7 cC8
cC9 cC10 cC11 cC12
cC13 cC14 cC15 cC16 }

Only a few operators appear in the <u>Principia Mathematica</u>:

$$P = \left\{ \begin{matrix} - & p \vee q & - & - \\ p \supset q & - & p \equiv q & p \,.\, q \\ p / q & - & - & - \\ - & - & - & - \end{matrix} \right\}$$

Other logicians have completed the scheme as the following:

$$P = \left\{ \begin{matrix} p \,\mathrm{T}\, q & p \vee q & p \subset q & p \\ p \supset q & q & p \equiv q & p \,.\, q \\ p / q & p \,\underline{\vee}\, q & -q & p \not\supset q \\ -p & p \not\subset q & p \swarrow q & p \,\mathrm{C}\, q \end{matrix} \right\}$$

6. A Notation for Dyadic Operators

Draw a Venn's Diagram in the form of two ellipses:

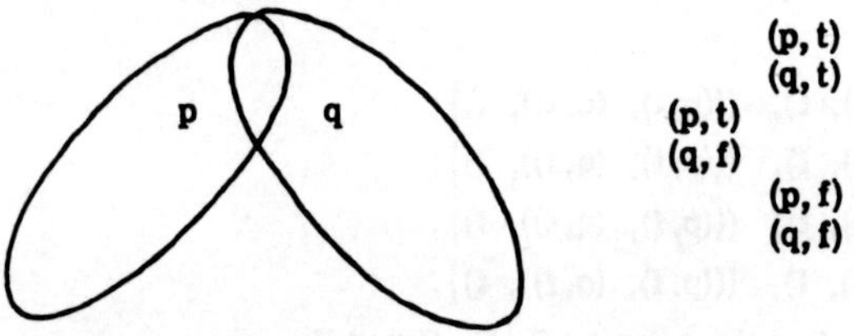

The matrix may be re-written as the following:

$$P = \begin{matrix} \begin{smallmatrix} & t & \\ t & & t \\ & t & \end{smallmatrix} & \begin{smallmatrix} & t & \\ t & & t \\ & f & \end{smallmatrix} & \begin{smallmatrix} & t & \\ t & & f \\ & t & \end{smallmatrix} & \begin{smallmatrix} & t & \\ t & & f \\ & f & \end{smallmatrix} \\ \begin{smallmatrix} & t & \\ f & & t \\ & t & \end{smallmatrix} & \begin{smallmatrix} & t & \\ f & & t \\ & f & \end{smallmatrix} & \begin{smallmatrix} & t & \\ f & & f \\ & t & \end{smallmatrix} & \begin{smallmatrix} & t & \\ f & & f \\ & f & \end{smallmatrix} \\ \begin{smallmatrix} & f & \\ t & & t \\ & t & \end{smallmatrix} & \begin{smallmatrix} & f & \\ t & & t \\ & f & \end{smallmatrix} & \begin{smallmatrix} & f & \\ t & & f \\ & t & \end{smallmatrix} & \begin{smallmatrix} & f & \\ t & & f \\ & f & \end{smallmatrix} \\ \begin{smallmatrix} & f & \\ f & & t \\ & t & \end{smallmatrix} & \begin{smallmatrix} & f & \\ f & & t \\ & f & \end{smallmatrix} & \begin{smallmatrix} & f & \\ f & & f \\ & t & \end{smallmatrix} & \begin{smallmatrix} & f & \\ f & & f \\ & f & \end{smallmatrix} \end{matrix}$$

Represent the operators by small circles, within which the presence or absence of a 'spoke' denotes respectively 't' or 'f':

P =

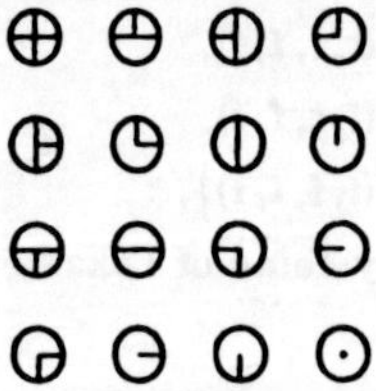

Let us classify the operators according to their characteristics:

NAME	NUMBER	CLASS SYMBOLS	INDIVIDUAL SYMBOLS
Symmetric operators	8		
Non-symmetric operators	8		
Even operators	8		
Odd operators	8		
Odd and symmetric	4		
Even and symmetric	4		
Odd and non-symmetric	4		
Even and non-symmetric	4		
Traverse operators	2		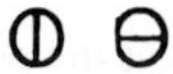
Non-traverse operators	14		All operators other than 
Limiting operators	2		
Non-limiting operators	14		All operators other than 
Negative operators	2		

Complementary operators. The following pairs are mutually complementary:

The above classification is based on the number and position of 'spokes'. The operators are called 'even', 'odd', 'limiting' and 'non-limiting' according to the number of spokes; they are called 'symmetric', 'non-symmetric', 'traverse' and 'non-traverse' according to the position of spokes. Two operators are 'complementary' when the total number of spokes is four, which is the maximum number possible.

The following is a comparison between the new notation and the old:

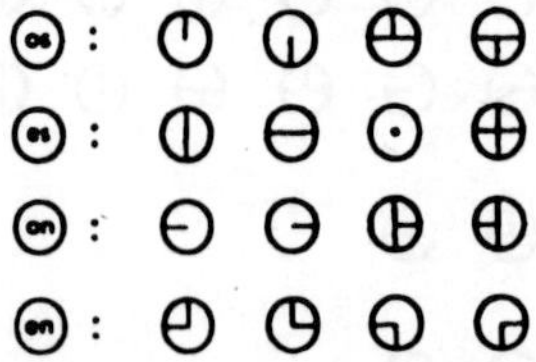

.	↓	V	/
≡	$\underline{v}$	C	T
⊅	⊄	⊃	⊂
p	q	-q	-p

The  group includes conjunction, bi-negation, inclusive disjunction and Sheffer stroke; the  group includes equivalence, exclusive disjunction, contradiction and tautology; the  group includes implication, reverse implication and their negation; the  group includes two components and their negation. In the last group, one of the two variables vanishes from the scene; a dyadic operation turns out to be monadic.

Logicians have defined these operators in terms of primitive operators in various ways:

a. One dyadic operator: conjunction '.', or disjunction 'V'.
One monadic operator: negation '-'.
Parentheses: '()'.

b. One dyadic operator: Sheffer stroke '/', or bi-negation '↓'.
Parentheses: '()'.

It seems that Sheffer stroke and bi-negation are more 'primitive' than other operators, because the monadic operator can be dispensed with. Russell has mentioned: "It should be stated that a new and very powerful method in mathematical logic has been invented by Dr. H. M. Sheffer. This method, however, would demand a complete re-writing of Principia Mathematica". (Principia Mathematica, 2nd ed. (1927) xv).

This is not quite the case. There are actually two monadic operators: assertion and negation, usually symbolized by the absence and presence of the sign '-'. The absence of a sign for assertion is merely for the sake of convenience in notation. However, because of such a notational matter, assertion has long been discarded as an operation altogether. Therefore, the absence of a negation sign actually means the presence of an implied assertion sign.

As a matter of fact, all the sixteen operators can be expressed in terms of eight 'odd operators' $\odot$ in two different patterns as follows:

$$p \ \textcircled{\scriptsize ,} \ q = \pm(\pm p \odot \pm q) \ \textcircled{\scriptsize ∞} \ \pm(\pm p \odot \pm q)$$

$$p \ \textcircled{\scriptsize i} \ q = \pm(\pm p \odot \pm q)$$

Here p and q can be any proposition, including tautology and contradiction, i.e. $(p = \pm T)$; p and q can either be distinct $(p \neq q)$ or identical $(p = q)$. The sign + means assertion and - means negation; they are completely equal in position in this topic. Sheffer stroke and bi-negation are two of the eight odd operators.

It is true that the two operators Sheffer stroke and bi-negation possess the feature of being able to remove the negation sign, thus a formula can be made purely assertive by the following process:

$$-p \equiv p \,/\, p \qquad \text{or} \qquad -p \equiv p \swarrow p.$$

However, the cost is extremely high. First, by eliminating one single negation sign, the formula has to be doubled in length. If the original formula is one inch long, the elimination of four or five negation signs would make it one foot long. Secondly, the new formula obtained would be beyond comprehension, because it is too remote from ordinary semantics. The practical application of this system is like reading binary digits in daily life. The few examples given by Russell are already enough to demonstrate this point.

The two forms given above are only patterns of the formulae but not the formulae themselves. There are altogether 16 x 8 = 128 such formulae, which should be formulated individually. Since it is easy to do so, they are omitted in this paper. One set of such formulae is given in Rudolf Carnap's <u>Formalization of Logic</u>, 1961. p. 82.

The notation of Peano-Russell and their followers has been adopted widely by logicians for a long time; consequently any new invention would seem to be a foreign language. Perhaps this is the reason why J. Łukasiewicz, the inventor of a new notation, sometimes applied the old notation in his own papers. For the same reason, the notation suggested above would be avoided as much as possible in this paper.

However, there are quite a few merits in the new notation apart from its being systematic. First, the properties of the operators can be directly shown in the shape of the symbols; this point has been clearly demonstrated in the classification on page lv. Secondly, the new notation is easier to be remembered than any arbitrary symbols. In the following examples, which are most frequently used, there is a close association between the shape and meaning of the symbols.

◴	either p or q or both	(inclusive disjunction)
⊖	either p or q, but not both	(exclusive disjunction)
◯	both p and q	(conjunction)
◯	neither p nor q	(bi-negation)
⦶	either 'both p and q' or 'neither p nor q'	(equivalence)
◷	an arrow pointing to the right	(implication)

7. The Meaning of a 'Truth Table'

The truth functions in propositional logic are usually defined by 'truth tables'. The derivation of operators in terms of sets is just a generalization of such tables. Both ways obviously convey the information about the assertion or negation of the four factors (p. q), (p. ~q), (~p. q) and (~p. ~q). But how the information of four individual factors is aggregated to form a single operator is not explicitly shown in a truth table.

For instance, the operator ⊃ is expressed in the form of sets as:

(((p, t), (q, t)), t), (((p, t), (q, f)), f), (((p, f), (q, t)), t), (((p, f), (q, f)), t));

or, in the form of truth table:

p	q	p ⊃ q
t	t	t
t	f	f
f	t	t
f	f	t

Does it mean that the information is aggregated together by means of a conjunction like the following:

(p ⊃ q) ≡ (p. q) . ~(p. ~q) . (~p. q) . (~p. ~q) ?

A simple test would tell that the above formula is wrong, but the following three ways are correct:

$$(p \supset q) \equiv (p.q) \vee (\sim p.q) \vee (\sim p.\sim q);$$

$$(p \supset q) \equiv \sim(p.\sim q);$$

$$(p \supset q) \equiv \sim(p.\sim q) \;.\; ((p.q) \vee (\sim p.q) \vee (\sim p.\sim q)).$$

The above shows that the information of all four factors is not necessary; either the negation of one or assertion of three would be enough to give an unambiguous information. The remaining fifteen operators may be expressed in a similar manner. First, let us classify the operators according to the number of t's and f's as following:

four-t, zero-f, or (4t) :	one operator,
three-t, one-f, or (3t) :	four operators,
two-t, two-f, or (2t) :	six operators,
one-t, three-f, or (1t) :	four operators,
zero-t, four-f, or (0t) :	one operator.

(4t) is equivalent to the disjunction of the assertion of all four factors.

(3t) is equivalent to the disjunction of the assertion of three factors,
or to the negation of one factor,
or to the conjunction of the above two.

(2t) is equivalent to the disjunction of assertion of two factors,
or to the conjunction of negation of two factors,
or to the conjunction of above two.

(1t) is equivalent to the assertion of one factor,
or to the conjunction of negation of three factors,
or to the conjunction of the above two.

(0t) is equivalent to the conjunction of the negation of all four factors.

The above statement may be symbolically expressed as the following, where '1' means 'true' and '0' means 'false':

	1st way	2nd way	3rd way
(4t)	(1 v 1 v 1 v 1)		
(3t)	(1 v 1 v 1)	(0)	(1 v 1 v 1).(0)
(2t)	(1 v 1)	(0 . 0)	(1 v 1).(0 . 0)
(1t)	(1)	(0 . 0 . 0)	(1).(0 . 0 . 0)
(0t)		(0 . 0 . 0 . 0)	

All the sixteen operators may be listed as follows:

1st way	2nd way	3rd way
(1 1 1 1)		(1 1 1 1)
(1 1 1)	(0)	(1 1 1 0)
(1 1 1)	(0)	(1 1 0 1)
(1 1)	(0 0)	(1 1 0 0)
(1 1 1)	(0)	(1 0 1 1)
(1 1)	(0 0)	(1 0 1 0)
(1 1)	(0 0)	(1 0 0 1)
(1)	(0 0 0)	(1 0 0 0)
(1 1 1)	(0)	(0 1 1 1)
(1 1)	(0 0)	(0 1 1 0)
(1 1)	(0 0)	(0 1 0 1)
(1)	(0 0 0)	(0 1 0 0)
(1 1)	(0 0)	(0 0 1 1)
(1)	(0 0 0)	(0 0 1 0)
(1)	(0 0 0)	(0 0 0 1)
	(0 0 0 0)	(0 0 0 0)

8. Two Ways of Interpretation in Class Logic

I. Molecular interpretation

A = classes

a_1 = class a

a_2 = class b

U = class identity

u_1 = 'being the class itself', e.g. 'a'

u_2 = 'being the complementary class of', e.g. '$\bar{a}$'

V = existence

v_1 = 'being non-empty', e.g. '$a \neq 0$'

v_2 = 'being empty', e.g. '$a = 0$'

$(a \not\subset b).(a \not\subset \bar{b})$ $(\bar{a} \not\subset b).(\bar{a} \not\subset \bar{b})$	$(\bar{a} \subset b)$	$(\bar{a} \subset \bar{b})$	$(a=U)$
$(a \subset b)$	$(b=U)$	$(a=b)$	$(a=b=U)$
$(a \subset \bar{b})$	$(a \subset \bar{b}).(\bar{a} \subset b)$	$(b=0)$	$(a \not\subset b)$
$(a=0)$	$(\bar{a} \not\subset \bar{b})$	$(a=b=0)$	$(a=b=\bar{a}=\bar{b}=0)$

The following primary operators have been used in the list:

'$\subset$'	=	'to be included in'	$(a\bar{b}=0)$
'$\not\subset$'	=	'not to be included in'	$(a\bar{b}\neq 0)$
'='	=	'to be equivalent to'	$(a\bar{b}=0).(\bar{a}b=0)$
'.'	=	conjunction in propositional logic	

II. Atomic Interpretation

A = classes

a_1 = class a

a_2 = class b

U = class identity

u_1 = 'being the class itself'

u_2 = 'being the complementary class of'

V = relevance

v_1 = 'being covered in the argument'

v_2 = 'not being covered in the argument'

U	$(a+b)$	$(a+\bar{b})$	a
$(\bar{a}+b)$	b	$(axb) + (\bar{a}x\bar{b})$	(axb)
$(\bar{a}+\bar{b})$	$(ax\bar{b}) + (\bar{a}xb)$	$\bar{b}$	$(ax\bar{b})$
$\bar{a}$	$(\bar{a}xb)$	$(\bar{a}x\bar{b})$	$\bar{U}$

In the above list, 'U' means the universe and '$\breve{U}$' means the empty universe. The following primary operators have been applied:

'+' = 'the sum of two classes';

'x' = 'the product of two classes'.

The two ways of interpretation are also possible in propositional logic. It may be specified that when the operators are expressed in terms of the four odd non-symmetric operators ' $\textcircled{on}$ '; including material implication ' $\supset$ ', the interpretation is 'molecular'; when they are expressed in terms of the four odd symmetric operators ' $\textcircled{os}$ ', including conjunction '.' and disjunction 'v', the interpretation is 'atomic'. The distinction between the two interpretations is not quite obvious, because the results of aggregation in both cases are propositions. The distinction becomes obvious in branches other than propositional logic, such as the logic of classes and the logic of relations, in which the aggregation according to the molecular interpretation yields propositions, while that according to the atomic interpretation does not.

In the establishment of truth table in propositional logic, fourteen operators out of the sixteen can be expressed in three different ways, as mentioned in p. lix. From this the following relationship can be established:

1. $-(-p.-q) \equiv ((p.q) \vee (p.-q) \vee (-p.q))$
2. $(-(-p.q).-(-p.-q)) \equiv ((p.q) \vee (p.-q))$
3. $(-(p.-q).-(-p.q).-(-p.-q)) \equiv (p.q)$

There are altogether four similar formulae in Group 1, six in Group 2, and four in Group 3. They show that the information of one part of the four factors can uniquely determine that information of the rest.

Such relationship does not apply to class logic according to molecular interpretation; the fact that certain sub-classes are empty does not imply that the remaining classes should be non-empty, and <u>vice versa.</u> Only for those who assume a non-empty universe, the fact that three sub-classes are empty implies that the remaining sub-class is non-empty, as mentioned by J. Venn. (<u>Symbolic Logic,</u> pp. 142-9). For instance, $(ab=0).(a\bar{b}=0).(\bar{a}b=0) \supset (\bar{a}\bar{b} \neq 0)$; the reverse is, of course, untrue.

The relationship does apply to class logic according to atomic interpretation, but it is too obvious and becomes superfluous. What is relevant is equivalent to what is mentioned; it would be absurd to say that among what is not mentioned, a part is relevant and a part is not.

In view of the above, the sixteen varieties of operators may be applicable to propositional logic, but it may be too 'rigid' for class logic. One way of solving the problem is to choose the 'most relevant sub-classes' for specific purposes. For instance, when 'syllogism' is concerned, the most relevant sub-classes are (ab) and ($a\bar{b}$). Therefore the number of operators can be reduced to four only: (11--), (10--), (01--) and (00--). The two less relevant classes ($\bar{a}b$) and ($\bar{a}\bar{b}$) are left 'unspecified'.

The choices of relevant sub-classes made by ancient Greek and Indian logicians differ from one another. While Aristotle was troubled by the ambiguty of his operators A, E, I and O on account of the uncertainty of his choice of relevant sub-classes, the Indians had made the most reasonable and convenient choice, which is precisely the same as the scheme mentioned above.

9. Two Ways of Interpretation in the Logic or Relations

I. Molecular interpretation

A = relations

a_1 = relation R

a_2 = relation S

U = identity

u_1 = 'being the relation itself', e.g. R

u_2 = 'being the complementary relation of', e.g. $\dot{-}$ R

V = existence

v_1 = 'being non-empty', e.g. $\exists!$ R

v_2 = 'being empty', e.g. $\not\exists!$ R

II. Atomic interpretation

A and U are the same as above.

V = relevance

v_1 = 'being covered in the argument'

v_2 = 'not being covered in the argument'

In the logic of relations, the following arguments and primary operators are introduced:

		definitions	analogous to class logic
Relation	R	$\hat{x}\hat{y}(xRy)$	a
Complementary relation	$\dot{-}R$	$\hat{x}\hat{y}(-xRy)$	$\bar{a}$
Universal relation	$\dot{V}$	$\hat{x}\hat{y}((x=x).(y=y))$	U
Contradictory relation	$\dot{\Lambda}$	$\hat{x}\hat{y}((x\neq x).(y\neq y))$	$\bar{U}$
Sum of relations	$R \dot{\cup} S$	$\hat{x}\hat{y}(xRy \vee xSy)$	$a+b$
Product of relations	$R \dot{\cap} S$	$\hat{x}\hat{y}(xRy . xSy)$	$a \times b$
Relation being non-empty	$\exists ! R$	$(Exy)xRy$	$a\neq 0$
Relation being empty	$\sim\exists ! R$	$\sim(Exy)xRy$	$a=0$
Inclusion	$R \dot{\subset} S$	$(xy)(xRy \supset xSy)$	$a \subset b$
Non-inclusion	$R \not\subset S$	$(xy)(xRy \not\supset xSy)$	$a \not\subset b$
Equivalence	$R \doteq S$	$(xy)(xRy \equiv xSy)$	$a=b$

The two lists are precisely analogous to those in class logic, they are therefore omitted in this paper.

10. The Mixed Interpretation

For practical purposes, an operator is interpreted in one way only, depending on whether the atomic or the molecular interpretation is the simpler. Let us call those operators whose atomic interpretation is simpler 'atomic operators', and call those whose molecular interpretation is simpler 'molecular operators'. The atomic operators are the eight even operators minus one of them; the molecular operators are the eight odd operators plus one even operator. Therefore there are seven atomic and nine molecular operators.

Symbols	Diagram
Propositional logic T = tautology C = contradiction ~ = negation . = conjunction V = disjunction	T (pVq) (p. q) (~pV~q) (p. ~q)V(~p. q) (~p. ~q) C
~ = negation ≡ = equivalence ⊃ = implication ⊅ = non-implication	(~p ⊃ ~q) p (p ⊃ q) q (p ≡ q) ~q (p ⊅ q) ~p (~p ⊅ ~q)
The logic of classes U = the universe $\bar{U}$ = the empty universe ‾ = complementation x = product + = sum	U (a+b) (axb) $(\bar{a}+\bar{b})$ $(a\text{x}\bar{b})+(\bar{a}\text{x}b)$ $(\bar{a}\text{x}\bar{b})$ $\bar{U}$
‾ = complementation = = equivalence ⊂ = inclusion ⊄ = non-inclusion	$(\bar{a} \subset \bar{b})$ a (a ⊂ b) b (a=b) $\bar{b}$ (a ⊄ b) $\bar{a}$ $(\bar{a} \not\subset \bar{b})$
The logic of relations $\dot{V}$ = Universal relation $\dot{\Lambda}$ = Contradictory relation $\dot{-}$ = complementation $\dot{\cap}$ = product $\dot{\cup}$ = sum	$\dot{V}$ $(R \dot{\cup} S)$ $(R \dot{\cap} S)$ $(\dot{-}R \dot{\cup} \dot{-}S)$ $(R \dot{\cap} \dot{-}S) \dot{\cup} (\dot{-}R \dot{\cap} S)$ $(\dot{-}R \dot{\cap} \dot{-}S)$ $\dot{\Lambda}$
$\dot{-}$ = complementation $\dot{\subset}$ = inclusion $\dot{\not\subset}$ = non-inclusion $\dot{=}$ = equivalence	$(\dot{-}R \dot{\subset} \dot{-}S)$ R $(R \dot{\subset} S)$ S $(R \dot{=} S)$ $\dot{-}S$ $(R \dot{\not\subset} S)$ $\dot{-}R$ $(\dot{-}R \dot{\not\subset} \dot{-}S)$

11. Analogous theorems

Analogy exists not only in operators but also in theorems. The following examples include deMorgan's law and the law of syllogism:

a. Atomic interpretation:

propositional logic	$-(p \vee q) \equiv (-p \;.\; -q)$
the logic of classes	$\overline{a + b} = \bar{a} \times \bar{b}$
the logic of relations	$\dot{-}(R \dot{\cup} S) \doteq \dot{-}R \dot{\cap} \dot{-}S$
quantificational logic	$-(Ex)(fx \vee gx) \equiv -(Ex)fx \;.\; -(Ex)gx$

b. Molecular interpretation:

propositional logic	$(p \supset q) \;.\; (q \supset r) \supset (p \supset r)$
the logic of classes	$(a \subset b) \;.\; (b \subset c) \supset (a \subset c)$
the logic of relations	$(R \dot{\subset} S) \;.\; (S \dot{\subset} T) \supset (R \dot{\subset} T)$
quantificational logic	$(x)(fx \supset gx) \;.\; (x)(gx \supset hx) \supset (x)(fx \supset hx)$

c. Mixed interpretation:

propositional logic	$(p \supset q) \equiv -(p \;.\; -q)$
the logic of classes	$(a \subset b) \equiv (a\bar{b} = 0)$
the logic of relations	$(R \dot{\subset} S) \equiv \nexists! \,(R \dot{\cap} \dot{-}S)$
quantificational logic	$(x)(fx \supset gx) \equiv -(Ex)(fx. -gx)$

12. The Group of Operators

The set of operators in propositional logic forms an abelian group with respect to the binary operation ⓘ, i.e. conjunction. The identity element is ⊙, i.e. contradiction. The inverse elements are the complementary operators mentioned in § 6. The characteristic property of this group is that the binary operation * of this group is itself one of the elements of the group, i.e. ⓘ.

The reason why the set can form an abelian group is as follows:

Consider the truth table of the conjunction

(p ① q) ⓘ (p ② q) ⓘ (p ③ q), where ①, ②, and ③ are any operators of the sixteen.

When all three factors are 't', the conjunction will be 't', irrespective of the association and sequence of the operation.

When at least one factor is 'f', the conjunction will always be 'f', irrespective of the association and sequence of the operation. Therefore the set is both associative and commutative with respect to the operation ⓘ.

CONCLUSION

By applying set theory we may establish a unified-field theory for several different systems of logic.[1] In the first stage of the theory, the multitude of symbols for operators: ⊂ , ⊃ , ≡ , +, x, &, ., v, ∧, /, ∪, ∩ , etc. etc., which appear disorderly in books of logic, can be arrayed, and they can form abelian groups. This primitive and trivial result happens to be originated from a study of an ancient system of logic, i.e. the Hetucakra of Dignāga and Uddyotakara.

In the rapid development of logic in our time, certainly we cannot expect too much from the study of an ancient system. Our modest result, which is not altogether disappointing, shows that to the gigantic system of modern logic, we still have something to add, from an archaic system which is even less advanced than the Aristotelian.

1. It is wrong, however, to think that a one-to-one correspondence of theorems in different systems, or something close to it, could be established. Such a correspondence is not possible because in many cases corresponding to existing theorems in one system, there is no counterpart in another.

PREFACE

Since last century Indian logic has been introduced to the west; a number of monumental works were written between 1920 and 1930 by S.C. Vidyabhusana, Gaṅgānātha Jhā, Th. Stcherbatsky, H.N. Randle, G. Tucci, A.B. Keith, etc.

There was a huge literature on Indian logic written by Chinese, Koreans and Japanese during the T'ang Dynasty. The surviving works, although they are merely a small fraction of the original collection, are still very voluminous. Not very much about the Chinese interpretation of Indian logic has been introduced to the west except a very defective book entitled '*Hindu Logic as Preserved in China and Japan*' by S. Sugiura.[1]

Recently symbolic logic has been applied in interpreting Indian logic. Professor Schayer first formulated the five-membered syllogism. Professors D.H.H. Ingalls, I.M. Bochenski and J.F. Staal used symbols to interpret definitions of '*vyāpti*' of the 'New School' of logic.[2] Attempts have been made to formulate the *Hetucakra* of Dignāga and the dialectic of Nāgārjuna.[3]

This work is primarily an interpretation of Indian logic preserved in China. The material is mainly taken from K'uei Chi's *Great Commentary on the Nyāyapraveśa*. It is not designed to be a comprehensive study of Indian logic in general, nor is it planned to be a complete exposition of K'uei Chi's work in particular. Its scope is confined to formal logic, therefore discussions on epistemological and historical problems, such as the theory of perception, the authorship of the *Nyāyapraveśa*, etc. will not be included. The reason is that these topics have been widely discussed by learned scholars in the last few decades. The author's intentions are to solve problems which have not yet been settled and to interpret theories which have not yet been clearly interpreted, instead of duplicating what other people have already done.

---

1. Sugiura 1.
2. Ingalls 1, Bochenski 3 and 4, Staal 3 to 5.
3. Sueki 1, Nakamura 1 and 2, Robinson 1.

There is a great difference in content between K'uei Chi's Great Commentary and this work. He devoted over one half of his book to the list of fallacies but paid much less attention to the fundamental principles of the Hetucakra and the Trairūpya. As a result his work has been considered for centuries to be a difficult book consisting of completely incomprehensible stuff.

In the present work, on the other hand, much more attention is paid to the fundamental principles but less attention is paid to the list of fallacies, in particular less to the over-elaboration, which does not make much sense either theoretically or practically. Through the new way of treatment, the list of fallacies becomes something simple and easy; it becomes evident even if no explanation is given. Since the over-elaborated part of the list of fallacies is reduced to a set of symbolic formulae and most of his illustrative cases are omitted, over one half of his book is reduced to a very short chapter.

In an examination of the principles of the Hetucakra and the Trairūpya, it is unavoidable that some non-Buddhist works are involved, i.e. without them the discussion of the theories would be incomplete. Therefore the theories of Uddyotakara, who was totally unknown to the early Chinese logicians, should be discussed.

In the course of interpretation I have found some critical remarks about early theories and contemporary interpretations unavoidable. My guiding principle has been to include only such criticisms as seemed necessary for the explanation of important theories concerned.

Besides interpretation of Indian theories, one chapter[1] is devoted to a discussion of possible consequences on western logic after Indian theories have been introduced and absorbed. This chapter is, of course, not an exposition of Indian logic itself.

Regarding symbolic notation, I generally follow that of the Principia Mathematica. One of the exceptions is the use of dots. First, I use '.' as symbol uniquely for conjunction but not for anything concerning association. Secondly, I have reversed Russell's convention and use the symbol '.' as a weaker connective than '⊃', i.e. when I write $p.q \supset r$,

1. 'What Do the Indian Theories of the Hetucakra and the Trairūpya Mean to Us?'

I mean (p . q)⊃r. The symbol '.' here is equivalent to the symbol ' & ' in many logic texts.

By the above alteration I have managed to get rid of the multiple use of either dots or brackets - both of them look very untidy. However, the new convention suits the present paper only and is not applicable in general, because the operations in this paper are very simple ones only.

A part of Aristotelian terminology, such as the names of premises, terms and moods, is used in this paper. However, neither in the five-membered nor in the three-membered syllogism were the major and the minor premises explicitly and separately stated as in the Aristotelian system. The conclusion in the three-membered Indian syllogism was stated in the form of the probandum, i.e. the first member of the syllogism. Therefore, the Aristotelian terminology is borrowed here as a substitute, and not the precise equivalent, for the sake of convenience only.

The Bibliography is in two parts:

Bibliography A. Oriental texts before +1800, arranged in alphabetical order of the titles.

Bibliography B. Books and articles after +1800, arranged in alphabetical order of the authors.

Works on western logic, except a few which particularly discuss Indian Logic, are not included in the Bibliography.

Bibliography B includes both works on the theory of logic and those on the application of logic to philosophy. Bibliography A includes works on the theory of logic only but not its application to Buddhist philosophy, because all these works[1] appear in the Taishō, the Supplementary Tripiṭaka and the Tōhoku Catalogues. It would be pointless to copy a very long list from the catalogues.

I must admit that the Bibliography is defective in various ways owing to the fact that the time for compilation is very short and should be revised later when time permits:

1. The Bibliography is far from being comprehensive, though it was designed to be so.

2. There is overlapping of entries in both Bibliography A and Bibliography B when there is either some European translation or European edition of an original text.

1. On Mādhyamika, Yogācāra, etc.

3. The information of the Bibliography is incomplete and is presented in a higgledy-piggledy manner. It should be rearranged in a systematic way and be presented in a standardized form.

Professor I. M. Bochenski wrote of: "le sentiment que les grands travaux de Stcherbatsky et des autres indianistes devraient être refaits par des logiciens".[1] If the present work, which is much inferior in scholarship and much narrower in scope than the encyclopaedic work of Stcherbatsky, can make any trifling contribution to a desirable result, it is only by serving as a medium between Stcherbatsky and more qualified logicians who may presently undertake a further study of the subject.

In conclusion I wish to acknowledge my debts of gratitude to the scholars who have rendered me help in the preparation of this work. I must first pay my respects to Professor W. Simon, F.B.A. of London University, Dr. A. Waley, C.H., Professor E.G. Pulleyblank of Cambridge University, Professor W. Kneale, F.B.A. of Oxford University and Dr. D. Friedman of London University for their help and encouragement, without which the present work would not have come into existence.

My thanks are also due to the librarians of the Universities of Oxford, Cambridge and London, of British Museum, of Indian Office and of Royal Asiatic Society for enabling me to have access to the rare books and manuscripts in their collections.

Oxford, 1963 R. S. Y. C.

I wish to acknowledge my deep gratitude to Professor A. N. Prior of Manchester University, Professor J. W. de Jong of the University of Leiden, Professor D. Hawkes of Oxford University and Dr. T. J. Smiley of Cambridge University for their kindness in offering valuable opinions on my manuscript. I am greatly indebted to Professor Sir Harold W. Bailey, F. B. A. of Cambridge University and the Editorial Board of Royal Asiatic Society for publishing this work in the distinguished learned society.

Oxford, 1964 R. S. Y. C.

I wish to express my thanks to Mrs. Grace Landers for her kindness in typing the Chinese characters.

Bloomington, 1968 R. S. Y. C.

1. Bochenski 2.

INTRODUCTION

The study of logic in China can roughly be divided into three periods, namely, the native product of the Pre-Ch'in dialectic, the first and the second importation of Indian logic.

It seems that the general opinion of ancient Chinese on logic was mostly unfavourable. The following criticisms on the Pre-Ch'in dialecticians can well illustrate the attitude of early philosophers and historians:

> "Dialecticians, like Ḥuan T'uan and Kung-sun Lung, tried to elaborate human thought and twist human minds. They could defeat men's words but not their minds".[1]
>
> "There were people who would not follow the early kings' ways, rejected convention and righteousness, but would like to indulge in fantastic arguments and to play with words. They were subtle but not realistic; critical but not pragmatic; they had much elaboration but little achievement. They were not good enough to do anything constructive, but they were harmful enough to deceive the ignorant masses, because their views seemed to be reasonable and their words seemed to be plausible".[2]
>
> "The logicians over-elaborated trivial matters in order to make their points irrefutable. Their judgement was merely based on words but contradicted human nature".[3]

In the Pre-Ch'in period, the logicians were opposed by most schools including the Confucianists and Taoists. After the great purge of all schools of thinkers during the Ch'in Dynasty, their enormous literature was lost and the surviving fragments were regarded as a matter of antiquity only.

The first import of Buddhist logic to China was the translation of a few Pre-Dignāgean works on logic. The translation was done by Indian missionaries during the fifth and sixth centuries. It seems that this period involved only introduction of texts so that a few more books were added to the stock-pile of the Chinese canon; because no significant

---

1. Chuang Tzu. SPPY edition. Vol. IV. fasc. 33. p. 22.
2. Hsün Tzu. SPPY edition. Vol. I. fasc. 3. Ch. 6. pp. 8-9.
3. Shih Chi. SPPY edition. Vol. XXIV. fasc. 130. p. 4.

response by the Chinese is known to us. The surviving works are:[1]

The Tarkaśāstra attributed to Vasubandhu, translated by Paramārtha during the Liang Dynasty.[2]

The Upāyahṛdaya attributed to Nāgārjuna, translated by Kekaya (?) during the Late Wei Dynasty.[3]

The Vigrahavyāvartanī by Nāgārjuna, translated by Vimokṣasena and Gautama ruci (?) during the Late Wei Dynasty.[4]

The second import of Buddhist logic brought about a quite different result. Although only a few short fragments were translated into Chinese during this period, the study of logic unexpectedly became a vogue of the day in the T'ang Dynasty in both China and Japan.

In this period Hsüan Tsang (+596-664) translated the Nyāyamukha and the Nyāyapraveśa; I Tsing (+635-713) translated the Pramāṇa-samuccaya, which was lost later. Such a collection seems to be rather poor when it is compared with the Tibetan Canon.

The Nyāyapraveśa was attributed to Śaṁkarasvāmin by Chinese but was attributed to Dignāga by Tibetans. The discussion of its authorship in our century became a controversy for a number of years. The scholars involved in this controversy are in two groups; the school following the Tibetan tradition and that following the Chinese tradition. Each of them criticized the other one for being inconclusive.[5]

It seems that certain scholars, particularly those belonging to the Tibetan school, did not care to touch the Chinese source materials. For instance, a very distinguished scholar said, "At least at the time of translation (i.e. re-translation from Chinese into Tibetan) Śaṁkarasvāmin as the author of the work was unknown not only in Tibet but also in China".

It is always dangerous to draw a conclusion like "Such-and-such is unknown to so-and-so", because it is difficult to prove but easy to refute. Incidently Śaṁkarasvāmin as the author was mentioned only shortly

---

1. Tucci 6.
2. Taishō 1633.
3. Taishō 1632.
4. Taishō 1631.
5. Vidhybhusana 21, Keith 4, V. Bhattacharya 1, Tucci 3, Tubianski 1, Mironov 1 and 2, Dhruva 1, etc., etc.

after the translation of this book from Sanskrit into Chinese, by K'uei Chi (+632-682) in his Great Commentary.

In this work I shall not continue this controversy but say only that the Nyāyapraveśa, as its title stands for, is an elementary textbook on logic. It does not resemble the great and original papers written by Dignāga.

Śaṁkarasvāmin's name is unfamiliar and his dates are not known. In view of the fact that some commentaries were written by non-Buddhists[1] one can say that this book must have been once very popular in India.

Although Hsüan Tsang was himself an extraordinary debater, it seems that he was not very keen in introducing the Indian tradition of debate to China, as happened later in Tibet. His intention can be revealed through observation of the following facts:

After his return to China, he worked with great industry and perseverance in the translation of Buddhist texts. He translated seventy-four books of 1,335 fasciculi, including the encyclopaedic works of the six hundred fasc. of the Mahāprajñāpāramitā, the two hundred fasc. of the Mahāvibhāṣā and the one hundred fasc. of the Yogācārabhūmi. The two short fragments on logic are merely one tenth of one per cent of his work of translation. Many important works by Dignāga were excluded, let alone the works of others.

In his translated works, we can find here and there controversies between Buddhists and non-Buddhists, between the Mahāyāna and the Hīnayāna, between schools within the Sarvāstivāda, but rarely between the Mādhyamika and Yogācāra within the Mahāyāna.

In his Biography[3] we can see that he was not quite co-operative to Nadī, a Mādhyamika scholar who carried 1,500 Buddhist texts from India to China. It is most likely that among the 1,500 texts there were some works like those of Candrakīrti, who was a most radical and uncompromising critic.

From the above it seems that he did not like to widen the gap between the two main streams of thought within the Mahāyāna. In his Biography

---

1. vṛtti by Haribhadra, pañjikā by Pārśvadevagaṇi, and ṭippana by Śrīcandra.
2. Dhruva 1.
3. Taishō 2060, pp. 458-9.

it was recorded that he had done something positive: he wrote Hui Tsung Lun (會宗論 Reconciliation of Sectarian Differences) in Sanskrit in India.

In Hsüan Tsang's time logic in India was mainly a tool for organised public debates. In China there was no such a tradition and public disputation was rare. As a result the application of logic in China was even more modest than that in India. It was not applied as a tool for actual debate, but as a key to the understanding of certain Indian texts in which debates were involved. In other words, certain Indian texts would be completely incomprehensible to one if one had not some knowledge of logic.

It was recorded in the Sung Kao Seng Chuan[1] that Hsüan Tsang gave personal tutorials to K'uei Chi on the Vijñaptimātratāsiddhi. The teaching was 'pirated' by a bright but cunning monk Yüan Ts'e, who bribed Hsüan Tsang's porter and hid himself in order to listen in to the teaching. Then he returned to his own temple to give a lecture on his newly acquired knowledge to his own audience.

Having discovered his mischief, Hsüan Tsang did not stop him coming, but taught K'uei Chi logic in strict secrecy. At last K'uei Chi received a most thorough teaching whereas Yüan Ts'ê remained an amateur.

The introduction of the two short texts met with unusual enthusiasm. It was recorded that several hundred commentaries on the Nyāyapraveśa were written by Chinese, Koreans and Japanese. Most of them were lost. But the surviving works collected in the Taishō and the Supplementary Tripiṭakas, the unpublished manuscripts and rare editions in private collections in Japan are still very voluminous. Long lists of titles can be found in the Dictionary of Buddhist Books[2] and Hotan's Commentary on the Nyāyapraveśa.[3]

Among these commentaries, K'uei Chi's, known as the 'Great Commentary', is the most important document on logic in Chinese. Many later works are sub-commentaries on the Great Commentary. The present work is mainly based on material from it.

---

1. Taishō 2061, pp. 725-7.
2. 佛書解說大辭典 Tokyo, 1934, pp. 182-206.
3. [illegible][illegible]因明論疏瑞源記 Shanghai, 1928.

According to his Biography[1] K'uei Chi was born in an aristocratic family, entered the order when he was seventeen, and joined the work on translation when he was twenty-five. He wrote one hundred commentaries on Indian texts and succeeded Hsüan Tsang as the leader of the Yogācāra School in China.

The enthusiasm for logic within the Buddhist order had also extended to a brilliant layman named Lü Ts'ai (+600-665), who was one of the Imperial Physicians. He was well versed in several sciences and arts, and was confident that he could understand any science if he wanted to.

Having been shown three commentaries on logic and been challenged by Ch'i Hsüan, an old friend of his, he studied the texts and wrote a book entitled Explanation and Diagrams on Logical Demonstration and Refutation, in which he raised forty points criticizing the three commentaries.[2]

His book brought about a serious controversy; finally he and Hsüan Tsang had a face-to-face confrontation, in which he was defeated and made his apology. The entire story was told in detail in Dr. A. Waley's The Real Tripitaka.[3]

It is most unfortunate that his book is lost, we cannot tell what his diagrams were like; possibly they were something like Euler's. About this controversy only his Preface and a few letters written by his friend and opponent survive. Unfortunately all these documents were written in an ornamental style which conveys not much sense.

His objection on terminology will be discussed in a later chapter.

Since logic was used in China merely for understanding Indian texts involving debates and not for practising actual debate in China, its application was very much limited. Indian original texts on logic translated into Chinese are extremely short, therefore its source material was also very much limited.

Therefore the prosperity of logic study was merely a vogue of the day because of curiosity; such a vogue can hardly last. Moreover, the science of logic itself was not favoured by the Chinese public, at least

---

1. Taishō 2061, pp. 725-6.
2. Taishō 2053, pp. 262-6; Hou, 1, Vol. 4a, pp. 108-40.
3. Waley 1, pp. 107-111.

not by the orthodox school of Confucianists, from a very early date. After the Buddhists were ruthlessly persecuted in the middle of the ninth century, the study of logic ceased and the entire literature was lost in China, including the most important work, the Great Commentary. All the works available today are preserved in Japan.

There were several commentaries on logic written during the Ming Dynasty; since all authoritative works had been lost at that time, the Ming commentaries have been considered as amateurish.

In our century the study of logic started again on a very limited scale in China. A number of commentaries were brough back from Japan; Pramaṇasamuccaya was translated for the second time from the Tibetan version by Lü Ch'eng[1]; a few original and critical works were written.[2]

Owing to lack of chronological record in India, the dates of the logicians are not certain. Estimates by various cholars often differ by as much as a century or even more. Since this work is not concerned very much with the historical aspect, it will perhaps be sufficient if the important persons involved in the study are dated roughly as follows:

Dignāga	+5 c.		
Śaṁkarasvāmin	+5-7 c.	Hsuan Tsang	+596-664
Dharmakīrti	+7 c.	K'uei Chi	+632-682
Uddyotakara	+7 c.		
Vācaspati Miśra	+10 c.		

1. Lü, 4.
2. Ch'en 1 and 2, Lü 1 and 2.

ABBREVIATIONS

BL-1	Th. Stcherbatsky: Buddhist Logic Vol. I, Leningrad, 1932.
BL-2	Th. Stcherbatsky: Buddhist Logic Vol. II, Leningrad, 1930.
FD	H. N. Randle: Fragments from Dignāga, London, 1926.
HIL	S. C. Vidyabhusana: A History of Indian Logic, Calcutta, 1921.
IL	H. N. Randle: Indian Logic in the Early Schools, London, 1930.
NB	The Nyāyabindu, ed. by P. Peterson. Bibliotheca Indica, Calcutta, 1889.
NBT	The Nyāyabinduṭīkā, Sanskrit edition as above.
NM	The Nyāyamukha, Chinese translation. Taishō Tripiṭaka No. 1628.
NPD	The Nyāyapraveśa, ed. by A. B. Dhruva, Gaekwad's Oriental Series, Baroda, 1930.
NPGC	K'uei-chi's Great Commentary on the Nyāyapraveśa. Taishō Tripiṭaka, No. 1840.
NPH	The Nyāyapraveśa, Chinese translation by Hsuan-tsang. Taishō Tripiṭaka, No. 1630.
NV	The Nyāyavārttika, ed. by V. P. Dvivedin (Dube), Bibliotheca Indica, 1887.
NVT	The Nyāyavārttikatātparyaṭīkā, ed. by G. S. Tailanga, Vizianagaram Sanskrit Series, Benares, 1898.
SPPY	The Ssu-pu pei-yau Edition of Chinese Classics, Shanghai.
VSC	K'uei-chi's Commentary on the Vijñaptimātratāsiddhi. Taishō Tripiṭaka, No. 1830.

CONTENTS

(For the section numbers, there should be a dot after the first digit on the left-hand side, e.g. 1.1, 1.11, 1.12, etc.; unfortunately the dots do not appear in the galley proof of subsequent pages, and it is too late to add them now.)

1. FUNDAMENTAL THEORIES

11. Dignāga's Hetucakra

111. Original Texts

Dignāga mentioned the hetucakra in both of his works the Pramāṇasamuccaya[1] and the Nyāyamukha.[2] He had also particularly written a short essay on the hetucakra titled the Hetucakradamaru.[3] Among them only the Nyāyamukha is preserved in Chinese and the other two, in Tibetan.

No Sanskrit original of the above texts survives. However, many lines in them were freely cited by Vācaspati miśra in the Nyāyavārttikatātparyaṭīkā; they were collected and interpreted by Prof. H.N. Randle in the Fragments from Diṅnāga.[4]

Pandit Vidyabhusana rendered the Hetucakra into English and included it in his History of Indian Logic,[5] which deviated in several points from its Tibetan version. Since then it has been rendered a number of times, either fully or partially, into European languages.[6]

The Nyāyamukha was rendered into English by Prof. G. Tucci; his text is based on the Chinese version and compared with the Tibetan version of the Pramāṇasamuccya and its vṛtti when there were occasions of correspondence between these two works.[7]

Both the Hetucakra and the Trairūpya were criticized by Uddyotakara in the Nyāyavārttika and then by Vācaspati miśra in the Nyāyavārttika tātparyaṭīkā. The former was rendered into English by Gaṅgānātha Jhā.[8]

The Trairūpya was modified by Dharmakīrti, whose work the Nyāyabindu was rendered by St. Stcherbatsky from Tibetan into English, accompanied by the ṭīkā by Dharmottara.[9]

---

1. Tōhoku No. 4203 and his own vṛtti, Tōhoku No. 4204
2. Taishō No. 1628
3. Tōhoku No. 4209
4. Randle 1
5. Vidyabhusana 21
6. e.g. Chatterji 3, Randle 1, 29-33, Randle 2, 225-229, etc. etc.
7. Tucci 2
8. Jhā 1
9. Stcherbatsky 12

Since Vidyabhusana wrote his History of Indian Logic, both the Hetucakra and the Trairūpya have been discussed in almost all books in European languages concerning Indian logic and in a number of articles. The notable works are Stcherbatsky (12), Randle (1, 2), Tucci (4, 10), Stasiak (1).

Prof. I.M. Bochenski is the first European logician who has included these two topics in the world history of logic. (Bochenski 4).

In recent decades attempts have been made to interpret these two topics by means of symbolic logic.[1] The present work is one of these attempts; it is merely tentative and is not regarded as anything final.

The text of the Hetucakraḍamaru is very brief; it does not occupy much space and I shall quote it in full.

Like many Indian philosophical works, the original was written in verse, although there is nothing poetic about it. It was so written for the sake of memorizing only.

Because of the extreme conciseness in the use of words, without adding a number of supplementary words it can hardly make sense in English, whether in verse or in prose. Therefore I might as well maintain its original form and render it in verse.

THE WHEEL OF REASONS

Homage to Mañjuśrīkumārabhūta.

Homage to the Omniscient One, who is
The destroyer of the snare of ignorance.
I am expounding the determination of
The probans with three-fold characteristics. (1)

Among the three possible cases of 'presence', 'absence' and 'both'
Of the probans in the probandum,
Only the case of its 'presence' is valid,
While its 'absence' is not. (2)

The case of 'both presence and absence' is inconclusive,
It is therefore not valid either.

1. Sueki 1, Nakamura 1, 2

The 'presence', 'absence' and 'both',
Of the probans in similar instances,
Combined with those in dissimilar instances,
There are three combinations in each of three. (3)

The top and the bottom are valid,
The two sides are contradictory.
The four corners are inconclusive through being too broad,
The centre is inconclusive through being too narrow. (4)

Knowable, produced, impermanent, (5)
Produced, audible, effort-made,
Impermanent, effort-made and incorporeal,
Are used to prove the properties of being:
Permanent, impermanent, effort-made,
Permanent, permanent, permanent,
Non-effort-made, impermanent, and permanent. (6)

When two tops or two bottoms meet,
The probans is valid,
When two corresponding sides meet,
It is contradictory. (7)

When corresponding corners meet,
It is inconclusive through being too broad,
When the centres of two crosses meet,
It is inconclusive through being too narrow. (8)

Since there are nine classes of probans,
Accordingly we have nine sets of examples:

Space-pot, pot-space, (9)
Pot-lightning-space,
Space-pot, (space-pot), space-pot-lightning,
Lightning-space-pot,
Pot-lightning-space,
Space-atom-action-pot. (10)

The above concerns the 'determined probans' only;
As regards the 'doubtful' ones,
There are also nine combinations of
'Presence', 'absence' and 'both'. (11)

The Treatise on the Wheel of Reasons by Ācārya Dignāga.[1]

---

1. Sde-dge Edition, Ce. fol. 93 (Tōhoku 4209)
Snarthan Edition, Ce. fol. 193-4 (IHQ IX, 1933, pp. 266-72)
Co-ne Edition, Ce. fol. 92.
English translation by D. Chatterji. IHQ IX, 1933. pp. 511-4.

The text is followed by a diagram:

I	II	III
1. Sound is permanent	1. Sound is impermanent	1. Sound is produced by effort
2. It is knowable	2. It is produced	2. It is impermanent
3. space	3. pot	3. pot
4. pot	4. space	4. lightning, space
5. presence in sapakṣa	5. presence in sapakṣa	5. presence in sapakṣa
6. presence in vipakṣa	6. absence in vipakṣa	6. both presence and absence in vipakṣa
7. inconclusive too broad	7. valid	7. inconclusive too broad

IV	V	VI
1. Sound is permanent	1. Sound is permanent	1. Sound is permanent
2. It is produced	2. It is audible	2. It is produced by effort
3. space	3. space	3. space
4. pot	4. pot	4. pot, lightning
5. absence in sapakṣa	5. absence in sapakṣa	5. absence in sapakṣa
6. presence in vipakṣa	6. absence in vipakṣa	6. both presence and absence in vipakṣa
7. contradictory	7. inconclusive too narrow	7. contradictory

VII	VIII	IX
1. Sound is not produced by effort	1. Sound is impermanent	1. Sound is permanent
2. It is impermanent	2. It is produced by effort	2. It is incorporeal
3. lighting, space	3. pot, lightning	3. atom, space
4. pot	4. space	4. action, pot
5. both presence and absence in sapakṣa	5. both presence and absence in sapakṣa	5. both presence and absence in sapakṣa
6. presence in vipakṣa	6. absence in vipakṣa	6. both presence and absence in vipakṣa
7. inconclusive too broad	7. valid	7. inconclusive too broad

The numerals are added for the sake of clarity, and are not included in the original text.

The lines of the verse in the Tibetan canon are wrongly paragraphed; perhaps the printers or even editors considered them not more comprehensible than Dhāraṇī. No wonder the Hetucakra was regarded by Stasiak as something 'mysterious' !

Vidyabhusana's translation from the Tibetan version shows some deviation from other versions. He put 'impermanent' for the predicate in the type V instead of 'permanent', and put 'corporeal' for the hetu in type IX instead of 'incorporeal'.[1]

The above deviations actually do not matter very much, what really matters is that he had confused the notion of 'like' and 'unlike' altogether. In fact, the so-called 'similar' and 'dissimilar' instances refer to the likeness to the major term but not to the middle term. As a result his translation is almost incomprehensible.

The numerals which I have put in the diagram denote the following:

1. the probandum
2. the probans
3. similar instances
4. dissimilar instances
5. whether presence or absence in sapakṣa
6. whether presence or absence in vipakṣa
7. validity

Prof. Tucci gave a much clearer picture of the Hetucakra by translating the Commentary on the Nyāyamukha by Shen-t'ai in a review On the Fragments from Dignāga.[2]

112. Explanatory text

The following is extracted from the Commentary on the Nyāyapraveśa by K'uei Chi:[3]

Type I: Presence in similar instances and presence in dissimilar instances. For instance, a Śābdika (Mīmāṁsaka) said: "Sound is permanent,

Because it is knowable,

Like space and unlike a pot".

The property of being knowable is present in both similar and dissimilar instances.

---

1. Vidyabhusana 21. p. 298.
2. Tucci 4. JRAS. 1928. pp. 384-7.
3. NPGC. Taishō 1840. pp. 104c-105a.

Type II: Presence in similar instances and absence in dissimilar instances. For instance, a Vaiśeṣika said:

"Sound is impermanent,
Because it is produced.
Like a pot and unlike space".

The property of being produced is present in similar instances and absent in dissimilar instances.

Type III: Presence in similar instances, both presence and absence in dissimilar instances. For instance, a Vaiśeṣika said:

"Sound is produced by effort,
Because it is impermanent,
Like a pot, and unlike lightning or space".

The property of being impermanent is present in similar instances; it is present in some dissimilar instances such as lightning, and is absent in some other dissimilar instances such as space.

Type IV: Absence in similar instances, presence in dissimilar instances. For instance, a Śābdika said:

"Sound is permanent,
Because it is produced.
Like space, and unlike a pot".

The property of being produced is absent in similar instances and is present in dissimilar instances.

Type V: Absence in similar instances and absence in dissimilar instances. For instance, a Śābdika said:

"Sound is permanent,
Because it is audible,
Like space, and unlike a pot".

The property of being audible is absent in both similar and dissimilar instances.

Type VI: Absence in similar instances, both presence and absence in dissimilar instances. For instance, a Śābdika said:

"Sound is permanent,
Because it is produced by effort,
Like space, and unlike lightning or a pot".

The property of being produced by effort is absent in similar instances; it is present in some dissimilar instances such as a pot and is absent in some dissimilar instances such as lightning.

Type VIII: Both presence and absence in similar instances, and presence in dissimilar instances. For instance, a Śābdika said:

"Sound is not produced by effort,

Because it is permanent,

Like lightning or space, unlike a pot".

The property of being impermanent is present in some similar instances such as lightning, and is absent in some similar instances such as space: it is present in dissimilar instances such as a pot.

Type VIII: Both presence and absence in similar instances, absence in dissimilar instances. For instance, a Vaiśeṣika said: "Sound is impermanent,

Because it is produced by effort,

Like lightning or a pot, unlike space".

The property of being produced by effort is present in some similar instances such as a pot, and is absent in some similar instances such as lightning; it is absent in dissimilar instances such as space.

Type IX: Both presence and absence in similar instances, both presence and absence in dissimilar instances. For instance, a Śābdika said to a Vaiśeṣika:

"Sound is permanent,

Because it is incorporeal,

Like an atom or space, unlike a pot or pleasure".

The property of being incorporeal is present in some similar instances such as space, and is absent in some similar instances such as an atom; it is present in some dissimilar instances such as pleasure, and is absent in some dissimilar instances such as a pot.

The above gives K'uei Chi's explanatory notes on the Hetucakra. Although he wrote "So-and-so said that ... " he did not really mean that all these syllogisms are a truly historical account of debate. Some of them are obviously constructed for the sake of providing illustrative cases in a logic text only.

The "So-and-so" and "So-and-so said to so-and-so" do not mean very much here; they will make sense only when the notion of 'acceptance' is introduced. This will be discussed in a later chapter on logical fallacies.

The nature of 'sound' is discussed in the Hetucakra throughout. In fact not the sound in general, but the words of the Veda, were regarded by Mīmāṁsa school as something eternal and of infallible authority.

113. Interpretations

1131. The Three-Operator System

The three expressions 'presence', 'absence' and 'both presence and absence' in the Chinese and Tibetan versions of the Prāmaṇasamuccaya, the Nyāyamukha and the Hetucakraḍamaru are all obscure, particularly the last expression: 'both presence and absence'.

The convenient Sanskrit formulae are those used in the Nyāya-vārttika, namely -vyāpaka, -avṛtti, and -ekadeśavṛtti. Let us render them roughly as 'pervasive presence', 'absence' and 'partial presence' respectively.

Before I interpret the terms 'presence' etc. I should like to introduce two different types of syllogism in Indian logic, namely (1) inherence and (2) causation, which are among the three types of Dharmakīrti's classification of logical formulae. (inherence, causation and negation).[1]

These two types can be illustrated by two famous cases as follows:

(1) Inherence: "Sound is impermanent because it is produced". This is to prove that a thing possesses the property A (being impermanent) by pointing out that it possesses the property B (being produced). In other words, from the presence of the property B in a thing one can infer the presence of the property A in it.

(2) Causation: "The hill is fiery because it is smoky". This is to prove the truth of a proposition A by pointing out the truth of a proposition B.

By adding their respective major premisses to the above, we can have two kinds of syllogism, namely: that of the restricted predicate logic (or the logic of classes) and that of propositional logic.

First let us formulate them in the form of the logic of classes:

$(a \subset b).(b \subset c) \supset (a \subset c)$, where '$\subset$' represents class inclusion.

This formula reads: " 'The class a is included in the class b' and 'the

1. Nyāyabindu. p.104.
Stcherbatsky 12. Vol.II. p.60.

class b is included in the class c' implies ' the class a is included in the class c' ".

Secondly let us formulate the syllogism in the form of the restricted predicate logic:

$$(x)(fx \supset gx).\ (x)(gx \supset hx) \supset (x)(fx \supset hx).$$

All the illustrative cases show that Dignāga's Hetucakra belongs to the first type. It mainly concerns the possession of properties, therefore it can be interpreted in terms of the logic of classes.

1. Pervasive presence: "The property b is present wherever the property a is present". This is class inclusion:

$a \subset b$, **or** $a\bar{b} = 0$

2. Absence: "The property b is absent wherever the property a is present". This is class exclusion:

$a \subset \bar{b}$, **or** $ab = 0$

3. Partial presence: "In some cases the property b is present when the property a is present, but in some cases it is absent when the property a is present". This is class overlapping:

$ab \neq 0$ **and** $a\bar{b} \neq 0$

The above can easily be converted into the restricted predicate logic by putting $a = \hat{z}(\phi z)$ **and** $b = \hat{z}(\psi z)$**; then we have:**

1. Pervasive presence: $(x)(\phi x \supset \psi x)$, **which reads: "For all x, 'x possesses the property** ϕ**' implies 'x possesses the property** ψ **'; or "For all x, if x is a** ϕ **, then x is a** ψ **".**

2. Absence: $(x)(\phi x \supset \sim \psi x)$, **which reads: "For all x, 'x possesses the property** ϕ**' implies 'x does not possess the property** ψ**' "; or "For all x, if x is a** ϕ**, then x is not a** ψ **".**

3. Partial presence: $(Ex)(\phi x.\ \psi x).\ (Ex)(\phi x.\ -\psi x)$, **which reads: "In some cases x possesses the property** ϕ **and the property** ψ**, but in some cases x possesses the property** ϕ **but not the property** ψ **".**

In Dignāgean logic the possibility of a null class is always examined in every individual case, therefore the existential import is explicitly stated.

Let a, e and u be the symbols of the respective operators 'pervasive presence', 'absence' and 'partial presence' (called by Uddyotakara '-vyāpaka', '-avṛtti' and '-ekadeśavṛtti'), and S and P be the term

variables, we may define the three operators as follows:

-vyāpaka: $S\ a\ P = (x)(\Phi x \supset \psi x). (Ex)(\Phi x)$ Df.

-avṛtti: $S\ e\ P = (x)(\Phi x \supset \sim\psi x). (Ex)(\Phi x)$ Df.

-ekadeśavṛtti: $S\ u\ P = (Ex)(\Phi x. \psi x). (Ex)(\Phi x. \sim\psi x)$ Df.

For the sake of convenience in derivation, the following forms are used:

$S\ a\ P = \sim(Ex)(\Phi x. \sim\psi x). (Ex)(\Phi x. \psi x)$

$S\ e\ P = (Ex)(\Phi x. \sim\psi x). \sim(Ex)(\Phi x. \psi x)$

$S\ u\ P = (Ex)(\Phi x. \sim\psi x). (Ex)(\Phi x. \psi x)$

In the logic of classes, we have:

$S\ a\ P = (a\bar{b} = o). (ab \neq o)$ Df.

$S\ e\ P = (a\bar{b} \neq o). (ab = o)$ Df.

$S\ u\ P = (a\bar{b} \neq o). (ab \neq o)$ Df.

They are, respectively, the same as the Aristotelian A form with existential import, E form with existential import and the conjunct of the I and O forms. Three operators form a logical triangle instead of a logical square.

Among the four regions of the universe of discourse, namely ab, $a\bar{b}$, $\bar{a}b$ and $\bar{a}\bar{b}$, the two regions ab and $a\bar{b}$ are the decisive factors for the condition of implication while the other two are not. They will tell whether S implies P, or non-P., or both, or neither.

One characteristic of the three-operator system is that the existential condition of both these regions is stated.

In the Aristotelian system, (1) for the I and O forms, the existential condition of only one region is stated; (2) for the A and E forms, sometimes the existential condition of both regions is stated, but sometimes that of only one region is stated. The operators A and E are not uniquely defined, sometimes the existential import is imposed and sometimes not.

Because of the ambiguity of their definitions there has been great difficulty in interpreting the Aristotelian system in terms of the restricted predicate calculus. Usually certain laws collapse under one way of interpretation, but certain other laws will collapse under another way of interpretation.[1]

---

1. P.F. Strawson: Introduction to Logical Theory, London, 1952. p. 167 ff.

It was mentioned in a certain textbook on logic:
"Every a is b" implies "some a is b";
"Some a is b" implies "some a is not b";
Therefore, "every a is b" implies "some a is not b".

The above was mentioned as a joke. But it can well illustrate what kind of consequence will follow when a definition is ambiguous.

Another characteristic of the three-operator system is that all three are mutully exclusive and independent; none of them is derivable from one another.

In the Aristotelian system, the region $a\bar{b}$ in the I form is not specified. It is either empty or non-empty and there is no third alternative. It it is empty, it will become A form; if not, it will become O form. Therefore the 'I' form is either a conjunct of A and I, or that of I and O; and there is no independent I form which is neither A nor O. There is a similar difficulty in the O form.

The three-operator system is quite near the system developed by a French mathematician J.D. Gergonne, who introduced a five-operator system in 1816 - fifty years after the introduction of L. Euler's diagrams and sixty years before those of J. Venn's.

The five operators are symbolized by H (est hors de), X (s'entre-croise avec), I (est identique à), C (est contenu dans) and Ɔ (contiens). Let us compare them with the three operators a, e and u as follows:

(S H P) = (S e P) No S is P;
(S X P) = (S u P). (P u S) Some S is P, some S is not P and some P is not S;
(S I P) = (S a P). (P a S) Every S is P, and every P is S;
(S C P) = (S a P). (P u S) Every S is P, and some P is not S;
(S Ɔ P) = (S u P). (P a S) Some S is not P, and every P is S.

In the three-operator system, two regions are specified; in the five-operator system, three regions are specified. Therefore Dignāga's system is narrower than Aristotle's, and Gergonne's system is narrower than Dignāga's. This point can easily be illustrated by the following diagrams:

(S e P) = (S H P)
(S a P) = (S I P) V (S C P)
(S u P) = (S Ɔ P) V (S X P)

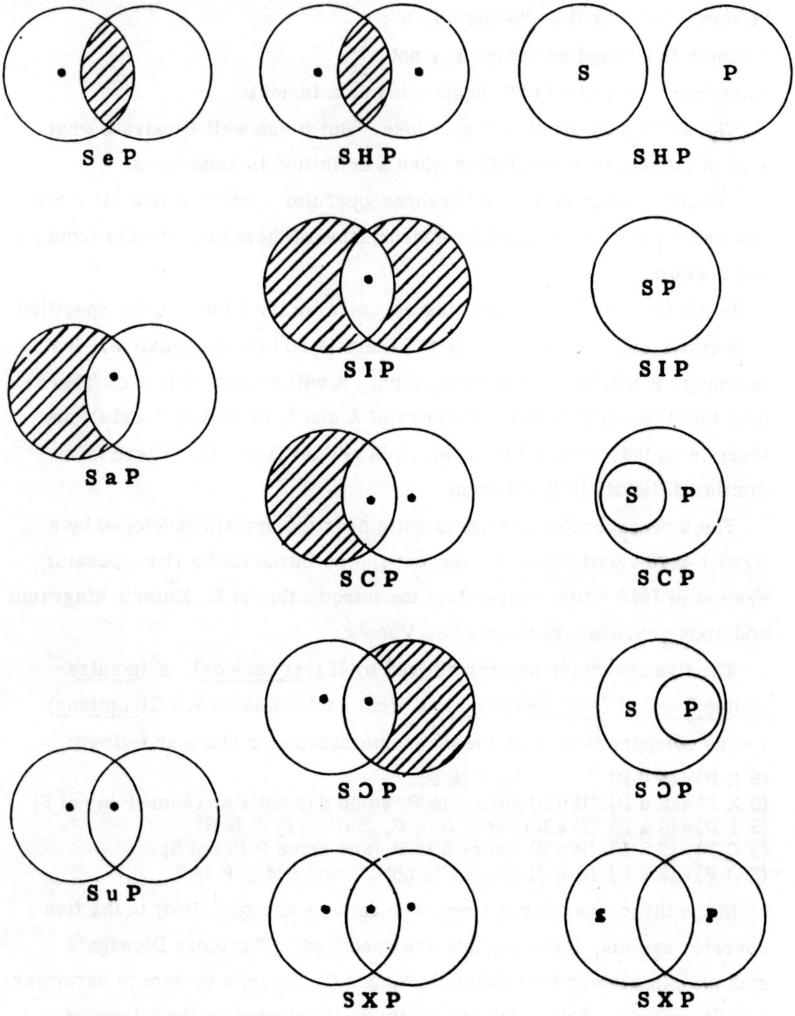

Venn's diagrams **Euler's diagrams**

1132. The Four Classes

Before we carry on the discussion on Indian logic, let us shift our attention for a moment to another point, namely the syllogism in the mood of 'Barbara'. In this mood, a minor premiss may assume two possible forms: it may be a singular proposition, such as "Socrates is a man"; or it may be a universal proposition, such as "Greeks are men" Let us call them respectively the 'Barbara-A' and 'Barbara-B' forms.

First let us formulate them in the form of the logic of classes:

Barbara-A: $(a \epsilon b).(b \subset c) \supset (a \epsilon c)$,
Barbara-B: $(a \subset b).(b \subset c) \supset (a \subset c)$, where ϵ denotes class membership, and $\subset$ denotes class inclusion.

The above reads:

Barbara-A: 'a is a member of the class b' and 'the class b is included in the class c' imples 'a is a member of the class c'.

Barbara-B: 'The class a is included in the class b' and 'the class b is included in the class c' implies 'the class a is included in the class c'.

Secondly let us formulate them in the form of the restricted predicate calculus:

Barbara-A: $gy. (x)(gx \supset hx) \supset hy$,

Barbara-B: $(x)(fx \supset gx). (x)(gx \supset hx) \supset (x)(fx \supset hx)$

The above reads:

Barbara-A: For every x, if x is g, then x is h. But y is g, therefore y is h.

Barbara-B: For every x, is x is g, then x is h. And for every x, if x is f, then x is g. Therefore, for every x, if x is f, then x is h.

These two forms had been wrongly identified in the west, e.g. by William of Ockham, but were distinguished by Frege and Peano.

In fact there are two points which are common to singular and universal affirmative propositions, namely: that neither of them can be negative, and that neither of them can be particular.

Therefore a singular proposition can be expressed in the form of a universal proposition. For instance, "Socrates is a man" can be expressed as "For every x, if x is Socrates, then x is a man". Both propositions can exclude "Socrates is not a man" and "Socrates is partly a man and partly not a man".

Now let us turn back to Dignāga. In his works these two forms were neither identified as one, nor very clearly distinguished.

His formulation of the minor premiss was brief and obscure. "... because it is produced" is something like 'gz' which reads 'z is g'. Whatever form this formulation may take, he did not really mean that the minor premiss of this illustrative case was a singular proposition, although there was no universal quantifier explicitly stated. As a matter of fact, throughout his works the minor premisses were almost always non-singular propositions.

The above can be explained by the fact that the distinction between singular and universal propositions, and the distinction between quantified and un-quantified variables was extremely obscure at his time.

Perhaps this is the reason why Uddyotakara raised his objection to the first clause of the Trairūpya by giving an illustrative case: "Atoms are impermanent because they are odorous"[1] in which the minor premiss is a particular proposition, because according to Indian tradition only 'earth atoms' are odorous while other kinds of atoms are not.

His illustrative case shows that if the quantifier of the minor premiss is not explicity stated, the minor premiss may turn out to be a particular proposition. Thus the syllogism will be invalid in the Barbara mood.

It was Dignāga who introduced the notion of quantification to Indian logic. In the Hetucakra he stressed very much the major premiss and not the minor premiss.

In the Hetucakra he rejected the type V, in which the middle term and the minor term have the same extension, as invalid because of 'being too narrow'. Let us call this fallacy 'petitio principii with respect to extension'.

From the above it will follow that the major premiss should never be a singular proposition, irrespective of whether the minor premiss is universal or singular.

Therefore, the problem which Ockham raised about the syllogism "Socrates is white, every man is Socrates, therefore every man is white" will not arise.

Perhaps this is one of the reasons why Dignāga stressed the major

1. NV. I.1.5. p.58.
IL. pp. 250-1.

premiss so much but left the minor premiss without clearly specifying whether it should be a universal or singular proposition.

In the second verse of the Hetucakra, he mentioned that among the three possible cases of 'presence', 'absence' and ' both' of the probans in the probandum, only the first case is valid.

The statement is very vague and obscure. He was talking about what kind of proposition a minor premiss should be. The three cases 'presence', 'absence' and 'both' actually mean affirmative, negative and particular propositions. Among the three, only the first one, the affirmative, is valid. An affirmative proposition includes both universal affirmative and singular affirmative ones.

In so far as the exclusion of negative and particular propositions is concerned, the universal and singular propositions are virtually the same.

Practically the form Barbara-B was almost always used in Indian logic. Since the symbolic formulations of Barbara-A and of Barbara-B are different, in this work I shall include both.

Here I should like to mention an important point concerning interpretation of Indian logic. Neither the five-membered nor the three-membered syllogism can coincide precisely with the familiar form of syllogism with a minor premiss, a major premiss and a conclusion.

It is not impossible to coin a new set of symbols and formulae for Indian logic, if we stick to the syntactic structure of Indian syllogism; but it will be extremely inconvenient, cumbersome and pointless. There is no reason why we should not use the current language, terminology and symbolism to interpret it.

Therefore in my formulation I do not actually translate the Indian authors' words into symbols, but express what they meant to say - i.e. what they would have said if they had used precisely the same language and symbols as we do.

Similarly in my derivation, many steps are not the words explicitly stated by the Indian authors, but are those which ought to be intuitively taken for granted by them as true, even if they were not aware of some theorems that had been applied.

Dignāga introduced the notions of 'similar instances' and 'dissimilar instances'. They are used to donote either the classes or the members of the classes. Two very important points concerning them are stated as follows:

First, the word 'similar' refers to the likeness to the subject in its possessing the property denoted by the predicate, and not the property denoted by the middle term. Vidyabhusana has made mistakes in his interpretation of the Hetucakraḍamaru because he failed to realize this point.

Secondly, the similar instances are only similar to, but not identical with, the subject. Therefore the subject itself should be excluded from the membership of the similar instances.

The term 'dissimilar instances' was defined by Dharmakīrti "A case which is not similar is dissimilar - it can be different from it, contrary to it, or its absence".[1]

Since its 'difference' and its 'contrariety' are included in its 'absence', the last definition is the proper one. Or, we may say: "Dissimilar instances are dissimilar to the subject in their not possessing the property denoted by the predicate".

Different authors employed various terms to denote the similar and dissimilar instances; perhaps they held slightly different opinions.

The 'similar instance' was called by Dignāga 'tattulya', by Dharmakīrti 'sapakṣa', by Praśastapāda 'tatsamānajatīya' and by Uddyotakara 'tajjātīya', etc. The 'dissimilar instance' was called by Dharmakīrti 'asapakṣa' and by Uddyotakara 'vipakṣa'.

Let us use the familiar terms 'sapakṣa' and 'vipakṣa'. Let us symbolize the four classes respectively hetu, pakṣa, sapakṣa and vipakṣa by H, P, S and V.

1. First let us define them in terms of the class variables a, b and c in the logic of classes. In the Barbara-A and the Barbara-B form of syllogism, i.e.

$(a \epsilon b).(b \subset c) \supset (a \epsilon c)$ and
$(a \subset b).(b \subset c) \supset (a \subset c)$, they can be defined as follows:

$H = b$ Df.
$P = a$ Df.
$S = \bar{a}c$ Df.
$V = \bar{c}$ Df.

---

1. Nyāyabindu, translated by Stcherbarsky. Stcherbatsky 12, p. 59
Nyāyabindu. p. 104.

2. Secondly let us define them in terms of the predicate variables f, g and h in the restricted predicate logic. In this system they are defined differently in the Barbara-A and the Barbara-B forms as follows:

Barbara-A: $gy . (x)(gx \supset hx) \supset hy$

$$
\begin{array}{lll}
H = \hat{z}(gz) & & \text{Df.} \\
P = y & & \text{Df.} \\
S = \hat{z}(hz . z \neq y) & & \text{Df.} \\
V = \hat{z}(-hz) & & \text{Df.}
\end{array}
$$

Barbara-B: $(x)(fx \supset gx) . (x)(gx \supset hx) \supset (x)(fx \supset hx)$

$$
\begin{array}{lll}
H = \hat{z}(gz) & & \text{Df.} \\
P = \hat{z}(fz) & & \text{Df.} \\
S = \hat{z}(-fz . hz) & & \text{Df.} \\
V = \hat{z}(-hz) & & \text{Df.}
\end{array}
$$

The Barbara-B form can be illustrated by the following diagrams:

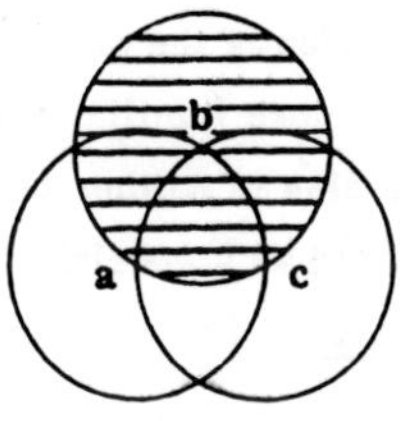

Hetu = b = $\hat{z}(gz)$

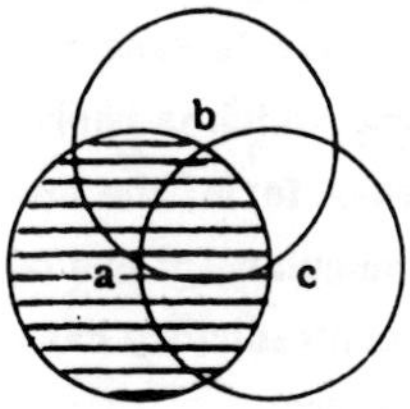

Pakṣa = a = $\hat{z}(fz)$

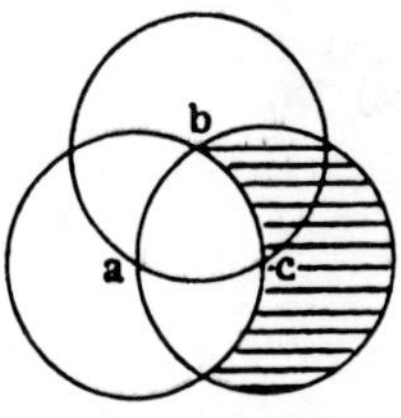

Sapakṣa = $\bar{a}c$
= $\hat{z}(-fz . hz)$

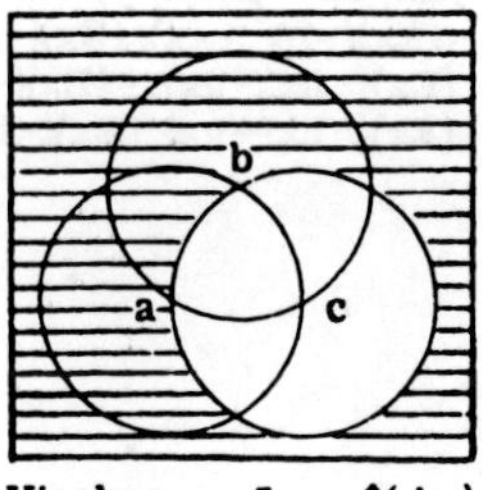

Vipakṣa = $\bar{c}$ = $\hat{z}(-hz)$

1133. The Nine Types of Premisses

Since there are three operators and four classes, if we take three classes operating against the class of hetu, there will be nine possible combinations. For instance, when the hetu pervades the pakṣa (called 'sādhya' in Uddyotakara's formulation of the hetucakra) or P a H, then by substituting the predicate variables f and g for ϕ and ψ in the operator 'a' (called by Uddyotakara -vyāpaka), we have

$$(P\ a\ H) = -(Ex)(fx. -gx).(Ex)(fx. gx) \quad Df.$$

The following is the list of all types of premisses in the Barbara-B form:

1. Sādhyavyāpaka: $(P\ a\ H) = -(Ex)(fx. -gx).(Ex)(fx. gx)$ Df.
2. Sādhyāvṛtti: $(P\ e\ H) = (Ex)(fx. -gx). -(Ex)(fx. gx)$ Df.
3. Sādhyaikadeśavṛtti: $(P\ u\ H) = (Ex)(fx. -gx).(Ex)(fx. gx)$ Df.
4. Sapakṣavyāpaka: $(S\ a\ H) = -(Ex)(-fx. hx. -gx).(Ex)(-fx. hx. gx)$ Df.
5. Sapakṣāvṛtti: $(S\ e\ H) = (Ex)(-fx. hx. -gx). -(Ex)(-fx. hx. gx)$ Df.
6. Sapakṣaikadeśavṛtti: $(S\ u\ H) = (Ex)(-fx. hx. -gx).(Ex)(-fx. hx. gx)$. Df.
7. Vipakṣavyāpaka: $(V\ a\ H) = -(Ex)(-hx. -gx).(Ex)(-hx. gx)$ Df.
8. Vipakṣāvṛtti: $(V\ e\ H) = (Ex)(-hx. -gx). -(Ex)(-hx. gx)$ Df.
9. Vipakṣaikadeśavṛtti: $(V\ u\ H) = (Ex)(-hx. -gx).(Ex)(-hx. gx)$ Df.

I follow Uddyotakara's Sanskrit formulation of the premisses except the term 'tajjātīya' which is replaced by a more familiar term 'sapakṣa'.

In the Barbara-A form, the minor premiss is neither universal nor particular, but singular. It can be regarded as a special case of 'vyāpaka' and a contradictory case of 'avṛtti'. The premisses can be formulated as follows:

1. $(P\ a\ H) = gy$ Df.
2. $(P\ e\ H) = -gy$ Df.
3. $(P\ u\ H) =$ not applicable.
4. $(S\ a\ H) = -(Ex)(hx. -gx)(x \neq y).(Ex)(hx. gx)(x \neq y)$ Df.
5. $(S\ e\ H) = (Ex)(hx. -gx)(x \neq y). -(Ex)(hx. gx)(x \neq y)$ Df.
6. $(S\ u\ H) = (Ex)(hx. -gx)(x \neq y).(Ex)(hx. gx)(x \neq y)$ Df.
7. $(V\ a\ H) = -(Ex)(-hx. -gx).(Ex)(-hx. gx)$ Df.
8. $(V\ e\ H) = (Ex)(-hx. -gx). -(Ex)(-hx. gx)$ Df.
9. $(V\ u\ H) = (Ex)(-hx. -gx).(Ex)(-hx. gx)$ Df.

The form Barbara-B can be expressed in terms of the logic of classes as follows:

1. $(P\ a\ H) = (a\bar{b} = O).(ab \neq O)$ Df.
2. $(P\ e\ H) = (a\bar{b} \neq O).(ab = O)$ Df.
3. $(P\ u\ H) = (a\bar{b} \neq O).(ab \neq O)$ Df.

4. $(S\ a\ H) = (\bar{a}\bar{b}c = O).(\bar{a}bc \neq O)$ Df.
5. $(s\ e\ H) = (\bar{a}\bar{b}c \neq O).(\bar{a}bc = O)$ Df.
6. $(S\ u\ H) = (\bar{a}\bar{b}c \neq O).(\bar{a}bc \neq O)$ Df.

7. $(V\ a\ H) = (\bar{b}\bar{c} = O).(b\bar{c} \neq O)$ Df.
8. $(V\ e\ H) = (\bar{b}\bar{c} \neq O).(b\bar{c} = O)$ Df.
9. $(V\ u\ H) = (\bar{b}\bar{c} \neq O).(b\bar{c} \neq O)$ Df.

The nine types of premisses in the Barbara-B form are illustrated as follows, where the shaded portion means empty classes and the portion with asterisks means non-empty classes. The portion with neither means unknown classes which require further information.

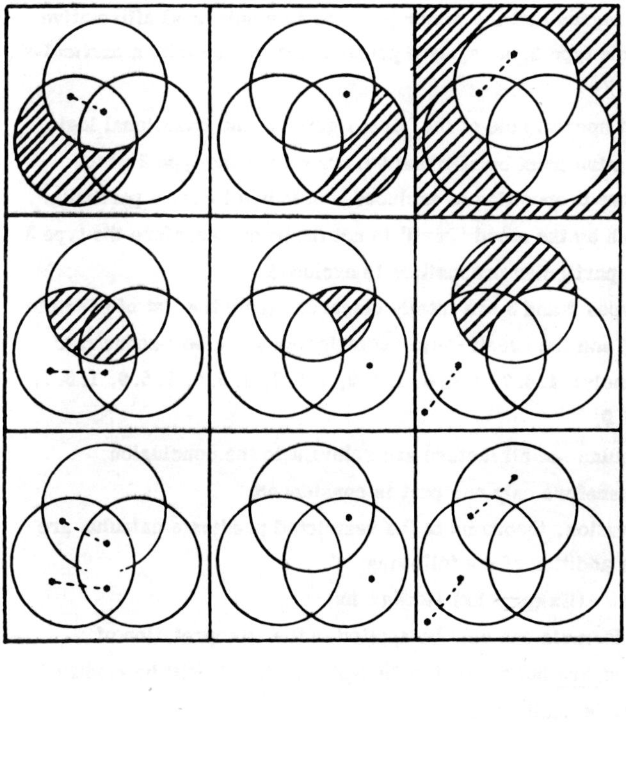

PaH SaH VaH

PeH SeH VeH

PuH SuH VuH

1134. The 'Wheel', Possible Combinations of Premisses

From here onwards I shall use the numerals 1 to 9 to denote the nine types of premisses, i.e. Sādhyavyāpaka, Sādhyāvṛtti, etc., which are defined in previous chapter in both the restricted predicate logic and the logic of classes.

The combinations of the numerals, e.g. 1.4.7, 1.4.8, etc. will denote the possible types in the Hetucakra. I use the new notation 1.4.7 etc. instead of the Roman numerals I, II, III etc. of Dignāga's sequence because Uddyotakara's order is different from Dignāga's.

If we classify the nine kinds of premisses into three groups, namely 1, 2 and 3, which show the relation between the hetu and the pakṣa, 4, 5 and 6, which show the relation between the hetu and the sapakṣa, 7, 8 and 9 which show the relation between the hetu and the vipakṣa; and take one from each group and combine them; then we shall have 3^3 or twenty-seven possible combinations.

The type 1 means that the minor premiss is a universal affirmative proposition; the type 2, a negative proposition; the type 3, a particular proposition.

By the first special rule of the 'first figure' in the traditional logic, the minor premiss must be affirmative; therefore the type 2 which denotes negative proposition is excluded. In Indian logic, a particular conclusion such as the mood 'Darii' is not desired; therefore the type 3 which denotes particular proposition is excluded.

Then the types 2 and 3 are totally discarded from the list of possible combinations, and the twenty-seven combinations are now reduced to nine only, namely: 1.4.7, 1.4.8, 1.4.9, 1.5.7, 1.5.8, 1.5.9, 1.6.7, 1.6.8 and 1.6.9.

In the formulae not all factors are relevant to the conclusion $(x)(fx \supset hx)$, therefore only one part is considered.

In the derivation, theorems of the restricted predicate calculus are used, with the addition of the following:

$(x)(gx \supset hx) \equiv \sim(Ex)(gx. \sim hx).(Ex)(gx. hx)$

The above formula can only be applied in the interpretation of Dignāga's hetucakra but not that of Uddyotakara's. It will be modified when the latter is dealt with.

It is important that the relation $(x)(gx \supset hx) \equiv -(Ex)(gx. -hx)$ does not hold here. According to Dignāga's convention, only $(x)(gx \supset hx) \supset -(Ex)(gx. -hx)$ or $(Ex)(gx. -hx) \supset -(x)(gx \supset hx)$ holds; while its reverse does not. Therefore a sign of implication is used instead of that of equivalence.

For the sake of convenience, let us omit all the apparent variable x's and use U and E to denote the universal and existential quantifiers respectively, such that

$U(\phi \supset \psi) = (x)(\phi x \supset \psi x)$ Df.

$E(\phi. \psi) = (Ex)(\phi x. \psi x)$ Df.

Now let us examine the nine types of the Hetucakra one by one, first in the Barbara-B form in terms of the restricted predicate calculus:

1.4.7

(P a H). (S a H). (V a H) =

$-E(f. -g). E(f. g). -E(-f. h. -g). E(-f. h. g). -E(-h. -g). E(-h. g)$ .... (i)

(i) implies $E(-f. h. g).$ $E(-h. g)$.... (ii)

(ii) implies $E(g. h).$ $E(g. -h)$.... (iii)

(iii) implies $-U(g \supset -h)$ $-U(g \supset h)$.... (iv)

Formula (iv) shows that g implies neither h nor -h, the syllogism is therefore not conclusive.

1.4.8

(P a H). (S a H). (V e H) =

$-E(f. -g). E(f. g). -E(-f. h. -g). E(-f. h. g). E(-h. -g). -E(-h. g)$ .. (i)

(i) implies $U(f \supset g). -E(f. -g). -E(-f. h. -g). -E(-h. g). E(h. g)$... (ii)

(ii) implies $U(f \supset g). -E(f. h. -g). -E(-f. h. -g). -E(g. -h). E(g. h)$. (iii)

(iii) implies $U(f \supset g). -E(h. -g). -E(g. -h). E(g. h.)$............. (iv)

(iv) implies $U(f \supset g). U(g \equiv h)$.................................(v)

(v) implies $U(f \supset h)$...................................(vi)

This type is valid for a universal affirmative conclusion.

1.4.9

(P a H). (S a H). (V u H) =

$-E(f. -g). E(f. g). -E(-f. h. -g). E(-f. h. g). E(-h. -g). E(-h. g)$.... (i)

Like the type 1.4.7, (i) implies $-U(g \supset -h). -U(g \supset h)$.

It is therefore inconclusive.

1.5.7

(P a H). (S e H). (V a H) =

$-E(f. -g). E(f. g). E(-f. h. -g). -E(-f. h. g). -E(-h. -g). E(-h. g)$... (i)

(i) implies $-E(-f. g. h).$ $E(g. -h)$... (ii)

The region (f. g. h) is unknown, therefore we have

$E(f. g. h) \vee -E(f. g. h)$............ (iii)

Combining (iii) and (ii) we have

(- E(- f. g. h). E(g. - h)). (E(f. g. h) V - E(f. g. h)) .... (iv)

(iv) implies (E(g. h). E(g. - h)) V (- E(g. h). E(g. - h)) ...... (v)

(v) implies (- U(g ⊃ - h). - U(g ⊃ h)) V U(g ⊃ - h) .... (vi)

The formula (vi) shows that if the region (f. g. h) is non-empty, the syllogism is inconclusive; if it is empty, the conclusion is negative. The latter case is equivalent to the mood of 'Celarent', which contradicts what is 'desired to prove'; it is therefore called 'contradictory'.

1.5.8

(P a H). (S e H). (V e H) =

- E(f. - g). E(f. g). E(- f. h. - g). - E(- f. h. g). E(- h. - g). - E(- h. g). ... (i)

(i) implies - E(- f. g. h). - E(g. - h). ... (ii)

The region (f. g. h) is unknown, therefore we have

E(f. g. h) V - E(f. g. h). .... (iii)

Combining (ii) and (iii) we have

(- E(- f. g. h). - E(g. - h)). (E(f. g. h) V - E(f. g. h)). .... (iv)

(iv) implies (- E(g. - h). E(g. h)) V (- E(g. h). - E(g.- h)). .... (v)

The formula (v) shows that if (f. g. h) is non-empty, the syllogism is valid; if it is empty, it is inconclusive.

But if we examine the minor premiss, and the factor - E(g. - h),

E(f. g). - E(g.- h) ⊃ E(g.h). .... (vi)

Combining (ii) and (vi), we have

E(g. h). - E(- f. g. h) ⊃ E(f. g. h). .... (vii)

The formula (vii) shows that the region (f. g. h) is non-empty, therefore the syllogism should be valid and not inconclusive.

1.5.9

(P a H). (S e H). (V u H) =

- E(f. - g). E(f. g). - E(- f. h. g). E(- f. h. - g). E(- h. g). E(- h. - g). .... (i)

Like the type 1.5.7, (i) implies (- U(g ⊃ - h). - U(g ⊃ h)) V U(g ⊃ - h)

It is therefore contradictory.

1.6.7

(P a H). (S u H). (V a H) =

- E(f. - g). E(f. g). E(- f. h. g). E(- f. h. - g). - E(- h. - g). E(- h. g). .... (i)

Like the type 1.4.7, (i) implies - U(g ⊃ - h). - U(g ⊃ h).

It is therefore inconclusive.

1.6.8

(P a H). (S u H). (V e H) =

- E(f. - g). E(f. g). E(- f. h. g). E(- f. h. - g). - E(- h. g). E(- h. - g). .... (i)

(i) implies U(f ⊃ g). E(g. h). - E(g. - h). .... (ii)

(ii) implies U(f ⊃ g). U(g ⊃ h). .... (iii)

(iii) implies U(f ⊃ h). .... (iv)

This type is valid for a universal affirmative conclusion.

1.6.9

$(P\ a\ H).(S\ u\ H).(V\ u\ H) =$

$-E(f.-g).E(f.g).E(-f.h.g).E(-f.h.-g).E(-h.g).E(-h.-g)\ldots\ldots(i)$

(i) implies $-U(g \supset -h).-U(g \supset h)$, like the type 1.4.7.

It is therefore inconclusive.

According to our usual syllogistic, the type 1.4.8 and the type 1.5.8 are of the following forms:

$(x)(fx \supset gx).(x)(gx \equiv hx) \supset (x)(fx \supset hx)$ and

$(x)(fx \equiv gx).(x)(gx \supset hx) \supset (x)(fx \supset hx)$.

The difference between them is whether the major or the minor premiss is a formal equivalence. They should be equally valid; why did Dignāga accept the former but reject the latter?

An old criticism, repeated by J.S. Mill, charged the Aristotelian syllogistic of being faulty on account of <u>petitio principii</u>. Dignāga's introduction of '<u>sapakṣa</u>' which is 'excluded type' of the major premiss seems to have managed to escape from Mill's objection.

The type 1.5.8 is a limiting case. In the syllogism "All men are mortal", etc., if the minor premiss is "Socrates is the only man in the universe", the difficulty will be more obvious.

Let us consider this problem from both points of view of intension and of extension. First, all the minor, middle and major terms should differ from one another in intension; otherwise the syllogism will be pointless because of lacking of practical inference.

Both Dignāga and Mill are reasoning from the point of view of extension. Is it necessary that the minor term and the middle term should differ in extension?

Instead of using Indian illustrative cases such as 'sound', let us use traditional cases such as 'featherless bipeds', to demonstrate this point as follows:

1. All men are featherless bipeds,
   All featherless bipeds are mortal,
   Therefore all men are mortal.
2. All men are unicorns,
   All unicorns are mortal,
   Therefore all men are mortal.
3. All unicorns are squared-circles,
   All squared-circles are mortal,
   Therefore all unicorns are mortal.

The above examples are, unfortunately, very odd ones; a few assumptions, therefore, should be added, namely:

1. that the three conclusions are unknown;

2. that the existence of men and of featherless bipeds and the non-existence of unicorns and of squared-circles are known;

3. that the premisses may be true or false.

Example 1 seems to be valid. In example 2, gx does not exist; in example 3, both gx and hx do not exist. One cannot make a mistake in the major premiss without simultaneously making a mistake in the minor premiss also. In other words, the mistakes in the non-existence of gx in the major premiss should not happen if the minor premiss is free from mistakes.

However, in Dignāga's system, the subject is excluded from the <u>spakṣa</u>. If we take only the 'excluded major premiss' into consideration:

1a. No non-human featherless biped is not mortal;
2a. No non-human unicorn is not mortal;
3a. No non-unicorn squared-circle is not mortal;

it will be difficult to find the difference between 1a and the other two; because non-human featherless biped, non-human unicorn and non-unicorn squared-circle are equally non-existent.

Their corresponding contrary premiss will be equally true or equally false:

1b. No non-human featherless biped is mortal;
2b. No non-human unicorn is mortal;
3b. No non-unicorn squared circle is mortal;

because none of them exists. Therefore the type 1. 5. 8 is considered as inconclusive.

Secondly let us express the <u>hetucakra</u> in the Barbara-A form in terms of the restricted predicate calculus:

1.4.7
gy. - (Ex)(hx. - gx)(x≠y). (Ex)(hx. gx)(x≠y).- (Ex)(- hx. - gx). (Ex)(- hx. gx)

1.4.8
gy. - (Ex)(hx. - gx)(x≠y). (Ex)(hx. gx)(x≠y). (Ex)(- hx. - gx). - (Ex)(- hx. gx)

1.4.9
gy. - (Ex)(hx. - gx)(x≠y). (Ex)(hx. gx)(x≠y). (Ex)(- hx. - gx). (Ex)(- hx. gx)

1.5.7
gy. (Ex)(hx. - gx)(x≠y). - (Ex)(hx. gx)(x≠y). - (Ex)(- hx. - gx). (Ex)(- hx.gx)

1.5.8

gy. (Ex)(hx. - gx)(x≠y). - (Ex)(hx. gx)(x≠y). (Ex)(- hx. - gx). - (Ex)(- hx. gx)

1.5.9

gy. (Ex)(hx. - gx)(x≠y). - (Ex)(hx. gx)(x≠y). (Ex)(- hx. - gx). (Ex)(- hx. gx)

1.6.7

gy. (Ex)(hx. - gx)(x≠y). (Ex)(hx. gx)(x≠y). - (Ex)(- hx. - gx). (Ex)(- hx. gx)

1.6.8

gy. (Ex)(hx. - gx)(x≠y). (Ex)(hx. gx)(x≠y). (Ex)(- hx. - gx). - (Ex)(- hx. gx)

1.6.9

gy. (Ex)(hx. - gx)(x≠y). (Ex)(hx. gx)(x≠y). (Ex)(- hx. - gx). (Ex)(- hx. gx)

The nine types can be classified into four groups, namely:

A. The four types 1.4.7, 1.4.9, 1.6.7 and 1.6.9 contain two factors in common:
(Ex)(gx. hx)(x≠y) and (Ex)(gx. - hx).
By dropping the restriction (x≠y), we have
(Ex)(gx. hx) and (Ex)(gx. - hx), which imply
- (x)(gx ⊃ - hx) and - (x)(gx ⊃ hx).
They are therefore inconclusive.

B. The two types 1.4.8 and 1.6.8 contain two factors in common:
(Ex)(gx. hx)(x≠y) and - (Ex)(gx. - hx).
By dropping the restriction (x≠y) we have
(Ex)(gx. hx) and - (Ex)(gx. - hx), which imply
(x)(gx ⊃ hx).
They are therefore valid.
The only difference between these two types is that 1.4.8 is actually (x)(gx ≡ hx).

C. The two types 1.5.7 and 1.5.9 contain two factors in common:
- (Ex)(gx. hx)(x≠y) and (Ex)(gx. - hx), which imply
(x)(gx ⊃ -hx)(x≠y).
In this case the restriction (x≠y) cannot be freely dropped.
The conjunct gy. (x)(gx ⊃ - hx)(x≠y) yields no result. Only when the restriction (x≠y) can be ignored, it will give

gy. (x)(gx ⊃ - hx) ⊃ - hy.

However, it is safe to say that the conclusion can be negative but can never be affirmative, if there is any conclusion at all. It is in this sense that it is called 'contradictory'.

D. The type 1.5.8 contains two factors:
- (Ex)(gx. hx)(x≠y) and - (Ex)(gx. - hx).
Neither of them can yield a universal affirmative conclusion with existential import. One can also say that they can yield both a universal affirmative and a universal negative conclusion without existential import simultaneously. This is also called 'inconclusive'.

The four groups of the nine types can be described as follows:

B. When a desired universal affirmative conclusion can be inferred, the syllogism is valid.

C. When an undesired negative conclusion can be inferred, or is likely to be inferred; while the desired universal affirmative conclusion cannot possibly be inferred, the syllogism is called 'contradictory'.

A. When neither of them can be inferred, it is called 'inconclusive because of being too broad'; i.e. the class of the hetu is broader than the class denoted by the major term.

D. When both an affirmative and a negative conclusion (without existential import) can be inferred, it is called 'inconclusive because of being too narrow'; i.e. the class of the hetu either can cover the class denoted by the minor term only, or cannot even cover it.

From the above we can see that the sense of validity (prāmānya) in the Dignāga's system is much narrower than that in traditional western logic. It should be defined in a way which seems to be quite alien to the west:

A syllogism is said to be valid if the universal affirmative conclusion which it is desired to prove can be inferred, otherwise it is said to be invalid. This will exclude the following cases:

1. First, it excludes any syllogism with a negative conclusion; because such a conclusion contradicts what it is desired to prove.

2. Secondly, it excludes any syllogism with a particular conclusion. But this case does not actually happen, because in the 'first figure' a mood like IAI is impossible.

3. Thirdly, it naturally excludes cases when no conclusion can be inferred.

4. Lastly, it also excludes the case when the extension of the middle term is not bigger than that of the minor term.

How about the case when a nagative conclusion is desired? Instead of saying 'S is not P', 'S is non-P' is used. Therefore a negative proposition can be expressed in an alternative affirmative form, and the negative proposition can be dispensed with.

We can see from the above that among the many factors in the syllogism, two factors are decisive:

A. 'inconclusive' (too broad): $(Ex)(gx.\,hx)$ and $(Ex)(gx.\,{\sim}hx)$,

B. 'valid': $(Ex)(gx.\,hx)$ and ${\sim}(Ex)(gx.\,{\sim}hx)$,

C. 'contradictory': ${\sim}(Ex)(gx.\,hx)(x{\neq}y)$ and $(Ex)(gx.\,{\sim}hx)$,

D. 'inconclusive' (too narrow): ${\sim}(Ex)(gx.\,hx)(x{\neq}y)$ and ${\sim}(Ex)(gx.\,{\sim}hx)$.

If we put $+ = (Ex)(gx.hx)$ and $- = \sim(Ex)(gx.\sim hx)$, we have:

A. 'inconclusive' (too broad): + +

B. 'valid': + -

C. 'contradictory': - +

D. 'inconclusive' (too narrow) - -

The same result may be derived by applying Boole's algebra, if we put the nine types in the form of the logic of classes according to the definitions mentioned in the chapter on the nine types of premisses (1133):

1. $(P\ a\ H) = (a\bar{b} = O).(ab \neq O)$ Df. etc. etc., we shall have

$1.4.7 = (a\bar{b} = O).(ab \neq O).(\bar{a}\bar{b}c = O).(\bar{a}bc \neq O).(\bar{b}\bar{c} = O).(b\bar{c} \neq O).$

etc. etc.

If we classify the sixteen types into four groups, we can see that only the Group B of the following list can derive the unique conclusion of $(a\bar{c} = O)$; the procedure of derivation is omitted here because it is analogous to that in the restricted predicate logic.

Group A. (1.4.7, 1.4.9, 1.6.7, and 1.6.9): $(\bar{a}bc \neq O).(b\bar{c} \neq O)$

Group B. (1.4.8 and 1.6.8): $(\bar{a}bc \neq O).(b\bar{c} = O)$

Group C. (1.5.7 and 1.5.9): $(\bar{a}bc = O).(b\bar{c} \neq O)$

Group D. (1.5.8); $(\bar{a}bc = O).(b\bar{c} = O)$

The results are as follows:

Group A. $(a\bar{c} \neq O).(ac \neq O).$

Group B. $(a\bar{c} = O).(ac \neq O)$

Group C. $(a\bar{c} \neq O).(ac = O)$ or $(a\bar{c} \neq O).(ac \neq O)$

Group D. $(a\bar{c} = O).(ac \neq O)$ or $(a\bar{c} = O).(ac = O)$

Strictly speaking, the four groups should be branded as:

Group A. inconclusive,
Group B. valid,
Group C. either contradictory or inconclusive,
Group D. either valid or inconclusive.

Dignāga's term for the four were prepared to 'err on the safe side':

Group A. inconclusive,
Group B. valid,
Group C. contradictory,
Group D. inconclusive.

The nine types of syllogism can be expressed in Venn's diagrams as follows, where all empty regions are shaded and non-empty regions are marked. The central region is neither shaded nor marked; it is the unknown part.

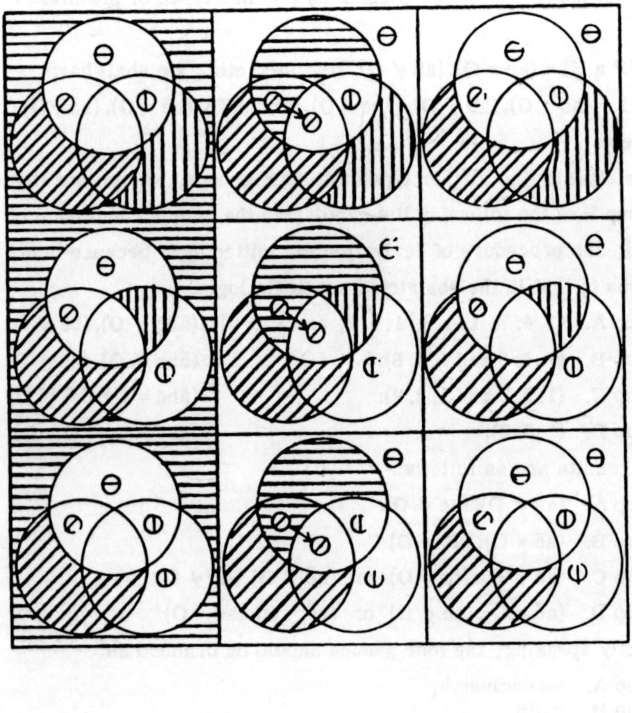

The order:

1.4.7	1.4.8	1.4.9
1.5.7	1.5.8	1.5.9
1.6.7	1.6.8	1.6.9

The signs:	1st premiss P x H	2nd premiss S x H	3rd premiss V x H
non-empty	⊘	⦶	⊖
empty		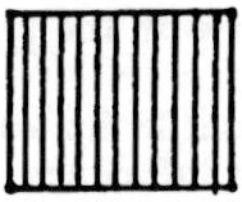	

In the types 1. 4. 8, 1. 5. 8 and 1. 6. 8, the region ab is non-empty according to the 1st premiss, but the part $ab\bar{c}$ is shaded according to the 3rd premiss. The result is that the part abc becomes known as non-empty, as discussed in the above.

In a faulty syllogism such as (1. 4. 7) "Sound is permanent because it is knowable", what is the cause of error? Is it being inconsistent with the empirical fact, or is it committing a logical mistake in formulation?

If the disputant meant to establish it in the Barbara form:

All knowable things are permanent,
Sound is knowable,
Therefore sound is permanent;

then he was making the error of assuming something inconsistent with the empirical fact, because some knowable things are not permanent.

If he meant to have known that some knowable things are permanent and some are not, and tried to establish a syllogism:

Some knowable things are permanent, (although some knowable things are not permanent),
Sound is knowable,
Therefore sound is permanent;

then he was committing a logical mistake. The syllogism is not of the form Barbara but a combination of IA- and OA- in which there is no inference because it infringes the rule of the first figure that the major premiss should be universal.

Although both cases can be the cause of error, we are concerned with the second case only.

12. The Trairūpya

121. Formulations by Dignāga and Dharmakīrti

An important verse was cited by Praśastapāda as follows:

> "What is conjoined with the probandum, and has been found in what possesses it,
> And is always absent in its absence, is the mark (liṅga) which brings about inference.
> What differs from this in one or two aspects is lacking of the mark,
> Being either contradictory, untrue or inconclusive. Said the son of Kaśyapa"[1]

This verse is extremely close to Dignāga's Trairūpya. Dignāga's own version in the Pramāṇasamuccaya was cited by Uddyotakara as follows:

anumeye 'tha tat-tulye sadbhāvo nāstitā' sati.[2]

It was later modified in the Nyāyabindu by Dharmakīrti as follows:

anumeye sattvam eva,
sapakṣa eva sattvam,
asapakṣe cāsattvam eva.

The Chinese rendering in the Nyāyapraveśa is closer to Dharmakirti's formulation:

遍是宗法性，同品定有性，異品遍無性.

I should like to quote the renderings of a few writers before I render the above into English. The two formulae are rendered by Prof. Randle as follows:

Dignāga's: "Existence in the probandum, and in what is like the the probandum, absence in what is not".

Dharmakīrti's: "Existence only (never non-existence) in the subject or things denoted by the minor term;
Existence in things which resemble the subject only (never in things which do not resemble the subject, i.e. in vipakṣas);
Only non-existence (never existence) in things which do not resemble the subject".[3]

Prof. Stcherbatsky rendered the two versions as follows:

Dignāga's

"1. Its presence on the subject of the inference;

---

1. Vaiśeṣika bhāṣya (Padārthadharmasaṁgraha) Benares. p.200.
2. Nyāyavarttika I.1.5. p.58.
3. Randle 2. p.181.

2. Its presence in similar instances;
3. Its absence in dissimilar instances".

Dharmakīrti's version was rendered in three stages:

A.

1. The presence of reason in the subject, its presence, 'just', i.e. never absence.
2. Its presence in similar instances, 'just' in similars, i.e. never in dissiliamrs, but not in the totality of the similars.
3. Its absence from dissimilar instances, its absence 'just' i.e. never presence, absence from the totality of the dissimilar instances.

B.

1. The necessary presence of the reason in the subjects totality.
2. Its necessary presence in similars only, although not in their totality.
3. Its necessary absence from dissimilars in their totality.

C.

1. In subject wholly;
2. In similars only;
3. In dissimilar never.[1]

Because of the extreme economy on the use of words, the lack of explanation by Dignāga himself, and the ambiguity in terminology, the interpretation of the Trairūpya has been controversal throughout the ages, and has remained vague even as late as the time of Stcherbatsky, as it is shown in the previous paragraph.

122. Uddyotakara's objections

The Trairūpya seems to have been respected as one of the most important doctrines in Indian logic, and yet the elaborate interpretations of distinguished scholars can hardly convey any sense to their readers.

The discussions recorded in surviving documents are lengthy. Some were made by commentators who tried hard to give plausible verbal interpretations without caring very much what Dignāga should have meant to say; some others were made by Dignāga's opponents such as Uddyotakara, who seemed to have understood what Dignāga really meant to say, but deliberately twisted his words in order to attack him.

Uddyotakara's attitude was biased in the very beginning. In the opening lines of his Nyāyavārttika, he wrote:

---

1. Stcherbatsky 12. pp. 244-5.

"Akṣapāda, the most eminent sage, expounded
A Treatise for the peace of the world.
I am writing a commentary on it, in order
To remove the errors veiled by quibblers".[1]

By the word 'quibblers' he meant Buddhist philosophers Nāgārjuna, Vasubandhu, Dignāga, etc., and the last one, called by him 'bhadanta' (a venerable Buddhist monk), was the main target of his attack.

Uddyotakara, though extremely brilliant, was not quite a scholarly personality. Rude expressions such as 'lunatic' appear more than once in his work.

He had in fact taken advantage of the briefness and obscurity of Dignāga's words; first deliberately interpreted Dignāga's words in a way which Dignāga did not really mean, then attacked him according to the twisted interpretation.

It is most unlikely that a brilliant character like Uddyotakara could possibly fail to understand what Dignāga actually meant to say, irrespective of the briefness and obscurity of the text.

The reason why Uddyotakara was so indignant against a philosopher who was over one century prior to his birth was not merely a matter of difference of opinions on logic. In fact logic was only the secondary issue, the means and not the end.

The primary factor of the controversy was the difference in religious doctrines. The Buddhist theories of the voidness of the empirical ego and that of substantiality were as intolerable to his mind as the Copernican theory to the mind of 'orthodox' schools in mediaeval Europe.

1221. Uddyotakara's criticism of the first clause:

He criticized the first clause in the unmodified form by raising an illustrative case of a minor premiss being a particular proposition:

"Atoms are impermanent because they are odorous".[2]

His objection was based on Indian tradition that the 'earth atoms' are odorous while other atoms are not.

---

1. NV. I.1.1. p.1.
   HIL. p.125.
   FD. p.1.
2. NV. I.1.5. p.58.
   IL. 250-1.

Although Dignāga had pointed out in the Hetucakradamaru (the Tibetan version) that there are three possible cases for a minor premiss, namely: presence (affirmative), absence (negative) and both presence and absence (particular) and that only the first is valid; his Trairūpya was not clearly defined in quantified form. Thus he left it open to the obvious criticism by Uddyotakara.

Then he criticized the first clause in the modified form with the restrictive word 'only'. Before I introduce his opinion let us first clarify the meaning of this word:

(1) Only b is present in a = every a is b
= no non-b is a.

(2) b is present in a only = every b is a
= no non-a is b.

(3) only b is absent in non-a = every a is b
= every non-b is non-a = no non-b is a.

(4) b is absent in non-a only = every b is a
= every non-a is non-b = no non-a is b.

Uddyotakara examined two ways of interpretation, namely

(1a) the hetu is present in the subject-only,
(1b) the hetu is only-present in the subject.[1]

Interpretation (1a) is equivalent to our Form (2). It is $(x)(gx \supset fx)$ instead of $(x)(fx \supset gx)$. The restrictive word 'only' was put in a wrong place and gave an inverse implication. Moreoever, it also contradicts the second clause.

Interpretation (1b) gives $(Ex)(fx. gx)$, which excludes the negative proposition $-(Ex)(fx. gx)$ or $(x)(fx \supset -gx)$. However, it is not sufficient to exclude a particular proposition. Therefore the condition is necessary but not sufficient.

1222. Uddyotakara's criticism of the second clause:

He examined two ways of interpretations, namely:

(2a) the hetu is present in the similar-instances-only,
(2b) the hetu is present in all similar instances.[2]

Interpretation (2a) is equivalent to our Form (2). It is $(x)(hx \supset -fx. gx)$ instead of $(x)(-fx. gx \supset hx)$. This is again an inverse implication and it also contradicts the first clause.

1. NV. I.1.5. p. 58.
IL. p. 251.
2. NV. I.1.5. p. 58.
IL. p. 254.

Uddyotakara said: "To say 'the middle term is present in similar instances only, and also in the subject' is like saying 'feed Devadatta only, and Yajñadatta also'. This is the language of a lunatic!"[1]

Interpretation (2b) has restricted the syllogism to the form $(x)(fx \supset gx).(x)(gx \equiv hx) \supset (x)(fx \supset hx)$ which is merely a special case of implication, and excludes the more general case. Therefore this interpretation becomes sufficient but not necessary.

1223. Uddyotakara's criticism of the third clause:

He examined two ways of interpretations, namely:

(3a) only-the-hetu is absent in the dissimilar instances,[2]
(3b) the hetu is absent in the dissimilar-instances-only.

Interpretation (3a) is equivalent to our Form (3). It is $(x)(\sim hx \supset \sim gx)$, or $\sim(Ex)(gx.\sim hx)$. Uddyotakara's objection was that this clause was superfluous, because it was identical with the second clause.

Interpretation (3b) is equivalent to our Form (4). It is $(x)(\sim gx \supset \sim hx)$, or $\sim(Ex)(\sim gx.hx)$. It is again an inverse implication. Uddyotakara raised an illustrative case:

"This is a cow, because it has horns" which is obviously faulty.

1224. Uddyotakara's intention in the criticism

Although he critized all three clauses, the real point of controversy lay in the second one. When the Buddhist raised the final possible interpretation - that the hetu must be found in some, not necessarily in all, similar instances, in other words, the phrase 'only-present' means 'barely present'; which was most likely the true interpretation, Uddyotakara at once rejected it just by saying:

"The formula does not succeed in saying this - not even with the help of the restrictive word 'only'!"[3]

He understood very well that the formula was an ambiguous one, and this was the very reason why he himself had tried various ways of interpretation. And yet when a true interpretation was raised, he suddenly became very sure that the formula could not possibly mean this as if all the ambiguity had gone.

---

1. NV. I.1.5. p.59.
   IL. p.257.
2. NV. I.1.5. p.59.
   IL. p.256.
3. NV. I.1.5. p.58.
   IL. p.255.

When we put 'two and two together', analyse and compare all his own interpretations, his intention will become very clear:

First, his interpretation (1b) which is $(Ex)(fx.gx)$ can suit the second clause beautifully, i.e. $(Ex)(gx.hx)$.

Secondly, his interpretation (3a) can be written in two forms, namely either $(x)(\sim hx \supset \sim gx)$ or $(x)(gx \supset hx)$. The former one, $(x)(\sim hx \supset \sim gx)$, can remain as the third clause and becomes no longer redundant, because the second clause means something quite different. The latter one, $(x)(gx \supset hx)$ can well suit the first clause, i.e. $(x)(fx \supset gx)$.

The above illustrates my suggestion that he did understand what Dignāga really meant, but in his interpretation he tried every possible way but the correct one, and deliberately evaded it, so as to make all his interpretations just 'miss the boat'.

Uddyotakara's criticism was not for the search of truth, but 'criticism for the sake of criticism'. His aim was to point out whatever Dignāga had said was wrong and to condemn his work as a whole, even at the cost of twisting his word.

123. Dharmottara's interpretation of the second clause

Dharmakīrti's addition of the restrictive word 'only' was to clarify Dignāga's original version; unexpectedly his modification caused further ambiguity. Commentators in his own school, from Dharmottara up to Stcherbatsky, had taken great pains to interpret it, none of them had interpreted in a satisfactory way.

Strangely enough, Dharmottara's interpretation has much in common with Uddyotakara's. In order to avoid repetition, I should like to put my elucidation of Dharmottara's interpretation in a manner different from the previous section. In order to avoid ambiguity, I put down all nouns and refrain from the use of pronouns.

1. 'Only presence'

= Only presence of the quality of the <u>hetu</u> in similar instances but not otherwise;

= only presence of the quality of the <u>hetu</u> in similar instances but not its absence;

= only presence of the quality of the <u>hetu</u> in similar instances but not absence of the quality of the <u>hetu</u> in similar instances.

In short, he affirmed gx. hx and excluded - gx. hx. It will exclude the function of formal implication and as a result the major premiss of a syllogism will be confined to 'formal equivalence' only. That is, a major premiss should be $(x)(gx \equiv hx)$ and should not be $(x)(gx \supset hx)$. This interpretation is of course untenable.

2. 'Only similar'

= Only the similar instances possess the quality of the <u>hetu</u>, and no others possess it;

= only the similar instances possess the quality of the <u>hetu</u>, and dissimilar instances do not possess the quality of the <u>hetu</u>.

In short, he affirmed gx. hx and excluded gx. - hx. That is, a syllogism should be $(Ex)(gx. hx). -(Ex)(gx. -hx)$ and should not be $(Ex)(gx. -hx)$.

This interpretation is quite tenable. But then the second clause will be another way of saying the same thing of the third clause, and they should not be regarded as two independent conditions for validity.

Dharmottara was in a dilemma and had to express a preference between two evils, and he had chosen the interpretation of 'only-similar', rather reluctantly.

If I were to imitate Uddyotakara's tone, I might add: "only an idiot would say: 'I pay you one pound for feeding Devadatta only; then I pay you another pound for not feeding Yajñadatta'".

124. Controversy on the <u>Trairūpya</u> at the time of Vācaspati Miśra

There were many debates during the time of Vācaspati Miśra. Certain Buddhist logicians defended the doctrine of the <u>Traiūpya</u> because it was initiated by their prodecessor - Dignāga. Unfortunately what they defended was the misinterpreted doctrine, and what was refuted by Vācaspati miśra was also the misinterpreted one. Therefore the entire debate became utterly pointless.

However, it is an even harder job to defend a faulty doctrine than to defend a right one. More elaborate devices must be applied in order to keep the debate going. As a result, these meaningless debates turned out very fascinating consequences in the history of Indian logic. Something like de Morgan's law, the principle of double negation, and the law of simplification of logical product were applied by Buddhists.

The following debate is recorded in the Nyāyavārttika tātparyatika:

1. The Buddhist's defence:[1]

First he said that he did not mean "feed Devadatta only, and feed Yajñadatta also". He meant that there was a 'joing restriction' (Samuccīyamānāvadhāraṇa), like the case "he generated two sons, Nara and Nārāyaṇa only".

Here he was referring to:

$(gx \supset fx.\ hx).\ (gx \supset {\sim}fx.\ hx) \equiv (gx \supset (fx \vee {\sim}fx).\ hx) \equiv (gx \supset hx).$

He was committing the mistake of making the minor premiss an inverse implication, because the minor premiss should be $(x)(fx \supset gx)$ and not $(x)(gx \supset fx)$.

2. Vācaspati Miśra's rejection:[2]

Vācaspati Miśra's rejection was based on the fact that the clause 'the hetu exists in the subject only' involves two conditions, namely:

(1) the hetu does not fail to exist in the subject, or $(Ex)(gx.\ fx)$
(2) the hetu does not exist in what is not the subject, or ${\sim}(Ex)(gx.\ {\sim}fx)$.

The clause 'the hetu exists in similar instances only' also involves two conditions, namely:

(1) the hetu does not fail to exist in similar instances, or $(Ex)(gx.\ {\sim}fx.\ hx)$.
(2) the hetu does not exist in what is not the similar instances, or ${\sim}(Ex)(gx.\ {\sim}({\sim}fx.\ hx))$.

The conjunct of these two clauses is self-contradictory:

$(Ex)(gx.\ fx).\ {\sim}(Ex)(gx.\ {\sim}fx).\ (Ex)(gx.\ {\sim}fx.\ hx).\ {\sim}(Ex)(gx.\ {\sim}({\sim}fx.\ hx)).$

3. The Buddhist's defence:[3]

Then the Buddhist replied that by joint restriction he did not mean it in the sense of mutual exclusion of the subject and similar instances (fx and ${\sim}fx$ are mutually exclusive); he actually meant it in the sense of repudiation of the negative meaning (apoha) - both terms alike signified exclusion of dissimilar instances.

Since $hx \equiv {\sim}{\sim}hx$, $fx.\ hx \supset hx$ and ${\sim}fx.\ hx \supset hx$;
Then $fx.\ hx \supset {\sim}{\sim}hx$ and ${\sim}fx.\ hx \supset {\sim}{\sim}hx$.
or, $((fx.\ hx \supset {\sim}{\sim}hx).\ ({\sim}fx.\ hx \supset {\sim}{\sim}hx)) \equiv ((fx \vee {\sim}fx).\ hx \supset {\sim}{\sim}hx)$

1. NVT. 59.2. p.128.
IL. pp.257-8.
2. NVT. 59.3. p.129.
IL. p.261
3. NVT. 59.3. p.129.
IL. p.261.

4. Vācaspati Miśra's rejection:[1]

He said that if the Buddhist really meant to say that the subject and similar instances are identical simply because they both exclude the same negative class, i. e.

$(fx.\,hx \supset --hx).(-fx.\,hx \supset --hx) \supset (fx.\,hx \equiv -fx.\,hx)$;

then the following syllogism would be a valid one:

"A cow is a tree, because it is not an elephant".

Although a cow and a tree are alike in the aspect of excluding an elephant, it is absurd to say that a cow and a tree are identical:

$(Cx \supset -Ex).(Tx \supset -Ex) \supset (Cx = Tx)$.

125. Why was the Theory of the Trairūpya misinterpreted?

There are three main reasons for the misinterpretation of the theory of the Trairūpya:

1. Ambiguity in terminology: Indian terminology on logic is incredibly ambiguous and diversified. Very frequently many terms may represent precisely one and the same thing according to the preference of different authors. For instance, the term for 'similar instances' has almost half a dozen different versions. Also quite often one single term may represent a multiplicity of meanings, even when it is used by one and the same author in a single sentence. The word 'anumeya' is an example:

"Anumeya has the usual double-meaning - neither S nor P, but SP".[2]

"Anumeya is here used in two different senses - first as P and then as S - in one and the same clause. Similar cases of the ambiguous use of sādhya in a single clause could be quoted from Vātsyāyana".[3]

"We may take sādhya or anumeya as an ambiguous abbreviation for either sādhyadharma or sādhyadharmin; in which case the ambiguity of the term is an accident of language. Or we may suppose that the ambiguity was an ambiguity of thought natural to the earliest formulation of inference, and that this ambiguity was subsequently realised - and that

---

1. NVT. 59.3. p.129.
IL. p.262.

2. Randle 2, p.168, N-2

3. Randle 2, p.170, N-1

then the distinction between the sādhyadharma and the sādhyadharmin was drawn. The latter supposition seems to be the true one".[1]

However, there is such a paragraph in the Nyāyamukha: "Somebody may object: Since the word anumeya is defined as 'that which is to be proved', why is it that in the above kārikā you have used it to mean that subject of a proposition only? I reply that I am not mistaken, because the name of the whole is implied by that of a part; such as the case 'a garment is burning' which is implied by 'a part of the garment is burning'. There are cases in which the word anumeya is used to mean the predicate only".[2]

Here obviously the ambiguity had been realized, and even an objection had been expected at a very early time. It is really hard to explain why on earth the Indian logicians should use technical terms with such an economy, whereas in some other cases they use them with an extreme extravagance as well.

Prof. Bochenski gives a list of technical terms in his Formal Logic.[3] Although it contains a few examples only, it can show how much diversified Indian terminology is.

It is the ambiguity of this very term anumeya used by Dignāga which led his hostile opponent Uddyotakara to launch an attack on him by taking advantage of the ambiguity and deliberately misinterpreting it.

2. The Yogācāra School, after Dharmakīrti and Dharmapāla, was in the stage of decline, and became dogmatic. Dignāga's initiative and freshness had all gone. His works were respected as sacred books without being really understood.

In fact, all the theories on the Hetucakra, the Trairūpya, the use of exemplification as one necessary part of the syllogism, the treatment of null classes and the list of fallacies, are closely interrelated with one another like the links of a chain, and none of them can be dispensed with.

Dignāga's descendents at the later period failed to realize this point and his theories were treated as disconnected and isolated thought fragments.

---

1. Randle 2, p.185, N-1
2. Nyāyamukha Taishō 1628. p.1b.
3. Bochenski 4, Section 53

3. The third cause is the deliberate misinterpretation by Dignāga's opponents, particularly by Uddyotakara, as mentioned in the last section.

The controversy on the Trairūpya in the time of Uddyotakara and of Vācaspati Miśra is almost pointless, both the defenders and the critics deviated from genuine search of truth but indulged in a game of dogmatic and sectarian competition. But for a matter of historical interest, the discussion in the previous chapter would not have been included in this work.

Another point to mention is that all the materials on the debate are based on the Nyāyavārttika and the Nyāyavārttika tātparyaṭīkā. In view of Uddyotakara's ill treatment of Dignāga's theories, it is hard to believe that his record is free from bias. Therefore the accuracy of his record as a historical account is doubtful.

126. Interpretation of the Trairūpya

Before we interpret the Trairūpya in our way, let us examine the hetucakra again. We can find that among the nine possible combinations of the hetucakra there are two distinctly different groups, namely the group containing numbers 1. 4. 8, 1. 5. 8 and 1. 6. 8 and the group containing all the others.

For the sake of convenience, let us call them the Group I and the Group II respectively. The difference between them is that in the Group I, $\sim(Ex)(gx. \sim hx)$ or $b\bar{c} = O$; while in the Group II, $(Ex)(gx. \sim hx)$ or $b\bar{c} \neq O$.

The above means that one point in common to all combinations in the Group I is that in this group the syllogisms are free from a counter example.

Let us classify further. Among the three combinations in the Group I, let us call the combinations 1. 4. 8 and 1. 6. 8 the sub-group Ia, and the combination 1. 5. 8 the sub-group Ib. The difference between them is that in the former at least one similar instance exists, i. e. $(Ex)(\sim fx. gx. hx)$, or $\bar{a}bc \neq O$; while in the latter no similar instance exists, i. e. $\sim(Ex)(\sim fx. gx. hx)$ or $\bar{a}bc = O$.

The above means that one point in common to all combinations in the sub-group Ia is that in this sub-group there exists at least one similar example - a positive example.

The difference between 1. 4. 8 and 1. 6. 8 in the sub-group Ia is that in the former the middle term implies the major term and *vice versa*, i. e. $(x)(gx \supset hx)$ and $(x)(hx \supset gx)$, or $(x)(gx \equiv hx)$; while in 1. 6. 8 only the middle term implies the major term but not *vice versa*, i. e. $(x)(gx \supset hx)$. This difference means nothing but whether the class $\hat{x}(-gx.hx)$ is empty does not effect the validity of the syllogism.

From the above we can see at once that one rule excludes the Group II from the Group I, i. e. $-(Ex)(gx.-hx)$, and another rule excludes the sub-group Ib from the sub-group Ia, i. e. $(Ex)(-fx.gx.hx)$. These two rules, which are so easily derived, are precisely the 2nd and the 3rd clauses of the controversial '*Trairūpya*'.

The first clause is less obscure, although the term *anumeya* (or *pakṣa*) has been used by early logicians in ambiguous ways - sometimes it means the minor term, sometimes the major term and sometimes the *probandum*. It is most obvious that this word here should refer to the minor term and not anything else.

The word 'only' in the first clause should be put in a position such that

"Only the *hetu* (gx, not - gx) is present in the subject" $(x)(fx \supset gx)$.

It should neither be

"The *hetu* is present in the subject only" $(x)(gx \supset fx)$, nor be

"The *hetu* is only (barely) present in the subject" $(Ex)(fx.gx)$, as wrongly interpreted by Uddyotakara.

The above way of interpretation is not merely my personal speculation. The Chinese translation, although usually very poor, is accurate enough in the rendering of the *Trairūpya*. The word 遍 which means 'pervade' or 'pervasive' is used in the first and the third clauses; while the word 定 which means 'necessary' is used in the second clause. According to the Chinese rendering, the *Trairūpya* should be translated as follows:

The pervasive presence of the *hetu* in the subject;
The necessary presence of the *hetu* in some similar instances;
The pervasive absence of the *hetu* from dissimilar instances.

The phrase 'necessary presence' actually means 'assured presence', 'not failing to be present' or 'bare presence' and includes two possible cases, namely: the pervasive presence and the partial presence. (sapakṣavyāpaka and sapakṣaikadeśavṛtti). In symbolic notation:

$$(x)((-fx.\,hx)\supset gx).\,(Ex)(-fx.\,hx.\,gx)\ \mathrm{V}\ (Ex)(-fx.\,hx.\,gx).\,(Ex)(-fx.\,hx.\,-gx)$$
$$\equiv -(Ex)(-fx.\,hx.\,-gx).\,(Ex)(-fx.\,hx.\,gx)\ \mathrm{V}\ (Ex)(-fx.\,hx.\,gx).\,(Ex)(-fx.\,hx.\,-gx)$$
$$\equiv (Ex)(-fx.\,gx.\,hx).(-(Ex)(-fx.\,hx.\,-gx)\ \mathrm{V}\ (Ex)(-fx.\,hx.\,-gx))$$
$$\equiv (Ex)(-fx.\,gx.\,hx)$$

Let us define "pervasive presence of b in a" as

"b is present in any a", or
"every a is b", in contrast to "partial presence of b in a" which means
"some a, but not every a, is b", or
"at least one a, but not every a, is b".

The "necessary presence of b in a" includes both types of presence, pervasive and partial, and is defined as

"b is present in at least one a, at most in every a", or
"at least one a, at most every a, is b".

The "pervasive absence of b from a" is defined by the formula

"b is absent from every a" or
"every a is non-b", or
"no a is b", in contrast to "partial absence", which means
"b is absent from some a" or
"some a, but not every a, is non-b". The difference is like that between the E-form and the O-form.

The "pervasive presence and absence" correspond to univeral proposition. But particular proposition includes both "necessary" and "partial" presence.

In accordance with the above understanding, the Trairūpya may be interpreted as follows:

The first clause:

"The property g is present in everything which possesses the property f",
"Everything which possesses the property f possesses the property g",
"For every x, 'x is an f' implies 'x is a g'", or
"$(x)(fx \supset gx)$", or "$a\bar{b} = O$"

The second clause:

"There is at least one occasion in which the property g is present in a thing which possesses the property h, apart from the thing which possesses the property f, which remains to be proved",
"Apart from the thing which possesses the property f, at least one thing which possesses the property h possesses the property g",
"For some x which is not an f, x is both an h and a g", or
"$(Ex)(-fx.\,gx.\,hx)$", or "$\bar{a}bc \neq O$"

The third clause:

"There is no occasion in which the property g is present in things which possess the property of non-h",
"Nothing which possesses the property non-h possesses the property g",
"For no x, x is both a non-h and a g",
"For every x, 'x is non-h' implies 'x is non-g'", or
"$-(Ex)(gx. -hx)$", or "$(x)(-hx \supset gx)$", or "$b\bar{c} = O$".

Now it seems to be possible to solve Dharmottara's dilemma on the interpretation of the word 'only' in the second clause:

'Only presence'
= "only presence of the property of the *hetu* in similar instances but not otherwise",
= "only presence of the property of the *hetu* in similar instances but not utter absence of it in all similar instances",
= "the presence of the property of the *hetu* in at least one similar instance".

In other words,
$(Ex)(gx. hx)$ is affirmed and $(x)(gx \supset -hx)$ is negated, or
$(Ex)(gx. hx)$ is affirmed and $-(Ex)(gx. hx)$ is negated.

This explanation can manage to avoid the dilemma of either inconsistency or redundancy.

It seems that I have spoken too much concerning the *Trairūpya* which is so simple and clear. As a matter of fact I would not have done so had the wrong interpretation not dominated the Indian logic since the seventh century.

Not to mention Dharmottara's *Nyāyabinduṭīkā*, even in our century Prof. Stcherbatsky has written in his monumental work *Buddhist Logic* in very definite language as follows:

> "It is indeed impossible to infringe the second rule without, at the same time, infringing the third one. The second and the third rules are only two aspects of one and the same rule. If the reason is not present in similar instances only, it *eo ipso* is present, either wholly or partially, in dissimilar instances also".[1]

Finally, let us link the *Trairūpya* and the *Hetucakra* together as follows:

1. Stcherbatsky 12. p. 320.

Middle	Major	Example	Terminology used in Hetucakra	Terminology used in Trairūpya
(1. 4. 8)				
produced	impermanent			
yes	yes	pot	sapakṣavyāpaka[1]	
no	yes	---		sapakṣa eva sattvam[5]
yes	no	---	vipakṣāvṛtti[2]	
no	no	space		
(1. 6. 8)				
effort-produced	impermanent			
yes	yes	pot	sapakṣaikadeśavṛtti[3]	
no	yes	lightning		asapakṣe cāsattvam eva[6]
yes	no	---	vipakṣāvṛtti[4]	
no	no	space		

13. Uddytokara's Hetucakra

131. Interpretation

1311. The Four-operator System

After criticizing Uddyotakara's ill-natured refutation, I should like to praise him for his achievement in expanding the Hetucakra to a perfect form.

In Dignāga's system there are two important regions in the universe of discourse, namely a$\bar{b}$ and ab; and there are two possible conditions for each of them, namely empty and non-empty.

Since we have four possible combinations, there should be altogether four operators. However, in Dignānean system there are only three of

1. pervasive presence in similar instances
2. absence in dissimilar instances
3. partial presence in similar instances
4. absence in dissimilar instances
5. unfailing presence in similar instances
6. necessary absence in dissimilar instances

them, two possible types of presence and only one possible type of absence, namely:

Pervasive presence:	$a\bar{b} = O,\ ab \neq O$
partial presence:	$a\bar{b} \neq O,\ ab \neq O$
absence:	$a\bar{b} \neq O,\ ab = O$

How about the remaining one, in which both regions ab and $a\bar{b}$ are empty?

The last case may be discarded by Dignāga because it seems to be unimportant, perhaps. It was Uddyotakara who first introduced the four-operator system, in which a new operator 'avidyamāna-' (non-existence) was used. Let us use the small 'y' to denote this operator.[1]

$$
\begin{aligned}
S\ y\ P &= \sim(Ex)\Phi x \ \text{Df.} \\
&= \sim(Ex)(\phi x . \psi x) . \sim(Ex)(\phi x . \sim\psi x) \ \text{Df.} \\
&= (ab = O).(a\bar{b} = O) \ \text{Df.} \\
&= (\hat{z}(\phi z) = \Lambda) \ \text{Df.}
\end{aligned}
$$

Now we have a logical square again instead of a triangle, but this square is different from that of Aristotle. This operator can be illustrated by Venn's diagram but not by Euler's:

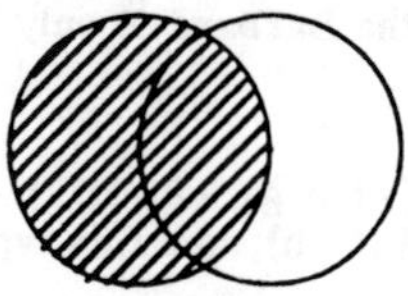

S y P

1312. Two Additional Premisses

Because of the introduction of one new operator, new premisses should be added. There are three classes operating against the class of hetu, there should be three more premisses. Since the hetucakra concerns mainly the major premiss, the following two are supplied by Uddyotakara:

1. I am using four vowels a, e, u and y for the four operators, in which u is the conjunct of Aristotelian i and o. The symbols used here are not the same as those of Hamilton and others who used additional symbols other than A, E, I and O.

10. <u>Avidyamānasapakṣa</u> S y H $= \sim(Ex)(\sim fx.\ hx)$ Df.
$= \sim(Ex)(\sim fx.\ hx.\ gx).\ \sim(Ex)(\sim fx.\ hx.\ \sim gx)$[1]

11. <u>Avidyamānavipakṣa</u> V y H $= \sim(Ex)(\sim hx)$ Df.
$= \sim(Ex)(\sim hx.\ gx).\ \sim(Ex)(\sim hx.\ \sim gx)$

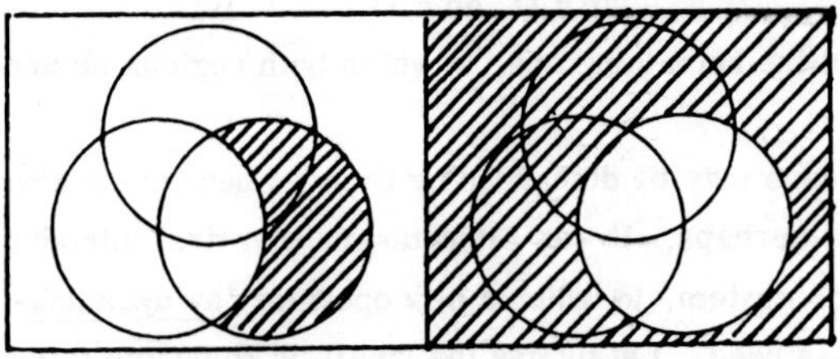

S y H V y H

1313. Uddyotakara's Wheel, with Sixteen Possible Combinations

If we take the premiss No. 1 as the minor premiss, and then take one from the group 4, 5, 6 and 10, to combine with one from the group 7, 8, 9 and 11, we shall have $1.\ 4^2$ or sixteen combinations. That is, we shall have seven new combinations.

Here I shall express them in the Barbara-B only as follows:

1. 4. 11
(P a H). (S a H). (V y H) =
$\sim E(f.\ \sim g).\ E(f.\ g).\ \sim E(\sim f.\ h.\ \sim g).\ E(\sim f.\ h.\ g).\ \sim E(\sim h.\ g).\ \sim E(\sim h.\ \sim g)$. . . . . (i)
Like the type 1. 4. 8, (i) implies $U(f \supset h)$, and this type is therefore valid.

1. 5. 11
(P a H). (S e H). (V y H) =
$\sim E(f.\ \sim g).\ E(f.\ g).\ E(\sim f.\ h.\ \sim g).\ \sim E(\sim f.\ h.\ g).\ \sim E(\sim h.\ g).\ \sim E(\sim h.\ \sim g)$. . . . . (i)
Like the type 1. 5. 8, this type is inconclusive because it is 'too narrow'.

1. 6. 11
(P a H). (S u H). (V y H) =
$\sim E(f.\ \sim g).\ E(f.\ g).\ E(\sim f.\ h.\ \sim g).\ E(\sim f.\ h.\ g).\ \sim E(\sim h.\ g).\ \sim E(\sim h.\ \sim g)$. . . . . (i)
Like the type 1. 6. 8, (i) implies $U(f \supset h)$ and this type is therefore valid.

The above three are not more than Dignāga's 1. 4. 8, 1. 5. 8 and 1. 6. 8, with the only difference of the non-existence of dissimilar instances.

Uddyotakara objected that "The middle 'being produced' is endowed with two characters for the person who does not admit the existence of any eternal object; and so is the middle 'being an effect of volition' and so these two middles would not be valid reasons" and "Either the

1. Premiss No. 10 was called by Uddyotakara '<u>avidyamānasajātīya</u>'

two arguments which the Buddhist gives as illustrations of valid syllogisms are not valid, or else he must admit that the purely positive is a valid type of syllogism".[1]

In fact, when Dignāga raised his illustrative case of "Sound is impermanent ... because it is produced" he avoided involving his own doctrine "everything is impermanent", which may not be accepted by his opponents. The example 'space' was used in a conventional sense. He should not be blamed simply because of his objective attitude.

Dignāga did put negative examples in the Hetucakra for the sake of illustration. But whether he had imposed the existence of dissimilar instances as a necessary condition in a syllogism is another question. But in view of the following facts, it seems most unlikely that he did.

First, he had never established a fourth clause in the Trairūpya like "necessary presence of dissimilar instances" as he did in the second clause. Secondly, in many of his works, a negative example was not always stated in syllogisms.

But Vācaspati Miśra held an opinion that the necessity of a dissimilar instance in a 'negative concomitance' is precisely the same as that of a similar instance in a 'positive concomitance'. If the Buddhist had accepted one, they should not reject the other.

At the first glance, his allegation seems to be plausible. If the premiss $(x)(gx \supset hx)$ is defined as $-(Ex)(gx.-hx).(Ex)(gx.hx)$, then by substituting $-hx$ for gx and $-gx$ for hx, the premiss $(x)(-hx \supset -gx)$ should be defined as $-(Ex)(-hx.--gx).(Ex)(-gx.-hx)$, or $-(Ex)(gx.-hx).(Ex)(-gx.-hx)$.

It seems that he was applying the law of simple contraposition $(x)(gx \supset hx) \equiv (x)(-hx \supset -gx)$ and concluded that $(Ex)(gx.hx)$ and $(Ex)(-gx.-hx)$ should be equally necessary or equally unnecessary.

His mistake is, the law of simple contraposition does not have existential import. If the two concomitances are defined in the following way:

$$(x)(gx \supset hx) = -(Ex)(gx.-hx).(Ex)(gx.hx) \quad Df.$$
$$(x)(-hx \supset -gx) = -(Ex)(-hx.gx).(Ex)(-gx.-hx) \quad Df.$$

the law of simple contraposition will no longer hold.

1. NV. I.1.35. p.132.
   IL. p.238.

In other words, the factor (Ex)(gx. hx) has no effect on (x)(- hx ⊃ - gx), and similarly the factor (Ex)(- gx. - hx) has not effect on (x)(gx ⊃ hx) either.

What the Buddhist used was the positive concomitance and not the negative one, and the negative example is not a necessity.

Even in the famous illustrative case in western traditional logic "Socrates is a man, etc.", the major premiss is definitely "All men are mortal" and not "All non-mortals are not men", irrespective of whether one regard these two propositions are equivalent.

Strictly speaking, the third clause of the Trairūpya should be - (Ex)(gx. - hx) and not (x)(- hx ⊃ - gx) if the latter is defined in the above way.

1.10.7
(P a H). (S y H). (V a H) =
- E(f. - g). E(f. g). - E(- f. h. - g). - E(- f. h. g). - E(- h. - g). E(- h. g). . . . . (i)
Like the type 1.5.7, this type is contradictory.

1.10.9
(P a H). (S y H). (V u H) =
- E(f. - g). E(f. g). - E(- f. h. - g). - E(- f. h. g). E(- h. - g). E(- h. g) . . . . . (i)
Like the type 1.5.9, this type is contradictory.

1.10.11
(P a H). (S y H). (V y h) =
- E(- f. g). E(f. g). - E(- f. h. - g). - E(- f. h. g). - E(- h. g). - E(- h. - g). . . . . (i)
Like the type 1.5.8, (i) implies - E(- f. h. g) and - E(- f. - h. g);
this type is therefore inconclusive because of being too narrow.

There is not much novelty in the above six types. The most interesting case is the type 1.10.8. This is the case which Uddyotakara considered as valid. His intention was to make use of this type to reject the second clause of the Trairūpya, i.e. without a similar instance (the class ābc is empty), the syllogism can still be valid.

Irrespective of whether this type is valid, he had unintentionally revealed one point, namely, that it is not the case that he failed to understand the second clause. For what he intended to reject by applying this type in the Hetucakra was precisely what Dignāga meant in the second clasue of the Trairūpya.

Let us examine whether this type is valid:

1.10.8

$(P\ a\ H).(S\ y\ H).(V\ e\ H) =$

$-E(f.-g).E(f.g).-E(-f.h.-g).-E(-f.h.g).-E(-h.g).E(-h.-g) \ldots (i)$

(i) implies $-E(-f.-g.h).-E(g.-h).E(-g.-h) \ldots \ldots (ii)$

The factor $-f$ cannot be dropped, even if he could, then

(ii) would become $-E(-g.h).-E(g.-h).E(-g.-h) \ldots \ldots (iii)$

(iii) implies $U(-g \supset -h).U(-h \supset -g)$, or $U(-g \equiv -h) \ldots \ldots (iv)$

Perhaps he was trying to apply the law of Inversion of Equivalence:

$U(g \equiv h) \equiv U(-g \equiv -h)$, without realizing that

$U(g \equiv h) = -E(g.-h).-E(-g.h).E(g.h)$ Df. and

$U(-g \equiv -h) = -E(g.-h).-E(-g.h).E(-g.-h)$ Df.

They are not identical if they are so defined, and the Law of Inversion of Equivalence does not hold.

Perhaps Uddyotakara would have defended himself by saying that he did not accept the concept of existential import in the first place, so he was not bound by the above definition.

If this is the case, why did he insist on giving a negative example $E(-g.-h)$ in the type 1.10.8; is it not an existential import? The type 1.10.8 was considered by him as valid; while the type 1.10.11 was not. The only difference lies in the existence of a negative example. Does the existential import not matter at all?

Perhaps he was trying to use the formula $U(f \supset -g).U(-g \equiv -h) \supset U(f \supset -h)$. This formula is correct. However, he was not justified to use this formula, because:

First, he wrote in the very beginning that $(x)(fx \supset -gx)$ or *sādhyāvṛtti* was invalid and therefore should be discarded from the list.

Secondly, granted the case *sādhyāvṛtti* can be allowed, it will become the same as 1.4.8 by substituting $-g/g$ and $-h/h$; and the type 1.10.8 will lose its meaning.

Thirdly, his illustrative case does not fit this formula. Repetition of negatives seems to have confused his contemporaries, perhaps including himself; but once symbols are applied, his mistakes immediately become obvious.

Uddyotakara's sequence is slightly different from Dignāga's:

1.4.7	1.4.8	1.4.9	1.4.11
1.5.7	1.5.8	1.5.9	1.5.11
1.6.7	1.5.8	1.6.9	1.6.11
1.10.7	1.10.8	1.10.9	1.10.11

Dignāga's:				Uddyotakar's:			
I	II	III	-	1	3	2	10
IV	V	VI	-	4	6	5	12
VII	VIII	IX	-	7	9	8	11
-	-	-	-	13	15	14	16

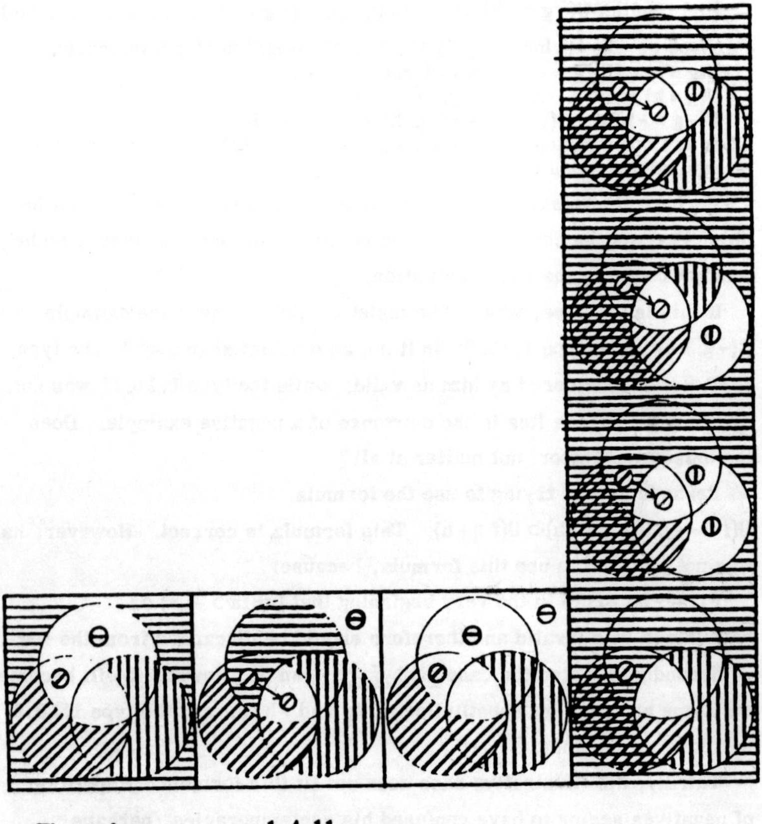

The order:

			1.4.11
			1.5.11
			1.6.11
1.10.7	1.10.8	1.10.9	1.10.11

1314. The Region (f.g.h)

Some doubt may arise about the condition of the central region (f.g.h) of the sixteen diagrams. In several types of the hetucakra (1.4.7, 1.5.7, 1.6.7, 1.10.7, 1.4.9, 1.5.9, 1.6.9 and 1.10.9) its existential condition is unknown. In the other types (1.4.8, 1.5.8, 1.6.8, 1.10.8, 1.4.11,

1.5.11, 1.6.11 and 1.10.11) we can see that in the diagrams there are arrows pointing from the area (f.g.-h) to the area (f.g.h), because the minor premiss has existential import. Does this mean that the area (f.g.h) becomes non-empty in these types?

Among these eight types, 1.4.8, 1.5.8 and 1.6.8 were introduced by Dignāga himself while all the others were introduced after his death by Uddyotakara. Dignāga accepted 1.4.8 and 1.6.8 but rejected 1.5.8. Following his rule of the trairūpya, we may reasonably assume that Dignāga would accept 1.4.11 and 1.6.11 but reject 1.5.11, 1.10.8 and 1.10.11, had these types been presented to him in his lifetime.

Suppose the area (f.g.h) of the eight types is non-empty, then all these eight types should be valid, why did Dignāga reject some of them?

It will be a long story to answer this question. Before I do so, it is necessary to consider another problem first, and then I shall return to this one again.

Let us leave the complexity of the central region (f.g.h) for a moment so that we may concentrate our attention on the characteristics of the major premiss only. As a matter of fact, in Dignāga's system, it is his handling of the major premiss alone, and not the complexity of the central region, which really interests me.

An isolated major premiss should not be called a major premiss any more, because it is no longer a part of a syllogism; we should therefore treat it as an independent quantified proposition. Graphically there will be two circles g and h, and the circle f disappears. Let us imagine that the circle f shrinks in such a way that it no longer overlaps either the two circles g and h or their complementary area: as a result the sixteen diagrams will appear much simpler, as shown in § 21.[1] A detailed discussion will be given in Chapter 2.

132. Uddyotakara's Illustrative Cases

1.4.11.
"Sound is impermanent, because it is produced" (everything is impermanent)

1.5.11
"Sound is impermanent, because it is audible" (everthing is impermanet)

1. Such a process of 'shrinking' is uni-directional, because the reverse process is impossible.

1.6.11
"Sound is impermanent, because it is an object of senses"
(everything is impermanent)

1.10.7
"Sound is permanent, because it is produced" (everything is impermanent)

1.10.8
"The living organism is not without a soul, because it is not without vital functions"

1.10.9
"Sound is permanent, because it is an object of senses"
(everything is impermanent)

1.10.11
"Everything is nameable, because it is knowable".

The types 1.4.11, 1.5.11, 1.6.11, 1.10.7, 1.10.9 are not very new to us, except that 'everything is impermanent' is imposed. Let us examine the illustrative case for the type 1.10.8:

Without the aid of symbols, he had taken great pains in establishing this type. Let us write his illustrative case in the following form:

"Everything that is without vital functions is without soul,
The living organism is not without vitalfunctions,
Therefore the living organism is not without soul".

Let Lx = x is living organism
Vx = x possesses vital functions
Sx = x possesses a soul

Granted that the exclusion of the subject can be neglected, the antecedent $(x)(Lx \supset \sim\sim Vx).(x)(\sim Vx \supset \sim Sx)$ is equivalent to $(x)(Lx \supset Vx).(x)(Sx \supset Vx)$, which cannot be assured equivalent to $(x)(Lx \supset Vx).(x)(Vx \supset Sx)$.

Vācaspati Miśra saw this point and wrote in the Nyāyavarttika tātparyaṭīkā that the major premiss should be 'converted' to the following form: (vyatyāsena yojanā)

"Everything that is without soul is without vital functions"[1]

In whatever system of logic, such a process of 'conversion' does not exist. Moreover, when the syllogism

$(x)(Lx \supset Vx).(x)(Vx \supset Sx) \supset (x)(Lx \supset Sx)$ can satisfy Vācaspati Miśra, the major premiss $(x)(Vx \supset Sx)$ was precisely the one which Uddyotakara tried to avoid in order to escape from the fallacy of petitio principii, because it was not accepted by the opponent.

---

1. NYT. 126.11. p.193.
IL. p.246.

Uddyotakara's intention was to 'smuggle' his sectarian dogma inside a text of logic. Consequently he had to commit a mistake of either one kind or of the other; i. e. either petitio principii, or infringing the law of simple contraposition:

$(x)(gx \supset hx) \equiv (x)(\sim hx \supset \sim gx)$, particularly since his earlier opponent Dignāga had announced a number of times in his works the illustrative case "If a thing is a product, it is impermanent; if it is not impermanent, it is not a product".

The last type 1. 10. 11 'pakṣavyāpaka-avidyamānasapakṣavipakṣa' (pakṣa pervasive, sapakṣa and vipakṣa non-existent) is a difficult one, because an illustrative case such that all regions g. h, g. ~h, ~g. h and ~g. ~h are empty is not as handy as those of the other fifteen types.

If we translate Uddyotakara 's illustrative case into a three-membered syllogism in the form of $U(f \supset g). U(g \supset h) \supset U(f \supset h)$, we have

Everything is knowable, (minor premiss)
Every knowable thing is nameable, (major premiss)
Therefore everything is nameable. (conclusion)

Being aware of the difficulty of this type, he managed to find out a case in which both sapakṣa and vipakṣa are empty. The subject 'everything' is exhaustive; its complement is empty. The sapakṣa, by definition, does not include the subject, therefore it is empty. The vipakṣa is empty, because nothing is not nameable.

At a prima facie observation, his case seems to be quite plausible. This is one more typical example of Uddyotakara's ingenuity, if it can be called so at all. If, however, we examine it carefully, we find the following faults:

1. In the diagram, the region (~f. g. h) is shaded simply because the complement of f is empty, i. e. ~E(~f). It is not the case that the region (g. h) is empty, i. e. ~E(g. h), which is actually demanded in this type. If the subject of the minor premiss is not 'everything' but 'a pot', the syllogism will be:

A pot is knowable, (minor premiss)
Everything knowable thing is nameable, (major premiss)
Therefore a pot is nameable. (conclusion).

Then the region (-f.g.h) will not be empty, and this case will belong to the type 1.4.11 and not 1.10.11.

Perhaps he had forgotten one thing, that the scheme of the hetucakra was designed to represent the variety, which should be complete and non-overlapping, of the major premiss. The major premiss of his illustrative case of type 1.10.11 actually belongs to the type 1.4.11; this is overlapping. The major premiss representing the empty universe lacks an illustrative case; this is incomplete.

2. He used 'everything' as the subject of the minor premiss, as if he tried to formulate this syllogism as $U(t \supset k). U(k \supset n) \supset U(t \supset n)$, where t = thing, k = knowable and n = nameable. The word 'everything' can certainly be the grammatical subject of a sentence, but its function in logic is a quantifier 'for every x, ... rather than a logical subject of a proposition. The formula of his illustrative case is no more a syllogism, but something like $Uk \,.\, U(k \supset n) \supset Un$.

It is most unsuitable to put such a formula in the list of the hetucakra, because it is something totally different from others, like 'a camel emerges from a group of sheep' in a Chinese proverb.

3. The premiss 'avidyamānavipakṣa' (vipakṣa non-existent) in this case is 'nothing is not nameable'. By a mere immediate inference of 'obversion' it can be changed into 'everything is nameable', which is exactly the required conclusion, without the necessity of adding any other premiss. We can say that his premiss 'avidyamānavipakṣa' is faulty on account of petitio principii, or his syllogism is pointless.

We can therefore conclude that Uddyotakara's illustrative case for the type 1.10.11 is a wrong one and cannot represent the formula 'pakṣavyāpaka-avidyamānasapakṣavipakṣa'.

2. WHAT DO THE THEORIES OF THE HETUCAKRA AND THE TRAIRŪPYA MEAN TO US?

This chapter is neither exposition nor interpretation of ancient Indian logic. It shows what the consequence to our system of logic will be after a few new notions in the Indian logic have been introduced.

In the present system of logic, we can find here and there analogous laws common to the logic of classes, the restricted predicate logic and the propositional logic.

They seem to be three different systems. But when the restricted predicate logic is monadic with one individual variable, the variable may be dispensed with and consequently the functions of the restricted predicate logic may be said to have the same meaning as functions of the logic of classes.[1]

The relation between the logic of classes and the propositional logic is quite a different one. Boole's logic of classes has been converted into the two-valued propositional logic swiftly by a very ingenious modification, namely, by imposing a condition that the class in question should either be universal or be empty, and by converting the universal class (V) and the empty class (Λ) into 'truth' and 'falsity'.

However, such a transformation is merely a kind of artificial expedience; the logic of classes and propositional logic are not really identical but 'analogous'. So are the restricted predicate logic and the propositional logic.

21. The Logic of Classes

As I have mentioned in the last chapter, let us consider the major premiss only and treat it as an independent quantified proposition. The first of the three variables disappears and there are two variables left.

1. Carnap: Symbolische Logik, p. 96

In terms of the logic of classes, the variables left are b and c. Accordingly we may call these types 4.7, 4.8, 4.9 etc. instead of 1.4.7, 1.4.8, 1.4.9, etc. We can be temporarily free from the cumbersom factors $\bar{a}$, -fx and $x \neq y$ in various systems. Let us list all instances, both positive and negative, in the <u>hetucakra</u>, as follows:

	bc	$\bar{b}c$	$b\bar{c}$	$\bar{b}\bar{c}$
4.7	space	pot	-	-
4.8	pot	-	-	space
4.9	pot	lightning	-	space
5.7	-	pot	space	-
5.8	-	-	space	pot
5.9	-	pot	space	lightning
6.7	lightning	pot	space	-
6.8	pot	-	lightning	space
6.9	space	pleasure	atom	pot
4.11	pot	-	-	-
5.11	-	-	space	-
6.11	pot	-	lightning	-
10.7	-	pot	-	-
10.8	-	-	-	pot
10.9	-	pot	-	lightning
10.11	-	-	-	-

Then let us put:

4 = (S a H), etc. etc.

+ = valid

- = contradictory

b = inconclusive because of being too broad

n = inconclusive because of being too narrow

(x = v) = there is at least one member in this class

(x = o) = there is no member in this class

CLASS FUNCTION NAME	DEFINITION				SEQUENCE according to		VALIDITY according to	
	bc	$b\bar{c}$	$\bar{b}c$	$\bar{b}\bar{c}$	Dig.	Udd.	Dig.	Udd.
c-6.9	v	v	v	v	9	8	b	b
c-6.7	v	v	v	o	7	7	b	b
c-4.9	v	v	o	v	3	2	b	b
c-4.7	v	v	o	o	1	1	b	b
c-6.8	v	o	v	v	8	9	+	+
c-6.11	v	o	v	o		11		+
c-4.8	v	o	o	v	2	3	+	+
c-4.11	v	o	o	o		10		+
c-5.9	o	v	v	v	6	5	-	-
c-5.7	o	v	v	o	4	4	-	-
c-10.9	o	v	o	v		14		-
c-10.7	o	v	o	o		13		-
c-5.8	o	o	v	v	5	6	n	n
c-5.11	o	o	v	o		12		n
c-10.8	o	o	o	v		15		+
c-10.11	o	o	o	o		16		n

The above table should be read as follows:

c-6.9 = (bc = v). ($b\bar{c}$ = v). ($\bar{b}c$ = v). ($\bar{b}\bar{c}$ = v),

c-6.7 = (bc = v). ($b\bar{c}$ = v). ($\bar{b}c$ = v). ($\bar{b}\bar{c}$ = o), etc. etc.

Let us express the above table in everyday language and in Venn's diagram as follows:

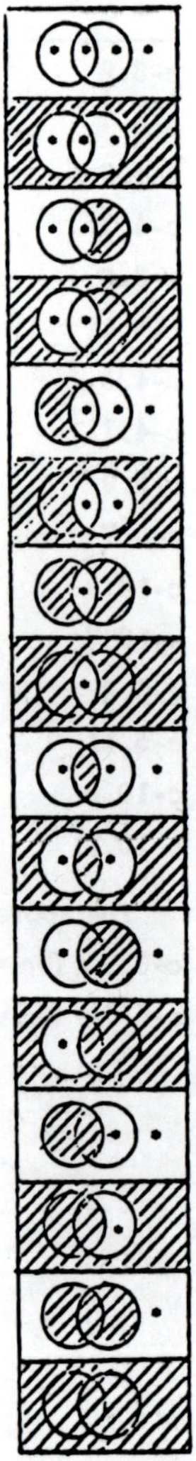

1. b and c are overlapping, $\bar{b}\bar{c}$ is non-empty.

2. " $\bar{b}\bar{c}$ is empty.

3. b includes c, $\bar{b}\bar{c}$ is non-empty.

4. " $\bar{b}\bar{c}$ is empty.

5. b is included in c, $\bar{b}\bar{c}$ is non-empty.

6. " $\bar{b}\bar{c}$ is empty.

7. b and c are equivalent, $\bar{b}\bar{c}$ is non-empty.

8. " $\bar{b}\bar{c}$ is empty.

9. b and c are mutually excluding, $\bar{b}\bar{c}$ is non-empty.

10. " $\bar{b}\bar{c}$ is empty.

11. c is empty, and b is not, $\bar{b}\bar{c}$ is non-empty.

12. " $\bar{b}\bar{c}$ is empty.

13. b is empty, and c is not, $\bar{b}\bar{c}$ is non-empty.

14. " $\bar{b}\bar{c}$ is empty.

15. both b and c are empty, $\bar{b}\bar{c}$ is non-empty.

16. " $\bar{b}\bar{c}$ is empty.

It is interesting to see that the above is a step further than Gergonne's attempt in finding out all possible relations between two classes concerning their extension. Gergonne gave five types of relations, under the condition that neither of the two classes should be null:

a C b (est contenu dans) = class inclusion
a Ɔ b (contiens) = inverse class inclusion
a I b (est indentique à) = class equivalence
a H b (est hors de) = class exclusion
a X b (s'entre-croise avec) = class overlapping

The date of Gergonne's paper was between the dates of introduction of Euler's and Venn's diagrams. The Hetucakra was designed as if it were an attempt of Gergonne formulated after the introduction of Venn's diagram.

Suppose we examine the relationship between two classes with respect to the universe of discourse, the universal and the null classes will inevitably enter in, and there must be sixteen types instead. Let us compare the Hetucakra and Gergonne's scheme as follows:

NUMBER	CLASS FUNCTION	GERGONNE'S SYMBOLS
1	c-6.9	b X c
2	c-6.7	b X c
3	c-4.9	b Ɔ c
4	c-4.7	b Ɔ c
5	c-6.8	b C c
6	c-6.11	b C c
7	c-4.8	b I c
8	c-4.11	b I c
9	c-5.9	b H c
10	c-5.7	b H c
11	c-10.9	
12	c-10.7	
13	c-5.8	
14	c-5.11	
15	c-10.8	
16	c-10.11	

From number 11 onwards, the empty classes enter in, therefore six types are not included in Gergonne's scheme. The five pairs from No. 1 to No. 10 correspond to Gergonne's five types. The reason why the number is doubled is that in the odd numbers there is no universal class; while in the even numbers universal classes enter in.

In Gergonne's scheme, no discrimination is made between the universal and non-universal classes.

In short, the Indian scheme of the Hetucakra is a generalized form of Gergonne's scheme.

As regards the total number of possible syllogisms, including both conclusive and inconclusive ones, let us use the following formula:

(the total number of possible syllogisms) =

(number of possible minor premisses) x

(number of possible major premisses) x

(number of possible conclusions).

Gergonn's: 5 x 5 x 5 = 125;
Dignāga's: 3 x 9 x 1 = 27; then reduced to 1 x 9 x 1 = 9;
Uddyotakara's: 3 x 16 x 1 = 48; then reduced to 1 x 16 x 1 = 16

In the Aristotelian system, there are the so-called 'weakened' moods, such as AAI. Although they are excluded from the list of valid syllogisms, they are not false either.

This is not true in Indian systems, because the mood 'AAU' is false. For instance,

AAA: All men are animals,
All animals are mortal,
Therefore all men are mortal.

AAI: All men are animals,
All animals are mortal,
Therefore there are men who are mortal.

AAU: All men are animals,
All animals are mortal,
Therefore, some men are mortal and some men are not.

Since AAI does not appear in Dignāgean syllogistic, and AAU is false, the only possible conclusion is AAA. That is to say, once the two premisses are stated, the conclusion is uniquely determined. Therefore the number of possible conclusions for a given pair of premisses is 1.

Their major premisses are derived from the conception of similar and dissimilar instances, therefore their major premisses are according to more detailed scheme than that of Gergonne. Their minor premisses do not concern similar and dissimilar instances, and have three forms only, namely A, E and U, therefore their minor premisses are less detailed than those of Gergonne.

Furthermore, since they have excluded E and U forms in their minor premisses, their number of minor premisses is further reduced from 3 to 1.

22. The Restricted Predicate Logic

Corresponding to the sixteen 'class relation functions' in the logic of classes, we can derive sixteen functions in the restricted predicate logic, or quantified calculus, defined in the following ways:

q-6.9 = E(g.h).E(g.~h).E(~g.h).E(~g.~h) Df.
q-6.7 = E(g.h).E(g.~h).E(~g.h).~E(~g.~h) Df., etc. etc.

where the letter 'q' denotes 'quantificational'. By putting the definitions in the form of a table, we have:

FUNCTION NAMES	DEFINITIONS			
	g.h.	g.~h	~g.h	~g.~h
q-6.9	E	E	E	E
q-6.7	E	E	E	-E
q-4.9	E	E	~E	E
q-4.7	E	E	~E	~E
q-6.8	E	-E	E	E
q-6.11	E	-E	E	~E
q-4.8	E	-E	~E	E
q-4.11	E	-E	~E	~E
q-5.9	-E	E	E	E
q-5.7	-E	E	E	~E
q-10.9	-E	E	~E	E
q-10.7	-E	E	~E	~E
q-5.8	-E	-E	E	E
q-5.11	-E	-E	E	~E
q-10.8	-E	-E	~E	E
q-10.11	-E	-E	~E	~E

The above list can be translated into everyday language as follows:

1. Something is g and something is non-g; something is h and something is non-h.
2. Nothing is both non-g and non-h; all other combinations are realized.
3. Nothing is both non-g and h; all other combinations are realized.
4. Everything is non-g; something is h and something is non-h.
5. Nothing is both g and non-h; all other combinations are realized.

6. Something is g and something is non-g; everything is non-h.

7. Nothing is both g and non-h and nothing is both non-g and h; all other combinations are realized.

8. Everything is both g and h, but not otherwise.

9. Nothing is both g and h; all other combinations are realized.

10. Nothing is both g and h, and nothing is both non-g and non-h; all other combinations are realized.

11. Something is g and something is non-g; everything is non-h.

12. Everything is both g and non-h, but not otherwise.

13. Everything is non-g; something is h and something is non-h.

14. Everything is both non-g and h; but not otherwise.

15. Everything is both non-g and non-h; but not otherwise.

16. There is neither g nor non-g, neither h nor non-h.

221. Implication and equivalence

A few functions in the list of the previous chapter may be expressed in a more familiar language as follows:

5. "All g is some h", which is implication;

3. 'Some g is all h', which is inverse implication;

7. "All g is all h", which is equivalence.

Among the sixteen functions, those of implication and equivalence are the most important ones. It is necessary to define them clearly according to various conditions.

First, we have so far four different kinds of implication:

1. $(x)(gx \supset hx) = -(Ex)(gx.-hx)$ Df.
$= (b\bar{c} = 0)$ Df.

The first definition is the usual 'formal implication' with no existential import. It does not exclude empty classes such as involved in 'all unicorns can square a circle".

2. $(x)(gx \supset' hx) = -(Ex)(gx.-hx).(Ex)(gx.hx)$ Df.
$= (b\bar{c} = 0).(bc = v)$ Df.

The second definition introduces existential import. This form is derived from the second and third clauses of the <u>Trairūpya</u>. Empty classes are excluded in this type.

3. $(x)(gx \supset'' hx) = -(Ex)(gx.-hx).(Ex)(gx.hx).(Ex)(-gx.hx)$ Df.
$= (b\bar{c} = 0).(bc = v).(\bar{b}c = v)$ Df.

The previous definition includes both cases of implication and equivalence. The third definition excludes the latter. This form is derived from Dignāga's <u>hetucakra</u> No. 1.6.8.

4. $(x)(gx \supset''' hx) = -(Ex)(gx.-hx).(Ex)(gx.hx).(Ex)(-gx.hx).(Ex)$ $(-gx.-hx)$ Df.

$$= (b\bar{c} = 0).(bc = v).(\bar{b}c = v).(\bar{b}\bar{c} = v) \quad \text{Df.}$$

The previous definition cannot discriminate implication from the type 6.11, i.e. 'everything is h'. The fourth definition can exclude the latter. This form is derived from Uddyotakara's <u>hetucakra</u> No. 1.6.8.

Secondly, we have three different kinds of equivalence:

1. $(x)(gx \equiv hx) = -(Ex)(gx.-hx).-(Ex)(-gx.hx)$ Df.

$$= (b\bar{c} = 0).(\bar{b}c = 0) \quad \text{Df.}$$

The first definition is the usual 'formal equivalence' with no existential import. It does not exclude empty classes.

2. $(x)(gx \equiv' hx) = -(Ex)(gx.-hx).-(Ex)(-gx.hx).(Ex)(gx.hx)$ Df.

$$= (b\bar{c} = 0).(\bar{b}c = 0).(bc = v). \quad \text{Df.}$$

The second definition introduces existential import. This form is derived from Dignāga's <u>Hetucakra</u> No. 1.4.8. It can exclude empty classes.

3. $(x)(gx \equiv'' hx) = -(Ex)(gx.-hx).-(Ex)(-gx.hx).(Ex)(gx.hx).(Ex)$ $(-gx.-hx)$ Df.

$$= (b\bar{c} = 0).(\bar{b}c = 0).(bc = v).(\bar{b}\bar{c} = v) \quad \text{Df.}$$

The previous definition cannot distinguish equivalence from the type 1.4.11, i.e. "everything is both g and h" which can be called 'formal conjunction'. This definition can exclude the latter. This form is derived from Uddyotakara's <u>hetucakra</u> No. 1.4.8.

The function 'implication' is undoubtedly the most important function; it is the key of logical inference. The function 'equivalence' has particular significance in Indian logic in establishing 'definitions'.

In establishing a definition, the extension of the <u>definiend</u> and that of the <u>definiendum</u> should be precisely equal. This point has been discussed in a paper by Prof. Staal.[1]

The fourth definition of implication and the third definition of equivalence are the narrowest forms among all definitions. Let us call them respectively 'narrow implication' and 'narrow equivalence'.

---

1. Staal 6

23. The Propositional Logic

Let us now turn to the third system propositional logic. The relation between the logic of classes and the propositional logic is not so direct as that between the logic of classes and the restricted predicate logic. The laws in the logic of classes and the propositional logic are only loosely analogous.

However, by an ingenious modification of the logic of classes that the classes in question should be either universal or empty, Boole's logic of classes can be transformed into the propositional logic.

Such a transformation is not a fact but a purely artificial device. Through failure in appreciating this point, a number of commentators have wrongly identified Boole's logic of classes with a two-valued algebra, as pointed out by Prof. W. Kneale in the Development of Logic.[1]

Let us apply the above mentioned modification to the construction of a similar table in the propositional logic, and call the two possible cases respectively 'true' and 'false'.

The table so constructed will not be new to us. It is precisely the same as that made by Ludwig Wittgenstein in his Tractatus Logico-Philosophicus,[2] and is a particular case of the theory in the Introduction to a General Theory of Propositions by E.L. Post, both of them were published in 1921.

In the following table, the function names are borrowed from R. Carnap's Formalization of Logic.[3] The notations of J. Łukasiewicz, R. Carnap and Peano-Russell are all added for a matter of reference. By 'Peano-Russell' I mean their general pattern of symbolism only; a few new symbols were introduced after the publication of the Principia Mathematica, namely: '$\underline{\vee}$' for 'exclusive disjunction'; '$\subset$' for 'inverse implication', '$\downarrow$' for 'bi-negation', 'T' for 'tautology' and 'C' for 'contradiction'.

1. p.413.
2. Tractatus Logico Philosophicus. Eng. tr. by D.F. Pears. (1963). pp.74-5.
3. R. Carnap: Formalization of Logic. (1943) pp.12 and 82.

The sixteen dyadic truth functions of the propositional logic

FUNCTION NAME	DEFINITION				SYMBOLS USED		
(Carnap)	qr TT	qr TF	qr FT	qr FF	(Peano-Russell)	(Carnap)	(Łukasiewicz)
Tautology	T	T	T	T	q T r	cC1	Vqr
Disjunction	T	T	T	F	q V r	cC2	Aqr
Inverse implication	T	T	F	T	q ⊂ r	cC3	Bqr
First component	T	T	F	F	q	cC4	Iqr
Implication	T	F	T	T	q ⊃ r	cC5	Cqr
Second component	T	F	T	F	r	cC6	Hqr
Equivalence	T	F	F	T	q ≡ r	cC7	Eqr
Conjunction	T	F	F	F	q . r	cC8	Kqr
Exclusion	F	T	T	T	q / r	cC9	Dqr
Non-equivalence	F	T	T	F	q $\underline{\vee}$ r	cC10	Jqr
Negation of the second	F	T	F	T	- r	cC11	Gqr
First alone	F	T	F	F	q . ~r	cC12	Lqr
Negation of the first	F	F	T	T	-q	cC13	Fqr
Second alone	F	F	T	F	-q . r	cC14	Mqr
Bi-negation	F	F	F	T	q ↓ r	cC15	Zqr
Contradiction	F	F	F	F	q C r	cC16	Oqr

where T = true
F = false
q = antecedent
r = consequent

24. Three kinds of functions defined by matrices in uniform symbols

Let us call the three tables 'the class matrices', 'the quantificational matrices' and 'the truth matrices', and compare them as follows:

	the class matrices				the quantificational matrices				the truth matrices			
	bc	b$\bar{c}$	$\bar{b}$c	$\bar{b}\bar{c}$	g.h	g.~h	~g.h	~g.~h	qr TT	qr TF	qr FT	qr FF
1.	v	v	v	v	E	E	E	E	T	T	T	T
2.	v	v	v	o	E	E	E	~E	T	T	T	F
3.	v	v	o	v	E	E	~E	E	T	T	F	T
4.	v	v	o	o	E	E	~E	~E	T	T	F	F
5.	v	o	v	v	E	~E	E	E	T	F	T	T
6.	v	o	v	o	E	~E	E	~E	T	F	T	F
7.	v	o	o	v	E	~E	~E	E	T	F	F	T
8.	v	o	o	o	E	~E	~E	~E	T	F	F	F
9.	o	v	v	v	~E	E	E	E	F	T	T	T
10.	o	v	v	o	~E	E	E	~E	F	T	T	F
11.	o	v	o	v	~E	E	~E	E	F	T	F	T
12.	o	v	o	o	~E	E	~E	~E	F	T	F	F
13.	o	o	v	v	~E	~E	E	E	F	F	T	T
14.	o	o	v	o	~E	~E	E	~E	F	F	T	F
15.	o	o	o	v	~E	~E	~E	E	F	F	F	T
16.	o	o	o	o	~E	~E	~E	~E	F	F	F	F

Let us try to find a uniform notation for the three systems, to represent (1) the matrices as definitions of their functions, and (2) the respective functions.

First let us determine a uniform notation for their 'values'. There have been a number of ways to denote their 'values', which are listed as follows:

(a) The Logic of classes:

i. The class a is an empty class, i.e.

$a = \Lambda$, or $(x)(x \in \bar{a})$.

ii. The class a is a non-empty class, i.e.

$a = v$, or $(Ex)(x \in a)$.

iii. The class a is a universal class, i.e.

$a = V$, or $(x)(x \in a)$.

(b) The restricted predicate logic:

i. There is no x such that x is f, i.e.

$-(Ex)(fx)$.

ii. There is at least one x such that x is f, i.e.

(Ex)(fx).

iii. For all x, x is f, i.e.

(x)(fx).

(c) The propostional calculus:

i. P is false, i.e. -P.

ii. P is true, i.e. P.

There are two possibilities in the propositional calculus, but there are three possibilities for the other two kinds of logic. There are in fact two alternative ways to let all three systems match on another. The first way is, as I have mentioned above, to assume that the classes in question should be either universal or empty. The second way is treating 'existential' and 'non-existential' in the logic of classes and in the restricted predicate logic as 'values', corresponding to 'truth' and 'falsity' in propositional calculus.

The functions of the logic of classes may be said to have the same meaning as those of the restricted predicate logic, let us call the relation between these two systems 'being equivalent'.

The functions of the logic of classes do not have the same meaning as those of propositional logic, but they have similar structure in matrices; let us call the relation between these two systems 'being analogous'.

It is understood that the restricted predicate logic mentioned here is confined to the monadic form with one individual variable only, and that the propositional logic mentioned here is confined to two-valued logic.

Let us use the set of symbols (O, v) to represent respectively 'empty' and 'non-empty' in the logic of classes and in the restricted predicate logic, and the set of symbols (O, 1) to represent respectively 'false' and 'true' in propositional calculus. Then the three matrices may be re-written as following:

	the class matrices				the quantificational matrices				the truth matrices			
	bc	$b\bar{c}$	$\bar{b}c$	$\bar{b}\bar{c}$	gh	g-h	-gh	-g-h	qr TT	qr TF	qr FT	qr FF
1.	v	v	v	v	v	v	v	v	1	1	1	1
2.	v	v	v	o	v	v	v	o	1	1	1	o
3.	v	v	o	v	v	v	o	v	1	1	o	1
4.	v	v	o	o	v	v	o	o	1	1	o	o
5.	v	o	v	v	v	o	v	v	1	o	1	1
6.	v	o	v	o	v	o	v	o	1	o	1	o
7.	v	o	o	v	v	o	o	v	1	o	o	1
8.	v	o	o	o	v	o	o	o	1	o	o	o
9.	o	v	v	v	o	v	v	v	o	1	1	1
10.	o	v	v	o	o	v	v	o	o	1	1	o
11.	o	v	o	v	o	v	o	v	o	1	o	1
12.	o	v	o	o	o	v	o	o	o	1	o	o
13.	o	o	v	v	o	o	v	v	o	o	1	1
14.	o	o	v	o	o	o	v	o	o	o	1	o
15.	o	o	o	v	o	o	o	v	o	o	o	1
16.	o	o	o	o	o	o	o	o	o	o	o	o

241. The 'Narrow Functions' and the 'Universal Functions'

From the preceding chapter we can see that the logic of classes and the restricted predicate logic, in so far as the sixteen functions are concerned, are virtually equivalent; their differences are reduced to a matter of notation only.

What really matters is that there exist two different systems of functions, as illustrated in the 'formal implication' and the 'narrow implication'.

Let us give names for these systems. We have already sixteen dyadic 'truth functions' which are defined by 'truth matrices'.

Then we have sixteen functions which are formed by putting a universal quantifier in front of every truth function, for instance:
$(x)(gx \supset hx)$, or $U(g \supset h)$. These functions are not directly defined by a kind of matrices, but by truth functions.

For instance, in the case of 'formal implication' which is defined by putting a universal quantifier in front of a material implication, we have:

$(q \supset r) \equiv -(q \,.\, -r)$;
$(gx \supset hx) \equiv -(gx \,.\, -hx)$;
$(x)(gx \supset hx) \equiv (x)(-(gx \,.\, -hx))$;
$(x)(gx \supset hx) \equiv -(Ex)(--(gx. -hx))$;
$(x)(gx \supset hx) \equiv -(Ex)(gx. -hx)$.

Let us call the sixteen functions with a universal quantifier, including the formal implication, 'universal functions'.

In Chapter 2221, the fourth definition of implication, i.e. (x)(gx ⊃ '' 'hx) and the third definition of equivalence, i.e. (x)(gx ≡ ''hx) have one thing in common, namely, that both of them are defined by four existential conditions.

Let us call the existential conditions 'existential matrices' and call the sixteen functions defined by the existential matrices 'narrow functions'.

In order to get rid of the many apostrophes in (x)(gx ⊃ '' 'hx), I should like to introduce a new symbol N for the word 'narrow' and call it 'narrow quantifier' so as to distinguish it from the universal quantifier (x) or U.

The difference between these two functions can be shown by the following example.

1. $U(g \supset h) = -E(g. -h)$ Df.
2. $N(g \supset h) = -E(g. -h). E(g. h). E(-g. h). E(-g. -h)$ Df.

Expressed in the language of the logic of classes, we have:

1. $= (b\bar{c} = o)$ Df.
2. $= (b\bar{c} = o). (bc = v). (\bar{b}c = v). (\bar{b}\bar{c} = v)$ Df.

The above shows that the narrow functions are narrower in scope but give more information than the universal functions.

Let us make a small list of functions as follows:

Function	System	Defined by
Truth function	Propositional logic	Truth Matrix
Universal function	Res. Predicate logic	Quantifier and Truth function
" "	Logic of classes	Incomplete existential matrix
Narrow function	Res. Predicate Logic	Complete existential matrix
" "	Logic of classes	" "

Because of difference in definition, many laws in truth functions hold in universal functions but do not hold in narrow functions. For instance:

$(q \equiv r) \supset (q \supset r)$;	$U(g \equiv h) \supset U(g \supset h)$;
$(q \,.\, r) \supset (q \equiv r)$;	$U(g \,.\, h) \supset U(g \equiv h)$;
$(q \,.\, r) \supset q$;	$U(g \,.\, h) \supset U(g)$. etc. etc.

We can see that in the above examples there exists the following rule:

(a narrower proposition) ⊃ (a broader proposition), or
(a proposition giving more information) ⊃ (a proposition giving less information)

The few examples in the last paragraph hold in the case of universal functions because they do not necessarily have the same scope. These examples do not hold in the case of narrow functions because the information of four regions are given in all narrow functions.

The most significant consequence of the above reasoning is that the two paradoxial laws do not hold in the narrow functions:

$U(h) \supset U(g \supset h)$ and $U(\sim g) \supset U(g \supset h)$ are true;
$N(h) \supset N(g \supset h)$ and $N(\sim g) \supset N(g \supset h)$ are false.

We can conclude that the universal functions, which are defined by a universal quantifier and corresponding truth functions, follow the theorems of the propositional logic. The narrow functions, which are defined by existential matrices, do not follow theorems of the propositional logic.

242. Notation of the functions

The next step is notation. We have three kinds of functions, namely, the truth functions, the universal functions and the narrow functions; the two latter kinds should be expressed in both the restricted predicate logic and the logic of classes. There should be five sets of symbols, i.e. 5 x 16 = 80 in all. To find such a large number of symbols is quite a problem. Therefore a systematic planning is not only preferable, but also necessary.

The most ideal way is to use definitions as symbols. We can use:

(g vvvv h) or (g $\overset{vv}{vv}$ h) or (g -◇- h) for restricted predicate logic,
(q 1111 r) or (q $\overset{11}{11}$ r) or (q -◇- r) for propositional logic.

The second choice is to use numerals or alphabets according to a sequence of the functions, such as cC1, cC2, cC3, etc. used by Carnap, and Aqr, Bqr, Cqr, etc. used by Łukasiewicz.

The above methods are certainly systematic and have some advantage, yet the popularity of the Principia Mathematica has made the Peano-Russell symbolism a kind of 'mother tongue' of logicians, and all other notations seem to be inconvenient like foreign languages. This is the reason why I finally chose Peano-Russell notation.to denote all five sets of functions.

The symbols for sixteen dyadic functions are not completed in this system, because both Wittgenstein's and Post's papers on truth functions were published after the publication of the Principia. An important symbol '/', the Sheffer Stroke, was introduced after the first edition of the Principia. Therefore new symbols have to be added and some convention has to be modified.

The major modification of the convention is the abolition of all symbols for class functions, such as '∪', '∩', '⊂', etc. First, it is cumbersome to find sixteen symbols for the logic of classes. Secondly, the sixteen class functions are analogous to other sets of functions, there is no reason why we should not use the same set of symbols throughout.

1. The symbol '⊂' will be used for 'inverse class inclusion' instead of 'class inclusion' in the logic of classes. That is, 'b ⊂ c' means 'the class b includes the class 'c'.

'Class inclusion' will be symbolized by the sign '⊃'. That is, 'b ⊃ c' means 'the class b is included in the class c'.

The above alteration is just a reverse of convention. It will cause a confusion in the beginning, but it will be less confused when the five systems are considered as parallel topics.

2. The four functions 'first component' (1100), 'second component' (1010), 'negation of the first' (0011) and 'negation of the second' (0101) have been so far symbolized as 'q', 'r', '~q' and '~r' respectively.

Since the dyadic functions concern two variables, it will look odd when one of them disappears completely from the symbols, even when the truth value of one does not depend on that of the other.

I should like to introduce two new symbols '+' and '-', such that the four functions q, r, ~q and ~r can be expressed by (r + q), (q + r), (r - q) and (q - r) respectively. They are defined as follows:

$$(r + q) = -(-q.r).-(-q.-r) \quad \text{Df.}$$
$$(q + r) = -(q.-r).-(-q.-r) \quad \text{Df.}$$
$$(r - q) = -(q.r).-(q.-r) \quad \text{Df.}$$
$$(q - r) = -(q.r).-(-q.r) \quad \text{Df.}$$

In the propositional logic, the alteration is merely formal and there is no effect in meaning. The four definitions can easily be reduced to the following forms by applying de Morgan's law:

$$(r + q) = -((-q.r) \vee (-q.-r)) \equiv --q \equiv q, \text{ similarly}$$
$$(q + r) = r,$$
$$(r - q) = -q,$$
$$(q - r) = -r.$$

However, the same alteration means something substantial in the narrow functions. They are defined in the following way and cannot be further reduced:

$$N(h + g) = E(g.h).E(g.-h).-E(-g.h).-E(-g.-h) \quad \text{Df.}$$
$$N(g + h) = E(g.h).-E(g.-h).E(-g.h).-E(-g.-h) \quad \text{Df.}$$
$$N(h - g) = -E(g.h).-E(g.-h).E(-g.h).E(-g.-h) \quad \text{Df.}$$
$$N(g - h) = -E(g.h).E(g.-h).-E(-g.h).E(-g.-h) \quad \text{Df.}$$

From the above we can see that the appearance of both variables g and h is justified.

3. I should like to introduce three new symbols '⊄', '⊅' and 'X', and define them as follows:

$$(q \not\supset r) = (q.-r) \quad \text{Df.}$$
$$(q \not\subset r) = (-q.r) \quad \text{Df.}$$
$$(q \, X \, r) = (q.r) \quad \text{Df.}$$

I shall use the same set of symbols for all five kinds of functions, but use different alphabets to distinguish one kind from another. I shall use a, b, c for the logic of classes, f, g, h for the restricted predicate logic, and p, q, r for the propositional logic.

In the restricted predicate logic, I shall use two quantifiers U and N for universal functions and narrow functions respectively. Similarly I shall use small letters 'u' and 'n' for universal class functions and narrow class functions respectively.

For instance, for the particular function of '⊃ (implication)', we have:

$(q \supset r)$	truth function
$U(g \supset h)$	universal function (restricted predicate logic)
$N(g \supset h)$	narrow function (" " ")
$u(b \supset c)$	universal function (logic of classes)
$n(b \supset c)$	narrow function (" ")

Ludwig Wittgenstein wrote in his Tractatus Logico Philosophicus: "Tautology and contradiction are without sense. Tautology and contradiction are, however, not non-sensical; they are part of the symbolism, in the same way that 'O' is part of the symbolism of arithmetic". He was referring to the the two truth functions TTTT and FFFF in propositional logic.

In the restricted predicate logic, the function vvvv, i.e. either U(g T h) or N(g T h), is not without sense; on the contrary, it is the most common case. For instance, we have male students, male non-students, non-male (female) students and non-male non-students.

243. Definitions and characteristics of the functions

In beginners' course of logic, the truth functions are usually defined by 'truth matrices', such as

q	r	$q \supset r$
T	T	T
T	F	F
F	T	T
F	F	T

What does the above table mean? Does it mean:

"$(q \supset r) = (q.r).\sim(q.\sim r).(\sim q.r).(\sim q.\sim r)$ Df."?

If we test the formula "$(q \supset r) \equiv (q.r).\sim(q.\sim r).(\sim q.r).(\sim q.\sim r)$" by a truth matrix, we can easily tell that the above answer is wrong.

The following two formulae are tautologies:

$(q \supset r) \equiv \sim(q.\sim r)$;
$(q \supset r) \equiv \sim(q.\sim r).((q.r) \vee (\sim q.r) \vee (\sim q.\sim r))$.

Since the second part of the second formula is optional, we can use the first formula as the definition:

$(q \supset r) = \sim(q.\sim r)$ Df.

Let us try another example - the material equivalence:
$(q \equiv r) \equiv \sim(q.\sim r).\sim(\sim q.r)$;
$(q \equiv r) \equiv \sim(q.\sim r).\sim(\sim q.r).((q.r) \vee (\sim q.\sim r))$.

We can use the first formula as the definition of material equivalence:

$(q \equiv r) = \sim(q.\sim r).\sim(\sim q.r)$ Df.

From the above two definitions we can see that the numbers of factors used to define the two functions are different. The next question is: how many factors are required to define truth functions?

Since the number of dyadic functions is finite - only sixteen; we can work them out one by one as follows:

First let us classify the sixteen functions from a new point of view, according to the number of T's and F's in the truth matrix as follows:

4t functions,	one function.
3t and 1f functions,	four functions.
2t and 2f functions,	six functions.
1t and 3f functions,	four functions.
4f functions,	one function.

The following formulae show the relations between the functions and the four components:

$$(q\ T\ r) \equiv ((q.r) \vee (q.-r) \vee (-q.r) \vee (-q.-r))$$

$$(q \vee r) \equiv ((q.r) \vee (q.-r) \vee (-q.r)) . -(-q.-r)$$
$$(q \supset r) \equiv ((q.r) \vee (q.-r) \vee (-q.-r)) . -(-q.r)$$
$$(q \subset r) \equiv ((q.r) \vee (-q.r) \vee (-q.-r)) . -(q.-r)$$
$$(q\ /\ r) \equiv ((q.-r) \vee (-q.r) \vee (-q.-r)) . -(q.r)$$

$$(r + q) \equiv ((q.r) \vee (q.-r)) . (-(-q.r).-(-q.-r))$$
$$(q + r) \equiv ((q.r) \vee (-q.r)) . (-(q.-r).-(-q.-r))$$
$$(q \equiv r) \equiv ((q.r) \vee (-q.-r)) . (-(-q.r).-(q.-r))$$
$$(q\ \underline{\vee}\ r) \equiv ((q.-r) \vee (-q.r)) . (-(q.r).-(-q.-r))$$
$$(q\ \bar{-}\ r) \equiv ((q.-r) \vee (-q.-r)) . (-(q.r).-(-q.r))$$
$$(r - q) \equiv ((-q.r) \vee (-q.-r)).. (-(q.r).-(q.-r))$$

$$(q\ X\ r) \equiv ((q.r) . (-(q.-r).-(-q.r).-(-q.-r))$$
$$(q \not\supset r) \equiv (q.-r) . (-(q.r).-(-q.r).-(-q.-r))$$
$$(q \not\subset r) \equiv (-q.r) . (-(q.r).-(q.-r).-(-q.-r))$$
$$(q \downarrow r) \equiv (-q.-r) . (-(q.r).-(-q.r).-(q.-r))$$

$$(q\ C\ r) \equiv (-(q.r).-(q.-r).-(-q.r).-(-q.-r))$$

From the above formulae we can see that the right-hand sides of the equivalences are composed of the products of disjunctions of affirmative components and conjunctions of negative components.

If we separate the disjuncts and conjuncts apart, the following formulae are also tautologous:

(q T r) ≡ ((q. r) v (q. ~r) v (~q. r) v (~q. ~r))

(q v r) ≡ ((q. r) v (q. ~r) v (~q. r)) ≡ ~(~q. ~r)
(q ⊂ r) ≡ ((q. r) v (q. ~r) v (~q. ~r)) ≡ ~(~q. r)
(q ⊃ r) ≡ ((q. r) v (~q. r) v (~q. ~r)) ≡ ~(q. ~r)
(q / r) ≡ ((~q. r) v (q. ~r) v (~q. ~r)) ≡ ~(q. r)

(r + q) ≡ ((q. r) v (q. ~r)) ≡ (~(~q. r) . ~(~q. ~r))
(q + r) ≡ ((q. r) v (~q. r)) ≡ (~(q. ~r) . ~(~q. ~r))
(q ≡ r) ≡ ((q. r) v (~q. ~r)) ≡ (~(q. ~r) . ~(~q. r))
(q ⊻ r) ≡ ((q. ~r) v (~q. r)) ≡ (~(q. r) . ~(~q. ~r))
(q -̄ r) ≡ ((q. ~r) v (~q. ~r)) ≡ (~(q. r) . ~(~q. r))
(r - q) ≡ ((~q. r) v (~q. ~r)) ≡ (~(q. r) . ~(q. ~r))

(q X r) ≡ (q. r) ≡ (~(q. ~r) . ~(~q. r) . ~(~q. ~r))
(q ⊅ r) ≡ (q. ~r) ≡ (~(q. r) . ~(~q. r) . ~(~q. ~r))
(q ⊄ r) ≡ (~q. r) ≡ (~(q. r) . ~(q. ~r) . ~(~q. ~r))
(q ↓ r) ≡ (~q. ~r) ≡ (~(q. r) . ~(q. ~r) . ~(~q. r))

(q C r) ≡ (~(q. r) . ~(q. ~r) . ~(~q. r) . ~(~q. ~r))

These functions can be defined either by the disjunctive parts or by the conjunctive parts, except the tautology (q T r) which can be defined by disjunction only, and the contradiction (q C r) which can be defined by conjunction only.

Let us put all sets of functions and their definitions together in one list:

	Propositional Functions		Universal functions		Narrow functions	
1	(q T r)	1111	U(g T h) & u(b T c)		N(g T h) & n(b T c)	vvvv
2	(q v r)	o or 111	U(g v h) & u(b v c)	o	N(g v h) & n(b v c)	vvvo
3	(q ⊂ r)	o or 11 1	U(g ⊂ h) & u(b ⊂ c)	o	N(g ⊂ h) & n(b ⊂ c)	vvov
4	(r + q)	oo or 11	U(h + g) & u(c + b)	oo	N(h + g) & n(c + b)	vvoo
5	(q ⊃ r)	o or 1 11	U(g ⊃ h) & u(b ⊃ c)	o	N(g ⊃ h) & n(b ⊃ c)	vovv
6	(q + r)	o o or 1 1	U(g + h) & u(b + c)	o o	N(g + h) & n(b + c)	vovo
7	(q ≡ r)	oo or 1 1	U(g ≡ h) & u(b ≡ c)	oo	N(g ≡ h) & n(b ≡ c)	voov
8	(q x r)	ooo or 1	U(g x h) & u(b x c)	ooo	N(g x h) & n(b x c)	vooo
9	(q / r)	o or 111	U(g / h) & u(b / c)	o	N(g / h) & n(b / c)	ovvv
10	(q ⊻ r)	o o or 11	U(g ⊻ h) & u(b ⊻ c)	o o	N(g ⊻ h) & n(b ⊻ c)	ovvo
11	(q -̄ r)	o o or 1 1	U(g -̄ h) & u(b -̄ c)	o o	N(g -̄ h) & n(b -̄ c)	ovov
12	(q ⊅ r)	o oo or 1	U(g ⊅ h) & u(b ⊅ c)	o oo	N(g ⊅ h) & n(b ⊅ c)	ovoo
13	(r - q)	oo or 11	U(h - g) & u(c - b)	oo	N(h - g) & n(c - b)	oovv
14	(q ⊄ r)	oo o or 1	U(g ⊄ h) & u(b ⊄ c)	oo o	N(g ⊄ h) & n(b ⊄ c)	oovo
15	(q ↓ r)	ooo or 1	U(g ↓ h) & u(b ↓ c)	ooo	N(g ↓ h) & n(b ↓ c)	ooov
16	(q C r)	oooo	U(g C h) & u(b C c)	oooo	N(g C h) & n(b C c)	oooo

The above list is for comparison only. Let us take the case of the function '⊃'; it should actually be read as follows:

$(q \supset r) = -(q.-r)$ Df. or
$(q \supset r) = ((q.r) \vee (-q.r) \vee (-q.-r))$ Df.
$U(g \supset h) = -E(g.-h)$ Df.
$u(b \supset c) = (b\bar{c} = o)$ Df.
$N(g \supset h) = E(g.h).-E(g.-h).\underline{E}(-g.h).\underline{E}(-g.-h)$ Df.
$n(b \supset c) = (bc = v).(b\bar{c} = o).(\bar{b}c = v).(\bar{b}\bar{c} = v)$ Df.

Here we can find an important difference between the propositional logic and the logic of classes, etc. In the universe of discourse in the propositional logic, namely, qr, q. - r, - q. r and q. - r, the conjunction of negation of one part implies the disjunction of affirmation of the other part, and vice versa. We have fourteen such relations as follows:

$-(-q.-r) \equiv ((q.r) \vee (q.-r) \vee (-q.r))$
$-(-q.r) \equiv ((q.r) \vee (q.-r) \vee (-q.-r))$
$-(q.-r) \equiv ((q.r) \vee (-q.r) \vee (-q.-r))$
$-(q.r) \equiv ((q.-r) \vee (-q.r) \vee (-q.-r))$

$(-(-q.r) . -(-q.-r)) \equiv ((q.r) \vee (q.-r))$
$(-(q.-r) . -(-q.-r)) \equiv ((q.r) \vee (-q.r))$
$(-(q.-r) . -(-q.r)) \equiv ((q.r) \vee (-q.-r))$
$(-(q.r) . -(-q.-r)) \equiv ((q.-r) \vee (-q.r))$
$(-(q.r) . -(-q.r)) \equiv ((q.-r) \vee (-q.-r))$
$(-(q.r) . -(q.-r)) \equiv ((-q.r) \vee (-q.-r))$

$(-(q.-r) . -(-q.r) . -(-q.-r)) \equiv (q.r)$
$(-(q.r) . -(-q.r) . -(-q.-r)) \equiv (q.-r)$
$(-(q.r) . -(q.-r) . -(-q.-r)) \equiv (-q.r)$
$(-(q.r) . -(q.-r) . -(-q.r)) \equiv (-q.-r)$

These fourteen relations may be regarded as an extension of de Morgan's laws.

However, in the other two systems, the matrices concern existence and non-existence instead of truth and falsity. In the universe of discourse, namely, bc, b$\bar{c}$, $\bar{b}$c and $\bar{b}\bar{c}$, the existence of one part does not imply the non-existence of another. All four components are tightly connected by conjunctions and not by disjunctions.

From the above we know that we can have only one set of truth functions but more than one set of 'existential functions'. The two sets mentioned previously, namely, the 'universal' and the 'narrow' functions, do not exhaust all possibilities.

For instance, the 'formal implication' belongs to the 'universal functions' and Uddyotakara's Hetucakra is equivalent to the sixteen 'narrow functions'; but Dignāga's implication and equivalence belong to neither of them.

Dignāga's implication is defined by two components:

$(x)(gx \supset hx) = \sim(Ex)(gx. \sim hx).(Ex)(gx.hx)$ Df.

His equivalence is defined by three components:

$(x)(gx \equiv hx) = \sim(Ex)(gx. \sim hx). \sim(Ex)(\sim gx.hx).(Ex)(gx.hx)$ Df.

Therefore, between the universal functions and narrow functions there is still room for more varieties.

The universal functions give information of empty regions only therefore they are 'incomplete descriptions' of the universe of discourse. The narrow functions give information of both empty and non-empty regions, therefore they are 'complete descriptions' of the universe of discourse.

The narrow functions are defined by existential conditions; while the universal functions can be defined in two different ways: either by existential conditions of the universe of discourse, or by quantification of truth functions, which are defined by truth matrices.

Therefore, we may say that the narrow functions are 'directly' defined by existential matrices; the universal functions can either be 'directly' defined by existential matrices, or be 'indirectly' defined by truth matrices. Let us illustrate the two ways by the following example:

First definition: $U(g \supset h) = \sim E(g. \sim h)$ Df.

Second devinition: $U(g \supset h) = U(\sim(g. \sim h))$ Df.

Since $U(\sim(g. \sim h) \equiv \sim E(g. \sim h)$, these two definitions coincide.

Since universal and narrow functions are defined by existential functions, the former two are 'secondary functions' and the latter are 'primary functions'.

2431. The Meaning of the Word 'Or'.

One point should be clarified at this stage. Two functions $(q \vee r)$ and $(q \underline{\vee} r)$ in propositional logic are called inclusive and exclusive disjunctions and mean respectively "q or r" and "either q or r" in everyday language.

However, the meaning of the word 'or' disappears entirely in the functions $U(g \vee h)$, $N(g \vee h)$, $U(g \underline{\vee} h)$ and $N(g \underline{\vee} h)$. The reason is explained as follows:

In the sixteen dyadic functions of propositional logic, there are one 4-t function, four 3-t functions, six 2-t functions, four 1-t functions and one 4-f functions.

Among them the 4-t, 3-t, and 2-t functions have the meaning of 'or', while the other functions have not; let us express them in everyday language as follows:

$(q \; T \; r)$:	**either one or both or neither;**
$(q \vee r)$:	**either one or both;**
$(q \subset r)$:	**either not r or q;**
$(q \supset r)$:	**either not q or r;**
$(q \,/\, r)$:	**either one or neither;**
$(r + q)$:	**q, either r or not r;**
$(q + r)$:	**r, either q or not q;**
$(q \equiv r)$:	**either both or neither;**
$(q \underline{\vee} r)$:	**either q or r;**
$(q \bar{-} r)$:	**not r, either q or not q;**
$(r - q)$:	**not q, either r or not r.**

The above eleven functions can be defined by disjunctions of premisses as follows:

$(q \; T \; r) = (q.r) \vee (q.\sim r) \vee (\sim q.r) \vee (\sim q.\sim r)$ **Df.**

$(q \vee r) = (q.r) \vee (q.\sim r) \vee (\sim q.r)$ **Df.**
$(q \subset r) = (q.r) \vee (q.\sim r) \vee (\sim q.\sim r)$ **Df.**
$(q \supset r) = (q.r) \vee (\sim q.r) \vee (\sim q.\sim r)$ **Df.**
$(q \,/\, r) = (q.\sim r) \vee (\sim q.r) \vee (\sim q.\sim r)$ **Df.**

$(r + q) = (q.r) \vee (q.\sim r)$ **Df.**
$(q + r) = (q.r) \vee (\sim q.r)$ **Df.**
$(q \equiv r) = (q.r) \vee (\sim q.\sim r)$ **Df.**
$(q \underline{\vee} r) = (q.\sim r) \vee (\sim q.r)$ **Df.**
$(q \bar{-} r) = (q.\sim r) \vee (\sim q.\sim r)$ **Df.**
$(r - q) = (\sim q.r) \vee (\sim q.\sim r)$ **Df.**

The remaining five functions cannot be defined by disjunctions of premisses but can be defined by conjunctions of them:

$(q \times r) = (q.r)$ or $= \sim(q.\sim r).\sim(\sim q.r).\sim(\sim q.\sim r)$ **Df.**
$(q \not\supset r) = (q.\sim r)$ or $= \sim(q.r).\sim(\sim q.r).\sim(\sim q.\sim r)$ **Df.**
$(q \not\subset r) = (\sim q.r)$ or $= \sim(q.r).\sim(q.\sim r).\sim(\sim q.\sim r)$ **Df.**
$(q \downarrow r) = (\sim q.\sim r)$ or $= \sim(q.r).\sim(q.\sim r).\sim(\sim q.r)$ **Df.**
$(q \; C \; r) = \sim(q.r).\sim(q.\sim r).\sim(\sim q.r).\sim(\sim q.\sim r)$ **Df.**

From the above we know that all functions which possess the meaning of the word 'or' are those which can be defined by disjunctions of premisses and <u>vice versa</u>. That is to say, the sense of flexibility or freedom in the word 'or' comes from disjunction and not from conjunction.

By the same reasoning the meaning of the word 'or' does not occur in the narrow functions and the universal functions which can be defined only by conjunctions of existential conditions.

244. A Few Theorems on the Three Sets of Functions

For further simplication of symbolism, let us use the expressions 'T1, T2, T3 ... T16' for the truth functions, 'U1, U2, U3 ... U16' for the universal functions, and 'N1, N2, N3 ... N16' for the narrow functions. The sequence from 1 to 16 is the same as that arranged in Carnap's Formalization of Logic. For instance,

$$
\begin{aligned}
T5 &= (q \supset r) \quad \text{Df.} \\
&= \sim(q \, . \sim r) \quad \text{Df.}
\end{aligned}
$$

$$
\begin{aligned}
U5 &= U(g \supset h) \quad \text{Df.} \\
&= \sim E(g \, . \, \sim h) \quad \text{Df.} \\
&= \sim(Ex)(gx . \sim hx) \quad \text{Df.} \\
&= (b\bar{c} = o) \quad \text{Df.}
\end{aligned}
$$

$$
\begin{aligned}
N5 &= N(g \supset h) \quad \text{Df.} \\
&= E(g.h). \sim E(g. \sim h). E(\sim g. h). E(\sim g. \sim h) \quad \text{Df.} \\
&= (Ex)(gx. hx). \sim(Ex)(gx. \sim hx). (Ex)(\sim gx. hx). (Ex)(\sim gx. \sim hx) \quad \text{Df.} \\
&= (bc = v). (b\bar{c} = o). (\bar{b}c = v). (\bar{b}\bar{c} = v) \quad \text{Df.}
\end{aligned}
$$

Under the restrictions imposed previously, the logic of classes and the restricted predicate logic have the same meaning and therefore they are expressed by the same set of symbols.

We have now three sets of functions; therefore we can have three systems of logic, each of which can have its own theorems. The development of the three systems will be immense, and in this work only very simple cases are considered.

First, let us consider the simplest case with minimum number of variables but one. The simplest case is: among the sixteen functions, the truth of certain ones implies that of certain others; how are these functions related to one another?

Let us start with truth functions and examine such relations by putting the sign of material implication between two truth functions as follows:

A. 'To imply'; in Peano-Russell Notation:

1.

(q C r) ⊃ (q C r);
(q C r) ⊃ (q ↓ r);
(q C r) ⊃ (-q. r);
(q C r) ⊃ (-q   );
(q C r) ⊃ (q. - r);
(q C r) ⊃ (- r);
(q C r) ⊃ (q v r);
(q C r) ⊃ (q 7 r);
(q C r) ⊃ (q . r);
(q C r) ⊃ (q ≡ r);
(q C r) ⊃ (r);
(q C r) ⊃ (q ⊃ r);
(q C r) ⊃ (q   );
(q C r) ⊃ (q ⊂ r);
(q C r) ⊃ (q v r);

2.

(q ↓ r) ⊃ (q ↓ r); (-q. r) ⊃ (-q. r); (q . - r) ⊃ (q . - r); (q . r) ⊃ (q . r);
(q ↓ r) ⊃ (-q   ); (-q. r) ⊃ (-q   ); (q . - r) ⊃ (- r); (q . r) ⊃ (q ≡ r);
(q ↓ r) ⊃ (- r); (-q. r) ⊃ (q v r); (q . - r) ⊃ (q v r); (q . r) ⊃ (r);
(q ↓ r) ⊃ (q / r); (-q. r) ⊃ (q 7 r); (q. - r) ⊃ (q 7 r); (q . r) ⊃ (q ⊃ r);
(q ↓ r) ⊃ (q ≡ r); (-q. r) ⊃ (r); (q. - r) ⊃ (q   ); (q . r) ⊃ (q   );
(q ↓ r) ⊃ (q ⊃ r); (-q. r) ⊃ (q ⊃ r); (q. - r) ⊃ (q v r); (q . r) ⊃ (q ⊂ r);
(q ↓ r) ⊃ (q ⊂ r); (-q. r) ⊃ (q v r); (q. - r) ⊃ (q ⊂ r); (q . r) ⊃ (q v r);
(q ↓ r) ⊃ (q T r); (-q. r) ⊃ (q T r); (q. - r) ⊃ (q T r); (q . r) ⊃ (q T r);

3.

(-q   ) ⊃ (-q   ); (-r) ⊃ (-r); (q v̲ r) ⊃ (q v r);
(-q   ) ⊃ (q / r); (-r) ⊃ (q / r); (q v̄ r) ⊃ (q 7 r);
(-q   ) ⊃ (q ⊃ r); (-r) ⊃ (q ⊂ r); (q v̄ r) ⊃ (q v r);
(-q   ) ⊃ (q T r); (-r) ⊃ (q T r); (q v̄ r) ⊃ (q T r);

(q ≡ r) ⊃ (q ≡ r); (r) ⊃ (r); (q   ) ⊃ (q   );
(q ≡ r) ⊃ (q ⊃ r); (r) ⊃ (q ⊃ r); (q   ) ⊃ (q ⊂ r);
(q ≡ r) ⊃ (q ⊂ r); (r) ⊃ (q v r); (q   ) ⊃ (q v r);
(q ≡ r) ⊃ (q T r); (r) ⊃ (q T r); (q   ) ⊃ (q T r);

4.

(q / r) ⊃ (q / r); (q ⊃ r) ⊃ (q ⊃ r); (q ⊂ r) ⊃ (q ⊂ r); (q v r) ⊃ (q v r);
(q / r) ⊃ (q T r); (q ⊃ r) ⊃ (q T r); (q ⊂ r) ⊃ (q T r); (q v r) ⊃ (q T r);

5.

(q C r) ⊃ (q C r)

A. 'To imply'; in simplified notation:

1.

T16 ⊃ T16
T16 ⊃ T15
T16 ⊃ T14
T16 ⊃ T13
T16 ⊃ T12
T16 ⊃ T11
T16 ⊃ T10
T16 ⊃ T9
T16 ⊃ T8
T16 ⊃ T7
T16 ⊃ T6
T16 ⊃ T5
T16 ⊃ T4
T16 ⊃ T3
T16 ⊃ T2

2.

T15 ⊃ T15	T14 ⊃ T14	T12 ⊃ T12	T8 ⊃ T8
T15 ⊃ T13	T14 ⊃ T13	T12 ⊃ T11	T8 ⊃ T7
T15 ⊃ T11	T14 ⊃ T10	T12 ⊃ T10	T8 ⊃ T6
T15 ⊃ T9	T14 ⊃ T9	T12 ⊃ T9	T8 ⊃ T5
T15 ⊃ T7	T14 ⊃ T6	T12 ⊃ T4	T8 ⊃ T4
T15 ⊃ T5	T14 ⊃ T5	T12 ⊃ T3	T8 ⊃ T3
T15 ⊃ T3	T14 ⊃ T2	T12 ⊃ T2	T8 ⊃ T2
T15 ⊃ T1	T14 ⊃ T1	T12 ⊃ T1	T8 ⊃ T1

T13 ⊃ T13	T11 ⊃ T11	T10 ⊃ T10	T7 ⊃ T7	T6 ⊃ T6	T4 ⊃ T4
T13 ⊃ T9	T11 ⊃ T9	T10 ⊃ T9	T7 ⊃ T5	T6 ⊃ T5	T4 ⊃ T3
T13 ⊃ T5	T11 ⊃ T3	T10 ⊃ T2	T7 ⊃ T3	T6 ⊃ T2	T4 ⊃ T2
T13 ⊃ T1	T11 ⊃ T1	T10 ⊃ T1	T7 ⊃ T1	T6 ⊃ T1	T4 ⊃ T1

4.

T9 ⊃ T9	T5 ⊃ T5	T3 ⊃ T3	T2 ⊃ T2
T9 ⊃ T1	T5 ⊃ T1	T3 ⊃ T1	T2 ⊃ T1

5.

T1 ⊃ T1

B. 'To be implied'; in Peano-Russell Notation:

a.

(q T r) ⊃ (q T r);
(q v r) ⊃ (q T r);
(q ⊂ r) ⊃ (q T r);
(q   ) ⊃ (q T r);
(q ⊃ r) ⊃ (q T r);
(r) ⊃ (q T r);
(q ≡ r) ⊃ (q T r);
(q . r) ⊃ (q T r);
(q / r) ⊃ (q T r);
(q $\underline{v}$ r) ⊃ (q T r);
(~r) ⊃ (q T r);
(q . ~r) ⊃ (q T r);
(~q   ) ⊃ (q T r);
(~q. r) ⊃ (q T r);
(q ↓ r) ⊃ (q T r);

b.

(q v r) ⊃ (q v r); (q ⊂ r) ⊃ (q ⊂ r); (q ⊃ r) ⊃ (q ⊃ r); (q / r) ⊃ (q / r);
(q   ) ⊃ (q v r); (q   ) ⊃ (q ⊂ r); (r) ⊃ (q ⊃ r); (q $\underline{v}$ r) ⊃ (q / r);
(r) ⊃ (q v r); (q ≡ r) ⊃ (q ⊂ r); (q ≡ r) ⊃ (q ⊃ r); (~r) ⊃ (q / r);
(q . r) ⊃ (q v r); (q . r) ⊃ (q ⊂ r); (q . r) ⊃ (q ⊃ r); (q. ~r) ⊃ (q / r);
(q $\underline{v}$ r) ⊃ (q v r); (~r) ⊃ (q ⊂ r); (~q   ) ⊃ (q ⊃ r); (~q   ) ⊃ (q / r);
(q. ~r) ⊃ (q v r); (q.~r) ⊃ (q ⊂ r); (~q.r) ⊃ (q ⊃ r); (~q.r) ⊃ (q / r);
(~q. r) ⊃ (q v r); (q ↓ r) ⊃ (q ⊂ r); (q ↓ r) ⊃ (q ⊃ r); (q ↓ r) ⊃ (q / r);
(q C r) ⊃ (q v r); (q C r) ⊃ (q ⊂ r); (q C r) ⊃ (q ⊃ r); (q C r) ⊃ (q / r);

c.

(q   ) ⊃ (q); (r) ⊃ (r); (q ≡ r) ⊃ (q ≡ r);
(q . r) ⊃ (q); (q . r) ⊃ (r); (q . r) ⊃ (q ≡ r);
(q . ~r) ⊃ (q); (~q. r) ⊃ (r); (q ↓ r) ⊃ (q ≡ r);
(q C r) ⊃ (q); (q C r) ⊃ (r); (q C r) ⊃ (q ≡ r);

(q $\underline{v}$ r) ⊃ (q $\underline{v}$ r); (~r) ⊃ (~r); (~q   ) ⊃ (~q);
(q. ~r) ⊃ (q $\underline{v}$ r); (q . ~r) ⊃ (~r); (~q. r) ⊃ (~q);
(~q. r) ⊃ (q $\underline{v}$ r); (q ↓ r) ⊃ (~r); (q ↓ r) ⊃ (~q);
(q C r) ⊃ (q $\underline{v}$ r); (q C r) ⊃ (~r); (q C r) ⊃ (~q);

d.

(q . r) ⊃ (q . r); (q . ~r) ⊃ (q . ~r); (~q. r) ⊃ (~q. r); (q ↓ r) ⊃ (q ↓ r);
(q C r) ⊃ (q . r); (q C r) ⊃ (q . ~r); (q C r) ⊃ (~q. r); (q C r) ⊃ (q ↓ r);

e.

(q C r) ⊃ (q C r).

B. 'To be implied'; in simplified notation:

a.

T1 ⊃ T1
T2 ⊃ T1
T3 ⊃ T1
T4 ⊃ T1
T5 ⊃ T1
T6 ⊃ T1
T7 ⊃ T1
T8 ⊃ T1
T9 ⊃ T1
T10 ⊃ T1
T11 ⊃ T1
T12 ⊃ T1
T13 ⊃ T1
T14 ⊃ T1
T15 ⊃ T1

b.

T2 ⊃ T2 T3 ⊃ T3 T5 ⊃ T5 T9 ⊃ T9
T4 ⊃ T2 T4 ⊃ T3 T6 ⊃ T5 T10 ⊃ T9
T6 ⊃ T2 T7 ⊃ T3 T7 ⊃ T5 T11 ⊃ T9
T8 ⊃ T2 T8 ⊃ T3 T8 ⊃ T5 T12 ⊃ T9
T10 ⊃ T2 T11 ⊃ T3 T13 ⊃ T5 T13 ⊃ T9
T12 ⊃ T2 T12 ⊃ T3 T14 ⊃ T5 T14 ⊃ T9
T14 ⊃ T2 T15 ⊃ T3 T15 ⊃ T5 T15 ⊃ T9
T16 ⊃ T2 T16 ⊃ T3 T16 ⊃ T5 T16 ⊃ T9

c.

T4 ⊃ T4 T6 ⊃ T6 T7 ⊃ T7 T10 ⊃ T10 T11 ⊃ T11 T13 ⊃ T13
T8 ⊃ T4 T8 ⊃ T6 T8 ⊃ T7 T12 ⊃ T10 T12 ⊃ T11 T14 ⊃ T13
T12 ⊃ T4 T14 ⊃ T6 T15 ⊃ T7 T14 ⊃ T10 T15 ⊃ T11 T15 ⊃ T13
T16 ⊃ T4 T16 ⊃ T6 T16 ⊃ T7 T16 ⊃ T10 T16 ⊃ T11 T16 ⊃ T13

d.

T8 ⊃ T8 T12 ⊃ T12 T14 ⊃ T14 T15 ⊃ T15
T16 ⊃ T8 T16 ⊃ T12 T16 ⊃ T14 T16 ⊃ T15

e.

T16 ⊃ T16

From the above lists we can derive the following general theorems, which can be expressed in two ways, namely, A. 'to imply' and B. 'to be implied'.

A. 'to imply'	B. 'to be implied'
1. Every truth function implies itself.	1. Every truth function is implied by itself.
2. The 4-F function (i.e. contradiction) implies every function except tautology.	2. The 4-F function is not implied by other functions.
3. Every 1-T 3-F function implies eight functions (including itself and tautology).	3. Every 1-T 3-F function is implied by itself and contradiction only.
4. Every 2-T 2-F function implies four functions (including itself and tautology).	4. Every 2-T 2-F function is implied by four functions (including itself and contradiction).
5. Every 3-T 1-F function implies itself and tautology only.	5. Every 3-T 1-F function is implied by eight functions (including itself and contradiction).
6. The 4-T function (i.e. tautology) does not imply any other function.	6. The 4-T function is implied by every function, except contradiction.

The theorems A. 1 to 6 as a whole are equivalent to theorems B. 1 to 6. The theorem A. 1 is identical to the theorem B. 1; they are written in two ways for the sake of symmetry only.

The total number of theorems in the above list is

$1 \times 15 + 4 \times 8 + 6 \times 4 + 4 \times 2 + 1 \times 1 = 15 + 32 + 24 + 8 + 1 = 80.$

For a further simplification, let us use two small letters 'i' and 'j' to stand for the numbers of functions which appear respectively as antecedent and consequent of any formula in the list A. Then we can set a general formula for truth functions as the following:

$Ti \supset Tj$.

B. For universal functions, the following formula also holds:

$Ui \supset Uj$.

There are also 80 theorems of universal functions.

C. The case is different for narrow functions. The following formula does not hold.

$Ni \supset Nj$.

D. Let us now consider the relations between universal and narrow functions. The following formulae hold:

a. Ni ⊃ Uj;

b. Nk ⊃ Uk; where k stands for any number from 1 to 16.

There are 80 theorems for D.a and 16 theorems for D.b.

The above mentioned theorems can be proved as follows:

The theorems A (truth functions) can be verified by truth matrices. The process is easy and is omitted here.

The theorems B and D (universal and narrow functions) can be verified either by the predicate logic or the logic of classes. For instance:

To prove that U7 ⊃ U5:

$(b\bar{c} = o).(\bar{b}c = o) \supset (b\bar{c} = o)$; or
$-E(g.-h).-E(-g.h) \supset -E(g.-h)$.

To prove that N7 ⊃ U5:

$(b\bar{c} = o).(\bar{b}c = o).(bc = v).(\bar{b}\bar{c} = v) \supset (b\bar{c} = o)$; or
$-E(g.-h).-E(-g.h).E(g.h).E(-g.-h) \supset -E(g.-h)$.

To prove that N7 ⊃ U7:

$(b\bar{c} = o).(\bar{b}c = o).(bc = v).(\bar{b}\bar{c} = v) \supset (b\bar{c} = o).(\bar{b}c = o)$; or
$-E(g.-h).-E(-g.h).E(g.h).E(-g.-h) \supset -E(g.-h).-E(-g.h)$.

The formula (N7 ⊃ U5) can also be proved by the conjunction of (N7 ⊃ U7) and (U7 ⊃ U5).

Let us use capital D to represent dyadic functions and small v and w to denote variables in either propositional, restricted predicate or class logic. The symbol vDw is used to represent any one of the following: qDr, U(gDh), u(bDc), N(gDh) and n(bDc).

Alternatively let us use Fi to denote Ti, Ni or Ui, where i ranges from 1 to 16.

The capital D andF are used only for theorems common to all kinds of functions. Let us compare the notations as follows:

General:	vDw	Fi
Propositional:	qDr	Ti
Universal:	U(gDh) u(bDc)	Ui
Narrow:	N(gDh) n(bDc)	Ni

In the theorems $Ti \supset Tj$, $Ui \supset Uj$ and $Ni \supset Uj$, let us examine a few particular cases:

In the group A.b of theorems, we have the following sixteen sets of formulae:

$T5 \supset T5$,	$T9 \supset T9$
$T6 \supset T5$,	$T10 \supset T9$
$T7 \supset T5$,	$T11 \supset T9$
$T8 \supset T5$,	$T12 \supset T9$
$T13 \supset T5$,	$T13 \supset T9$
$T14 \supset T5$,	$T14 \supset T9$
$T15 \supset T5$,	$T15 \supset T9$
$T16 \supset T5$,	$T16 \supset T9$.

Using the notation qDr, we have:

$(q \supset r) \supset (q \supset r)$,	$(q \,/\, r) \supset (q \,/\, r)$
$(q + r) \supset (q \supset r)$,	$(q \underline{\vee} r) \supset (q \,/\, r)$
$(q \equiv r) \supset (q \supset r)$,	$(q - r) \supset (q \,/\, r)$
$(q \,.\, r) \supset (q \supset r)$,	$(q \not\supset r) \supset (q \,/\, r)$
$(r - q) \supset (q \supset r)$,	$(r - q) \supset (q \,/\, r)$
$(q \not\subset r) \supset (q \supset r)$,	$(q \not\subset r) \supset (q \,/\, r)$
$(q \downarrow r) \supset (q \supset r)$,	$(q \downarrow r) \supset (q \,/\, r)$
$(q \, C \, r) \supset (q \supset r)$,	$(q \, C \, r) \supset (q \,/\, r)$

In the above we can see that all functions T5, T6, T7 and T8 imply function T5; functions T9, T10, T11 and T12 imply the function T9; functions T13, T14, T15 and T16 imply both T5 and T9. The functions T1, T2, T3 and T4 are not present here, and they can easily be proved that they imply neither T5 nor T9.

The function $(q \,/\, r)$ is equivalent to $(q \supset \sim r)$, in which there is a sign of negation on the consequent r.

Let us re-write the above formulae as follows:

$T1 \supset \ldots$	$(q \, T \, r) \supset \ldots$	1.11
$T2 \supset \ldots$	$(q \, V \, r) \supset \ldots$	1.12
$T3 \supset \ldots$	$(q \supset r) \supset \ldots$	1.13
$T4 \supset \ldots$	$(r + q) \supset \ldots$	1.14
$T5 \supset T5$	$(q \supset r) \supset (q \supset r)$	1.21
$T6 \supset T5$	$(q + r) \supset (q \supset r)$	1.22
$T7 \supset T5$	$(q \equiv r) \supset (q \supset r)$	1.23
$T8 \supset T5$	$(q \,.\, r) \supset (q \supset r)$	1.24
$T9 \supset T9$	$(q \,/\, r) \supset (q \supset \sim r)$	1.31
$T10 \supset T9$	$(q \underline{\vee} r) \supset (q \supset \sim r)$	1.32
$T11 \supset T9$	$(q - r) \supset (q \supset \sim r)$	1.33
$T12 \supset T9$	$(q \not\supset r) \supset (q \supset \sim r)$	1.34
$T13 \supset T5.\ T9$	$(r - q) \supset (q \supset r).(q \supset \sim r)$	1.41
$T14 \supset T5.\ T9$	$(q \not\subset r) \supset (q \supset r).(q \supset \sim r)$	1.42
$T15 \supset T5.\ T9$	$(q \downarrow r) \supset (q \supset r).(q \supset \sim r)$	1.43
$T16 \supset T5.\ T9$	$(q \, C \, r) \supset (q \supset r).(q \supset \sim r)$	1.44

It is obvious that the sixteen functions are classified into four types, according to whether they imply $(q \supset r)$, or $(q \supset \sim r)$, or both, or neither.

Similar results can be obtained in the relations $Ui \supset Uj$ and $Ni \supset Uj$.

Let us consider another relation when the conjunction of two dyadic functions implies a third dyadic function, i.e.

$Ti \,.\, Tj \supset Tk.$

Let us consider a particular case when Ti is T4, and when Tk is T6 or T11, i.e.

$T4 \,.\, Tj \supset T6;$ $\qquad$ $T4 \,.\, Tj \supset T11.$

$T4 \,.\, T1 \supset \ldots$	$q \,.\, (q\, T\, r) \supset \ldots$	2.11
$T4 \,.\, T2 \supset \ldots$	$q \,.\, (q \vee r) \supset \ldots$	2.12
$T4 \,.\, T3 \supset \ldots$	$q \,.\, (q \subset r) \supset \ldots$	2.13
$T4 \,.\, T4 \supset \ldots$	$q \,.\, (q \quad\;) \supset \ldots$	2.14
$T4 \,.\, T5 \supset T6$	$q \,.\, (q \supset r) \supset r$	2.21
$T4 \,.\, T6 \supset T6$	$q \,.\, (\quad r) \supset r$	2.22
$T4 \,.\, T7 \supset T6$	$q \,.\, (q \equiv r) \supset r$	2.23
$T4 \,.\, T8 \supset T6$	$q \,.\, (q \,.\, r) \supset r$	2.24
$T4 \,.\, T9 \supset T11$	$q \,.\, (q \,/\, r) \supset \sim r$	2.31
$T4 \,.\, T10 \supset T11$	$q \,.\, (q \,\underline{\vee}\, r) \supset \sim r$	2.32
$T4 \,.\, T11 \supset T11$	$q \,.\, (\quad \sim r) \supset \sim r$	2.33
$T4 \,.\, T12 \supset T11$	$q \,.\, (q \not\supset r) \supset \sim r$	2.34
$T4 \,.\, T13 \supset T6.\ T11$	$q \,.\, (\sim q \quad) \supset r \,.\, \sim r$	2.41
$T4 \,.\, T14 \supset T6.\ T11$	$q \,.\, (q \not\subset r) \supset r \,.\, \sim r$	2.42
$T4 \,.\, T15 \supset T6.\ T11$	$q \,.\, (q \downarrow r) \supset r \,.\, \sim r$	2.43
$T4 \,.\, T16 \supset T6.\ T11$	$q \,.\, (q\, C\, r) \supset r \,.\, \sim r$	2.44

So far we have been dealing with functions of two variables. Let us now consider a special case of functions with three variables such that the conjunction of a function Ti with variables p and q and a function Tj with variables q and r implies a third function Tk with variables p and r; or

$Ti\,(p,q) \,.\, Tj\,(q,r) \supset Tk\,(p,r).$

There will be a large number of combinations; let us narrow our scope further by fixing Ti and Tk such that Ti = T5, Tk = T5 and also Tk = T9. Then we have

$T5\,(p,q) \,.\, Tj\,(q,r) \supset T5\,(p,r);$
$T5\,(p,q) \,.\, Tj\,(q,r) \supset T9\,(p,r).$

Note 1. The dots '. . . ' denote that there is no desired inference; it does not mean that there is no inference at all.

Note 2. The symbols 'q', 'r', '-q' and '~r' are used instead of 'r + q', 'q + r', 'r - q' and 'q - r' because the former are more meaningful in this paragraph.

Proceed as before, we have the following combinations:

T5(p, q) . T1(q, r) ⊃ . . .
T5(p, q) . T2(q, r) ⊃ . . .
T5(p, q) . T3(q, r) ⊃ . . .
T5(p, q) . T4(q, r) ⊃ . . .

T5(p, q) . T5(q, r) ⊃ T5(p, r)
T5(p. q) . T6(q, r) ⊃ T5(p, r)
T5(p, q) . T7(q, r) ⊃ T5(p, r)
T5(p, q) . T8(q, r) ⊃ T5(p, r)

T5(p, q) . T9(q, r) ⊃ T9(p, r)
T5(p, q) .T10(q, r) ⊃ T9(p, r)
T5(p, q) .T11(q, r) ⊃ T9(p, r)
T5(p, q) .T12(q, r) ⊃ T9(p, r)

T5(p, q) . T13(q, r) ⊃ T5(p, r) . T9(p, r)
T5(p, q) . T14(q, r) ⊃ T5(p, r) . T9(p, r)
T5(p, q) . T15(q, r) ⊃ T5(p, r) . T9(p, r)
T5(p, q) . T16(q, r) ⊃ T5(p, r) . T9(p, r)

(p ⊃ q). (q T r) ⊃ . . . 3.11
(p ⊃ q). (q V r) ⊃ . . . 3.12
(p ⊃ q). (q ⊂ r) ⊃ . . . 3.13
(p ⊃ q). (q   ) ⊃ . . . 3.14

(p ⊃ q). (q ⊃ r) ⊃ (p ⊃ r) 3.21
(p ⊃ q). (r) ⊃ (p ⊃ r) 3.22
(p ⊃ q). (q ≡ r) ⊃ (p ⊃ r) 3.23
(p ⊃ q(. (q . r) ⊃ (p ⊃ r) 3.24

(p ⊃ q). (q / r) ⊃ (p ⊃ ~r) 3.31
(p ⊃ q). (q v̲ r) ⊃ (p ⊃ ~r) 3.32
(p ⊃ q). (~r) ⊃ (p ⊃ ~r) 3.33
(p ⊃ q). (q ⊅ r) ⊃ (p ⊃ ~r) 3.34

(p ⊃ q). (~q   ) ⊃ (p ⊃ r). (p ⊃ ~r) 3.41
(p ⊃ q). (q ⊄ r) ⊃ (p ⊃ r). (p ⊃ ~r) 3.42
(p ⊃ q). (q ↓ r) ⊃ (p ⊃ r). (p ⊃ ~r) 3.43
(p ⊃ q). (q C r) ⊃ (p ⊃ r). (p ⊃ ~r) 3.44

For universal functions, we have:

U(f ⊃ g). U(g T h) ⊃ . . . 4.11
U(f ⊃ g). U(g V h) ⊃ . . . 4.12
U(f ⊃ g). U(g ⊂ h) ⊃ . . . 4.13
U(f ⊃ g). U(g   ) ⊃ . . . 4.14

U(f ⊃ g). U(g ⊃ h) ⊃ U(f ⊃ h) 4.21
U(f ⊃ g). U(h) ⊃ U(f ⊃ h) 4.22
U(f ⊃ g). U(g ≡ h) ⊃ U(f ⊃ h) 4.23
U(f ⊃ g). U(g . h) ⊃ U(f ⊃ h) 4.24

U(f ⊃ g). U(g / h) ⊃ U(f ⊃ ~h) 4.31
U(f ⊃ g). U(g v̲ h) ⊃ U(f ⊃ ~h) 4.32
U(f ⊃ g). U(~h) ⊃ U(f ⊃ ~h) 4.33
U(f ⊃ g). U(g ⊅ h) ⊃ U(f ⊃ ~h) 4.34

$U(f \supset g).U(\sim g \quad) \supset U(f \supset h).U(f \supset \sim h)$ 4.41

$U(f \supset g).U(g \not\subset h) \supset U(f \supset h).U(f \supset \sim h)$ 4.42

$U(f \supset g).U(g \downarrow h) \supset U(f \supset h).U(f \supset \sim h)$ 4.43

$U(f \supset g).U(g\ C\ h) \supset U(f \supset h).U(f \supset \sim h)$ 4.44

Several familiar laws in elementary logic are scattered in formulae listed above. For instance:

1.22 is equivalent to verum sequitur ad quodlibet;
1.41 is equivalent to ex falso sequitur quodlibet;
2.21 is equivalent to modus ponendo ponens;
2.31 is equivalent to modus ponendo tollens;
2.22 is equivalent to the law of a fortiori;
2.41 can be made equivalent to ex falso sequitur quodlibet $\sim q \supset (q \supset r)$ by applying the law of exportation and the law of a fortiori;
3.21 is equivalent to the law of syllogism;
3.22 can be made equivalent to verum sequitur quodlibet $r \supset (p \supset r)$ by applying the law of a fortiori;
4.21 is equivalent to the law of syllogism.

It is interesting that the laws, both familiar and unfamiliar, can be arranged in a sequence. They can be classified into four groups, A, B, C and D as follows:

1. A. $(q\ D\ r)$ implies neither $(q \supset r)$ nor $(q \supset \sim r)$;
   B. $(q\ D\ r)$ implies $(q \supset r)$;
   C. $(q\ D\ r)$ implies $(q \supset \sim r)$;
   D. $(q\ D\ r)$ implies both $(q \supset r)$ and $(q \supset \sim r)$.

   A. $U(g\ D\ h)$ implies neither $U(g \supset h)$ nor $U(g \supset \sim h)$;
   B. $U(g\ D\ h)$ implies $U(g \supset h)$;
   C. $U(g\ D\ h)$ implies $U(g \supset \sim h)$;
   D. $U(g\ D\ h)$ implies both $U(g \supset h)$ and $U(g \supset \sim h)$.

2. A. $q\ .\ (q\ D\ r)$ implies neither r nor $\sim r$;
   B. $q\ .\ (q\ D\ r)$ implies r;
   C. $q\ .\ (q\ D\ r)$ implies $\sim r$;
   D. $q\ .\ (q\ D\ r)$ implies both r and $\sim r$.

3. A. $(p \supset q).(q\ D\ r)$ implies neither $(p \supset r)$ nor $(p \supset \sim r)$;
   B. $(p \supset q).(q\ D\ r)$ implies $(p \supset r)$;
   C. $(p \supset q).(q\ D\ r)$ implies $(p \supset \sim r)$;
   D. $(p \supset q).(q\ D\ r)$ implies both $(p \supset r)$ and $(p \supset \sim r)$.

4. A. $U(f \supset g).U(g\ D\ h)$ implies neither $U(f \supset h)$ nor $U(f \supset \sim h)$;
   B. $U(f \supset g).U(g\ D\ h)$ implies $U(f \supset h)$;
   C. $U(f \supset g).U(g\ D\ h)$ implies $U(f \supset \sim h)$;
   D. $U(f \supset g).U(g\ D\ h)$ implies both $U(f \supset h)$ and $U(f \supset \sim h)$.

The four groups correspond respectively to Dignāga's 'inconclusive because of being too broad', 'valid', 'contradictory' and 'inconclusive because of being too narrow'.

In the Hetucakra and the Trairūpya, the judgement of correct inference is not quite the same as what we call 'validity' and is much narrower. For the sake of clarity, let us introduce the term 'correctness' instead of 'validity'.

Relating to 'correctness' two more notions should be introduced, namely, 'desirability' and 'uniqueness'.

Logic was used in India as a tool of debate, it was for defending oneself instead of opposing oneself. "A Syllogism is used to prove the probandum which is in accordance with the opinion of the disputant" said Dignāga in his Nyāyamukha.[1]

In accordance with the above principle, a syllogism with an undesirable conclusion is discarded as an incorrect one.

But how about a negative probandum? It is expressed in Dignāgean logic in the form of a positive one: "A is non-B" is used instead of saying "A is not B".

From the point of view of formal logic, if the conclusion contradicts the probandum, the fault lies on the probandum and not on the syllogism. We may therefore regard the 'contradictory' type as negative, which is valid.

Though we should not take the conception of 'desirability' seriously, the conception of 'uniqueness' is extremely important.

To say that the arguments in the group D are inconclusive does not mean that a conclusion cannot be inferred. No-one can refute the validity of the formula $(p \supset q).(\sim q) \supset (p \supset r)$. The trouble is, a conclusion $(p \supset q).(\sim q) \supset (p \supset \sim r)$ can also be inferred. The effect which we require to draw from the syllogism is cancelled by two conclusions which are contradictory to each other.

The formulae in the group D very much resemble the ex falso sequitur quodlibet, which is sometimes called the second paradoxical law. The group D is an extension of it; I therefore should like to call this group 'paradoxical'. Let us now list the four types as follows:

1. NM. Taishō 1628. p. 1. a.

Group	Characteristics	Indian view
A.	invalid	incorrect inference
B.	valid, affirmative	correct inference (unique and desirable)
C.	valid, negative	incorrect inference (unique but not desirable)
D.	valid, paradoxical	incorrect inference (not unique)

Now we can see what Dignāga regarded as 'correct inference' is a valid syllogism with an unique affirmative conclusion.

Let us consider the products of the contradictory factors:

1. $(p \supset r).(p \supset \sim r) \equiv (p\ C\ r)$.
2. $(r\ .\ \sim r)$, in the other notation, $(p + r).(p - r) \equiv (p\ C\ r)$.
3. The product $U(f \supset h).U(f \supset \sim h)$ is slightly different. By definition:

$U(f \supset h) = \sim E(f.\sim h)$;
$U(f \supset \sim h) = \sim E(f.h)$;
$U(f \supset h).U(f \supset \sim h) \equiv \sim E(f.\sim h).\sim E(f.h)$; therefore
$U(f \supset h).U(f \supset \sim h) \equiv \sim E(f)$

The above three formulae may be regarded as extended versions of the law of reductio ad absurdum. This type of argument was widely used by Buddhist philosophers, particularly the dialecticians (prāsaṅgika).

First, the opponent accepts that a thing f has the property h; i.e. $U(f \supset h)$. The disputant finds out a property g, which is accepted by the opponent, such that $U(f \supset g)$.

Then the disputant shows that the property g implies a property $\sim h$; i.e. $U(g \supset \sim h)$. Then the opponent is compelled to accept both $U(f \supset h)$ and $U(f \supset \sim h)$.

Then, if the thing f is existential, the conjunction $U(f \supset h).U(f \supset \sim h)$ is self-contradictory; or else the thing f is null:
$U(f \supset h).U(f \supset \sim h) \equiv \sim E(f)$.

25. What does the theory of the Trairūpya mean in Propositional Logic?

From the above we can see that the theory of the Hetucakra is very valuable to our knowledge of logic as a whole, even in the post-Russell Era. But how about the theory of the Trairūpya?

The Trairūpya is not so valuable as the Hetucakra, although it is not totally meaningless. The reason is that our logic today is no more a tool for debate, and therefore we are not much concerned with the conditions under which an unique affirmative conclusion can be inferred.

However, just for the sake of a comparative study, I should like to formulate a similar theory in propositional logic, despite its lack of practical value.

Let us find out the essential characteristics of the four groups by examining the definitions of the sixteen truth functions from the truth matrices:

	q r T T	q r T F	q r F T	q r F F
A	T	T	(these two columns	
B	T	F	are neglected	
C	F	T	because there is	
D	F	F	no essential effect	
			in the grouping)	

In the sixteen types only the four in the group B have been tested as valid in giving a unique affirmative conclusion. Then we can derive a set of rules which are analogous to Dignāga's Trairūpya as follows:

The counterpart (analogous formula) in propositional logic of the Form Barbara-A is the modus ponens; while that of the Form Barbara-B is the propositional syllogism. Let us deal with them separately as follows:

The conditions for a valid modus ponens in propositional logic with a unique affirmative conclusion are:

(1a) It is true that q;
(2a) when q and r are both true, the truth value of the function qr in the major premiss should be 'true';
(3a) when q is true and r is false, the truth value of the function qr in the major premiss should be 'false'.

The conditions for a valid propositional syllogism with a unique affirmative conclusion are:

(1b) p should materially imply q;
(2b) same as (2a);
(3b) same as (3a).

Condition (1) refers to the minor premiss and conditions (2) and (3) refer to the major premiss. It is understood that the term 'minor premiss' is used in its broader sense that it covers the premiss 'it is true that q' in the modus ponens, besides its conventional usage in syllogism.

The truth function which satisfies condition (1b) is material implication. Four truth functions among the sixteen can satisfy both conditions (2) and (3), namely: the material implication (q ⊃ r), the 'second component' (r), the material equivalence (q ≡ r) and the conjunction (q . r), because they are defined as follows:

	qr TT	qr TF	qr FT	qr FF
(q ⊃ r)	T	F	T	T
(r)	T	F	T	F
(q ≡ r)	T	F	F	T
(q . r)	T	F	F	F

The above shows that the minor premiss is confined to one truth function only while the major premiss can be one of the four functions mentioned above.

The reason why there is a discrimination between the major and the minor premisses is that there is some justification of this discrimination in the restricted predicate logic, such as the exclusion of the 'narrow equivalence' from the minor premiss in order to avoid 'inconclusiveness because of being too narrow'. Such a distinction does not exist in propositional logic.

Moreover, in the Hetucakra only the major premiss is stressed. Therefore in the propositional logic the condition (1) can be neglected.

26. The Problem of 'Inseparable Connection'

A. B. Keith wrote in his Indian Logic and Atomism[1] "But his (Vātsyāyana) logical doctrine is still meagre: inference is a mysterious thing, really argument from analogy, while Praçastpāda has a fully developed theory of invariable concomitance as the basis of inference".

Similarly H. N. Randle wrote in his Indian Logic in the Early Schools[2]: "It has been said that for Vātsyāyana inference was still really argument from analogy. It is true that Vātsyāyana's logic is more primative than Praśastapāda's".

1. Keith 1, p. 27.
2. Randle 2, p. 179.

After the introduction of the Trairūpya and the Hetucakra, the trend seems to have reversed. It was written by Randle [1] "For the present it is sufficient to point out that the Trairūpya, even as thus interpreted, makes the syllogism essentially an affair of examples - sapakṣas or concrete cases of P, and vipakṣas or concrete cases of the absence of P: and that there is nowhere to be found in it a statement of universal connection between M and P as abstract characters".

In the Nyāyavārttika Uddyotakara had definitely rejected the conception of 'inseparable connection' (avinābhāvena): "It may be suggested that smoke causes us to apprehend fire through 'inseparable connection'. That is, there is an 'inseparable connection' between smoke and fire. ... This view is wrong, because every interpretation of it that can be given turns out to be impossible. For what is meant by an inseparable connection between fire and smoke? Does it mean casual connection? or inherence (of both) in one thing, or of the one thing (in them both)? or simple relation of the one thing to the other thing? ... The answer is that this view is not tenable. We cannot infer relation between smoke and fire, because no such relation has been apprehended". [2]

If we turn back to the formation of the narrow functions, we find that they are defined by nothing else but the existential conditions for the four regions, or the emptiness and non-emptiness of the four sub-classes. The conception of the so-called 'invariable, or inseparable, or necessary or universal connection' does not enter in.

Now we have two obviously opposite trends: the change from 'argument from analogy' to 'inseparable connection', and the change from the 'inseparable connection' to existential conditions. If the former is a progress, should the second be a regress? Is the so-called 'an affair of examples' justified, i.e. a right inference?

From the point of view of the definition of the narrow functions, an example evidencing the existential condition is not only justified, but also necessary, unless it is otherwise defined.

I should like to say that both trends are progress. But how to reconcile the facts that they are both progress and opposite to each other?

1. Randle 2, p. 182.
2. NV. I. 1. 5. p. 53.
   IL. pp. 281-3.

The answer is: Dignāga had successfully resolved the major premiss into two components, namely the necessary presence of a positive example and the absence of a counter example.

In the first component, the presence of a positive example certainly cannot prove the truth of the major premiss, as the ancient logicians had wrongly attempted to do; but it is good enough to exclude the negative conclusion.

Let us use the symbol 'e' for a positive example. Then we have two ways of representing the existential condition in Barbara-A and Barbara-B, namely:

Barbara-A: $(ge.he).(e \neq y) \supset (Ex)(gx.hx)(x \neq y)$;
$(Ex)(gx.hx).(x \neq y) \supset (Ex)(gx.hx)$

Barbara-B: $(-fe.ge.he) \supset (Ex)(-fx.gx.hx)$;
$(Ex)(-fx.gx.hx) \supset (Ex)(gx.hx)$.

The premiss $(Ex)(gx.hx)$ certainly cannot prove the truth of $(x)(gx \supset hx)$, but it is good enough to prove the falsehood of $(x)(gx \supset -hx)$. i.e. $(Ex)(gx.hx) \supset -(x)(gx \supset -hx)$.

The second component is the non-existence of a counter example $-(Ex)(gx.-hx)$, because one single counter example raised by the opponent will be good enough to overthrow the disputant's conclusion. Let us use the symbol 'e'' for a counter example.

$(ge'.-he') \supset (Ex)(gx.-hx)$;
$(Ex)(gx.-hx) \supset -(x)(gx \supset hx)$.

By the use of the second component, the 'inseparable connection' can be dispensed with; because the major premiss can be defined simply by the existential conditions without reference to any inseparable connection.

However, the contraposition of the above formula

$(x)(gx \supset hx) \supset -(Ex)(gx.-hx) \supset -(ge'.-he')$

does not make sense. Therefore, from the practical point of view, the second component and the 'inseparable connection' are almost equally difficult to prove. To prove the non-existence of certain things and to assert the uniformity of a group of things are equally difficult.

The solution of the difficulty is to regard the factor $-(Ex)(gx.-hx)$ as a matter of convention instead of logical truth. The convention is: in so far as the opponent fails to provide with a counter example, the factor $-(Ex)(gx.-hx)$ will be conceded true, though only for the time of the debate.

Does this convention seem to be arbitrary? Does this mean that all kinds of truths so far are only relative?

Let us examine the debates practised today, such as parliament debates. When a cabinet minister gives a new promise and expresses his perfect confidence in its fulfillment, the members of the opposition usually try their best to find an example which the minister had promised previously and yet not fulfilled.

Let us also examine the history of human thought, particularly that of sciences. The development of a new theory usually started from a newly discovered fact which the old theory cannot cover. The old theory should therefore be modified and a new generalization would be made. The new theory is a better approximation to the truth than the older one.

Therefore the above-mentioned convention has so far dominated our judgement, whether we are aware of it or not.

27. Three Types of Connectives

We can see that in books on the logic of classes, three symbols occur very frequently: '$\subset$', '$\cup$', and '$\cap$' for 'class inclusion', 'logical sum of classes' and 'logical product of classes' repsectively. In fact these three symbols belong to two different types of connectives: (b $\subset$ c) means 'the class b is included in the class c'; (b $\cup$ c) means 'the logical sum of classes b and c'; (b $\cap$c) means 'the logical product of classes b and c'. The first formula is a proposition while the other two formulae are not.

There are three types of connectives, let us call them types A, B and C. Type A connectives connect propositions, such as (q $\supset$ r). Type B connectives form propositions, such as u(b $\supset$ c), n(b $\supset$ c), U(g $\supset$ h) and N(g $\supset$ h). Type C connectives connect classes, such as (b$\cap$ c); they cannot form propositions without being accompanied by other factors, e. g. 'the logical product of classes b and c' is not a proposition; but 'the logical product of classes b and c is empty' is a proposition.

We have used sixteen symbols to represent five different kinds of dyadic functions, all of which belong to the types A and B. The same set of symbols can also be used for the type C. Let us use the formula (b D c) for this type in order to distinguish it from universal and narrow functions.

1.	(b T c), the universe	16.	(b C c), the complement of 1.
2.	(b V c), the complement of 15.	15.	(b ↓ c), the product $\bar{b}\bar{c}$.
3.	(b ⊂ c), the complement of 14.	14.	(b ⊄ c), the product $\bar{b}$c.
4.	(c + b), the class b.	13.	(c - b), the complement of 4.
5.	(b ⊃ c), the complement of 12.	12.	(b ⊅ c), the product b$\bar{c}$.
6.	(b + c), the class c.	11.	(b - c), the complement of 6.
7.	(b ≡ c), the complement of 10.	10.	(b ⊻ c), the products b$\bar{c}$ and $\bar{b}$c.
8.	(b X c), the product bc.	9.	(b / c), the complement of 8.

From the above list we can see that the formula 1 to 8 are the respective complements of 16 to 9. The formula (b V c) is also called 'logical sum of b and c', (b C c) is also called 'the empty universe'. For the sake of simplicity, the term 'logical sum' is not applied, and we use two operators 'logical product' and 'logical complement' to express all sixteen functions.

We may treat the sixteen connectives as undefined symbols and apply them for dyadic functions other than those which have been mentioned by giving them new interpretations.

The main reason for using uniform notation of sixteen symbols in several different systems is that it is cumbersome to find as many as sixty-four different symbols, unless one is used to apply pictographs like Chinese characters. A disadvantage of using uniform notation is that it is easy to mix all things up. In order to prevent such a possible consequence once and for all, I should like to illustrate the different systems by following examples:

Type A.	(q ⊃ r)	'the truth of proposition q implies the truth of proposition r'.
Type B.	u(b ⊃ c)	'the class b is included in the class c'.
"	n(b ⊃ c)	'the class b is included in the class c; both classes and their complement are non-empty'.
"	U(g ⊃ h)	'nothing is both g and non-h'.
"	N(g ⊃ h)	'nothing is both g and non-h, all other combinations are realised'.
Type C.	(b ⊃ c)	'the complementary class of the logical product of b and $\bar{c}$'.

Type A.	(q V r)	'either the proposition q or the proposition r is true, or both propositions are true'.
Type B.	u(b V c)	'the logical product of classes $\bar{b}$ and $\bar{c}$ is empty.
"	n(b V c)	'the classes b and c are intersecting and are non-empty, their complement is empty'.
"	U(g V h)	'nothing is both non-g and non-h'.
"	N(g V h)	'nothing is both non-g and non-h, all other combinations are realised'.
Type C.	(b V c)	'the logical sum of classes b and c'.

28. A New Scheme of the Hetucakra

Not let us construct a new scheme of the sixteen types of syllogism by using U(f ⊃ g) as the minor premiss and sixteen dyadic functions, i.e. U(g D h), as major premisses. Then Venn's diagrams and corresponding formulae are as follows:

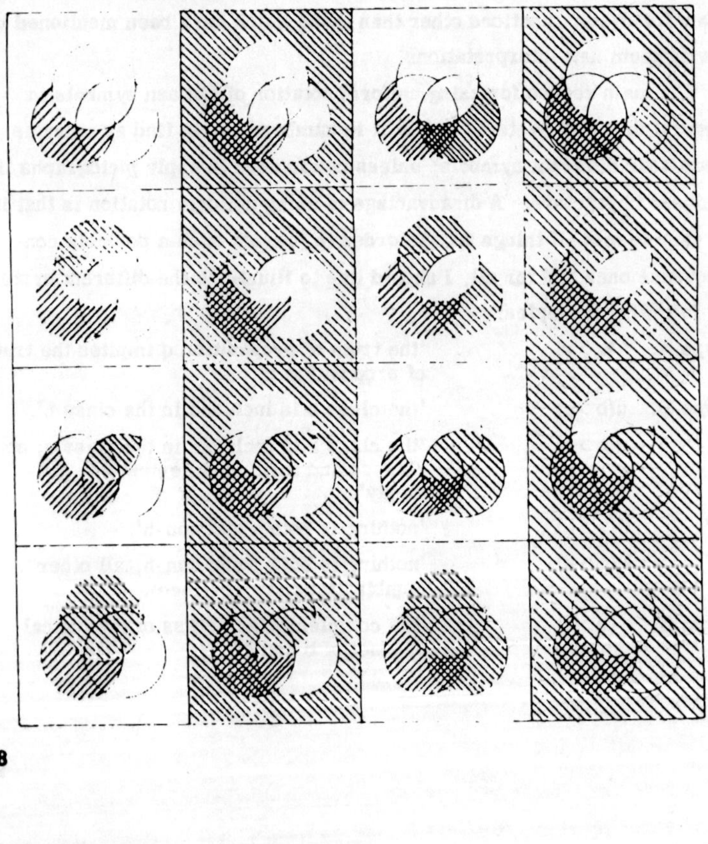

Row 1: $U(f \supset g).U(g\ T\ h) \supset .....$

$U(f \supset g).U(g\ V\ h) \supset .....$

$U(f \supset g).U(g \subset h) \supset .....$

$U(f \supset g).U(h + g) \supset .....$

Row 2: $U(f \supset g).U(g \supset h) \supset U(f \supset h)$

$U(f \supset g).U(g + h) \supset U(f \supset h)$

$U(f \supset g).U(g \equiv h) \supset U(f \supset h)$

$U(f \supset g).U(g\ X\ h) \supset U(f \supset h)$

Row 3: $U(f \supset g).U(g\ /\ h) \supset U(f \supset -h)$

$U(f \supset g).U(g\ \underline{v}\ h) \supset U(f \supset -h)$

$U(f \supset g).(g - h) \supset U(f \supset -h)$

$U(f \supset g).(g \not\supset h) \supset U(f \supset -h)$

Row 4: $U(f \supset g).U(h - g) \supset U(f \supset h).U(f \supset -h)$

$U(f \supset g).U(g \not\subset h) \supset U(f \supset h).U(f \supset -h)$

$U(f \supset g).U(g \downarrow h) \supset U(f \supset h).U(f \supset -h)$

$U(f \supset g).U(g\ C\ h) \supset U(f \supset h).U(f \supset -h)$

Alternatively we may use the formula $U(f \supset g).N(g\ D\ h)$ instead of $U(f \supset g).U(g\ D\ h)$. The difference between them is trivial. The diagrams of $U(f \supset g).N(g\ D\ h)$ will be similar to those of $U(f \supset g).U(g\ D\ h)$, except that all the unmarked regions become definitely existential.

Now let us re-arrange the old scheme of Dignāga-Uddyotakara's <u>hetucakra</u> in a sequence in agreement with our new scheme:

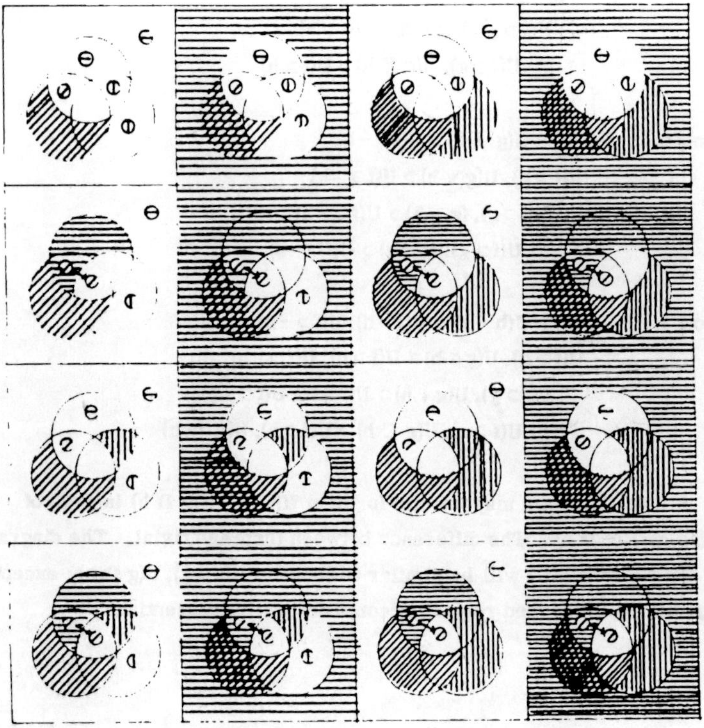

Row 1: 1.6.9 = PaH . SuH . VuH
1.6.7 = PaH . SuH . VaH
1.4.9 = PaH . SaH . VuH
1.4.7 = PaH . SaH . VaH

Row 2: 1.6.8 = PaH . SuH . VeH
1.6.11 = PaH . SuH . VyH
1.4.8 = PaH . SaH . VeH
1.4.11 = PaH . SaH . VyH

Row 3: 1.5.9 = PaH . SeH . VuH
1.5.7 = PaH . SeH . VaH
1.10.9 = PaH . SyH . VuH
1.10.7 = PaH . SyH . VaH

Row 4: 1.5.8 = PaH . SeH . VeH
1.5.11 = PaH . SeH . VyH
1.10.8 = PaH . SyH . VeH
1.10.11 = PaH . SyH . VyH

The two schemes are based on different theories: the old scheme is based on the variety of pakṣa-sapakṣa-vipakṣa combinations; while the new scheme is based on that of sixteen dyadic functions. Let us compare their diagrams:

In the first two rows there is no significant difference between them.

In the third row, the old scheme shows that the syllogism may either be contradictory or be inconclusive, because the central region is unknown. Dignāga called this type 'contradictory'. Although the use of this name may be explained by the reason that it was 'prepared for the worst'; logically speaking, 'either contradictory or inconclusive' should still be inconclusive, because a negative conclusion is not certain. In the new scheme all syllogisms in the third row can definitely yield negative conclusions which conform to Dignāga's 'contradictories'.

In the fourth row, the diagrams of the old scheme show that there is an arrow pointing from the region (f. g. - h) to the region (f. g. h), therefore the central region becomes non-empty, and these syllogisms should be valid and not 'inconclusive'. The diagrams of the new scheme show that they are inconclusive in the sense that two opposite conclusions can be yielded.

Let us summarize the result of examination in the following table:

	Dignāga-Uddyotakara's old scheme based on paksa-sapaksa-vipaksa combinations:	New scheme based on the sixteen dydadic functions:	Dignāga's examination on validity:
Row 1.	inconclusive	inconclusive	inconclusive
Row 2.	valid	valid	valid
Row 3.	either contradictory or inconclusive	negative	contradictory
Row 4.	valid	inconclusive	inconclusive

The above shows that the Dignāga-Uddyotakara's scheme of the hetucakra formulated by pakṣa-sapakṣa-vipakṣa combinations does not really fit in Dignāga's conditions of validity. A further investigation shows that the cause of the difficulty is two-fold:

First, the existential import of the minor premiss makes the central region (f. g. h) in Row 4 non-empty. Consequently these syllogisms become conclusive, and thus Dignāga's theory of validity is contradicted.

Secondly, the sapakṣa is by definition exclusive of the class of the subject itself. Therefore whether the region (-f. g. h) is empty is entirely irrelevant to whether the region (f. g. h) is empty, and logical inference becomes impossible. Consequently the syllogism in Row 3 become inconclusive although Dignāga called them 'contradictory'.

Our new scheme, being free from the above mentioned difficulties, can actually tally with Dignāga's standard of validity better than his own scheme. It seems that the hetucakra which was formulated by him according to pakṣa-sapakṣa-vipakṣa combinations and the hetucakra which was examined by him about the validity according to conditions of the trairūpya do not give exactly the same picture. We can imagine that while he formulated it he meant the former, and while he examined it he meant the latter. The one which was formulated and the one which was examined were so much alike that subtle differences between them could easily be ignored when many effective tools such as Venn's diagrams were lacking. Though his scheme based on paksa-sapaksa-vipaksa combinations is not a perfect one, it should be reckoned as a very close approximation. In his works he had never committed any serious and obvious mistakes, as Uddyotakara and Vacaspati Miśra had done very frequently.

The above is, of course, merely my personal speculation, as I am unable to assert what was definitely in the thinker's mind. It is actually my answer to a problem raised long ago in Chapter 1314: "Why did Dignāga reject the types 1.5.8, etc.?"

3. LIST OF FALLACIES

31. Śaṁkarasvāmin's List of Fallacies

311. Śaṁkarasvāmin's List and his Illustrative Cases

In India syllogistic was mainly applied as a tool for debate. The term ābhāsa means an erroneous though plausible argument. It has been so far translated as 'fallacy'.

In fact it does not mean precisely what we understand by 'logical fallacy'. It includes also other defects such as infringement of certain conventions which are artificially established for debates.

However, since this rendering has been widely and almost universally adopted, I shall use it also in this work with the above mentioned understanding.

The fallacies are numbered thirty-three in the Nyāyapraveśa. They are classified into three groups, namely:

1. the pakṣābhāsa, the fallacies of the probandum. They are fallacies which are pointed out in the probandum even before the reason is given.
2. the hetvābhāsa, the fallacies of the hetu. Because of the ambiguity of the term 'hetu', some of these fallacies are related to the minor premiss, and some to the major premiss.
3. the dṛṣṭāntābhāsa, the falacies of the exemplification. Also because of the ambiguity of the term 'dṛṣṭānta', some of these fallacies are related to the concrete examples, and some to the major premiss.

The ambiguity of these terms will be discussed later.

The above groups are classified further into sub-groups, and there are a few odd ones which do not belong to any one of the sub-groups. The sub-groups are:

A. Pakṣābhāsa, 似宗, 'fallacious probandum':

Viruddha, 相違, 'the contradictories', i.e. contradicting established fact or contradicting oneself.

Aprasiddha, 不極成, 'the unaccepted', i.e. failure to have major and minor terms accepted by both disputing parties.

B. <u>Hetvābhāsa,</u> 似因 , 'fallacious reasons':

<u>Asiddha,</u> 不成 , 'the unproved', i. e. the truth of the minor premiss is not proved.

<u>Anaikāntika,</u> 不定 , 'the uncertains', i. e. failure of the major premiss to yield a conclusive argument.

<u>Viruddha,</u> 相違 , 'the contradictories', i. e. the middle term leading to a conclusion contradictory to the desired <u>probandum.</u>

C. <u>Sādharmyadṛṣṭāntābhāsa,</u> 似同法喩 , 'fallacious positive exemplification':

<u>Asiddha,</u> 不成 , 'the undemonstrated', i. e. failure of the positive exemplification in demonstrating the desired properties.

D. <u>Vaidharmyadṛṣṭāntābhāsa,</u> 似異法喩 , 'fallacious negative exemplification:

<u>Avyāvṛtta,</u> 不遣 , 'the unexcluded', i. e. failure of the negative exemplification in excluding the undesired properties.

Indian logicians held different views regarding the classification of fallacious reasons. Akṣapāda gave an account of five types, Kaṇāda gave three. The latter was adopted by most Sāṁkhyas, Jaines and Buddhists.

The three types are <u>asiddha,</u> <u>viruddha</u> and <u>anaikāntika</u>. Praśastapāda divided the type of <u>anaikāntika</u> into two, namely <u>saṁdigdha</u> and <u>anadhyavasita.</u>

There is justification for <u>Praśastapāda's</u> modification. <u>Asiddha</u> is related to the minor premiss while the other three are related to the major premiss.

If we refer back to the list of sixteen varieties of the <u>Hetucakra,</u> we can find four groups A, B, C and D, in which the valid case fits the group B, whereas <u>saṁdigdha</u>, <u>viruddha</u> and <u>anadhyavasita</u> fit respectively the groups A, C and D. There is an essential difference between the groups A and D. In group D there can be two opposite conclusions, and the syllogism can be expressed in two tautological formulae. In group A there is no conclusion at all, and therefore the syllogism cannot be expressed by a tautological formula.

Uddyotakara had exerted the loudest voice in the anti-Dignāga campaign, but his modification of the sub-groups was not much more than a change of names. The following list gives the systems of fallacies of several Buddhists, Vaiśeṣikas and Naiyāyikas.

	Dignāga	Śaṁkara-svāmin	Praśasta-pāda	Bhāsarvajña	Uddyotakara	Gaṅgeśa
A1 A2 A3 A4 A5	pakṣā-bhāsa	pakṣā-bhāsa	pakṣā-bhāsa	bādhita	kālātīta	bādhita
A6 A7 A8 A9		pakṣā-bhāsa				
B1 B2 B3 B4	asiddha	asiddha	asiddha	asiddha	sādhyasama	sādhyasama
B5 B7 B8 B9	anaikān-tika	anaikān-tika	saṁ-digdha	anaikān-tika	savyabhi-cāra	savyabhi-cāra
B6	anaikān-tika	anaikān-tika	anadhy-avasita	anadhy-avasita		
B10	anaikān-tika	anaikān-tika	anadhy-avasita	satprati-pakṣa	prakaraṇa-sama	satprati-pakṣa
B11 B12 B13 B14	viruddha	viruddha	viruddha	viruddha	viruddha	viruddha

A. Pakṣābhāsa: 似宗 , 'fallacious probandum'[1]

Viruddha: 相違, 'the contradictories'

A1. Pratyakṣaviruddha, 現量相違, 'contradicting perception'. "Sound is not audible".

A2. Anumānaviruddha, 比量相違, 'contradicting inference'. "Pot, etc. are permanent".

A3. Āgamaviruddha, 自教相違, 'contradicting testimony' (of the disputant) A Vaiśeṣika says: "Sound is permanent".

A4. Lokaviruddha, 世間相違, 'contradicting convention'. "The Śaśi is not the moon". "A human skull is pure".

A5. Svavacanaviruddha, 自語相違, 'contradicting oneself'. "My mother is barren".

Aprasiddha: 不極成 , 'the unaccepted'.

A6. Aprasiddhaviśeṣaṇa, 能別不極成 'unaccepted predicate'. A Buddhist against a Sāṁkhya who held the view that when a thing disappears it becomes latent and is not perishable: "Sound is perishable".

A7. Aprasiddhaviśeṣya, 所別不極成 'unaccepted subject'. A Sāṁkhya against a Buddhist, who rejected the existence of a soul: "The soul is intellect".

A8. Aprasiddhobhaya, 俱不極成 ' unaccepted both' (terms) A Vaiśeṣika against a Buddhist, who accepted neither the existence of a soul nor that of a 'constitutive cause' (samavāyikāraṇa): "The soul is a 'constitutive cause'".

An odd one which does not belong to the two sub-groups:

A9. Prasiddhasaṁbandha, 相符極成 'being pre-established', i. e. the probandum is pointless because it has been accepted universally or at any rate by both the disputing parties. "Sound is audible".

B. Hetvābhāsa: 似因 'fallacious reasons'[2]

Asiddha: 不成 'the unproved'

B1. Ubhayāsiddha, 兩俱不成 'both untrue', i. e. the truth of the minor premiss is rejected by both parties. A Vaiśeṣika

1. NPD. pp. 2-3. NPH. Taishō 1630. p. 11 b-c.
2. NPD. pp. 3-5. NPH. Taishō 1930. p. 11c-12a.

against a Śābdika (Mīmāṁsā):
"Sound is impermanent because it is visible".

B2. Anayatarāsiddha, 隨一不成 'either untrue', i.e. the truth of the minor premiss is rejected by one of the disputing parties.
A Vaiśeṣika against a Śabdābhivyaktivādin,[1] who held the view that sound is not produced but manifested: "Sound is impermanent because it is a product".

B3. Saṁdigdhāsiddha, 猶豫不成 'being doubtful', i.e. the truth of the minor premiss is not certain.
"There is fire because there is mist".

B4. Āśrayāsiddha, 所依不成 'being unfounded'. The word 'unfounded' is used here in an unusual sense, it means that the minor premiss is not based on a subject accepted by both sides, i.e. at least one of the disputing parties rejects the existence of the subject. Since the subject is not accepted, the minor premiss will naturally be rejected. A Vaiśeṣika against a Sautrāntika, who rejected the existence of space: "Space is a substance, because it possesses qualities".

Anaikāntika: 不定 'the uncertains'

B5. Sādhāraṇa, 共不定 'being too broad', i.e. the syllogism is inconclusive because the scope of the middle term is too broad.
A Śābdika against a Buddhist: "Sound is permanent because it is knowable".

B6. Asādhāraṇa, 不共不定 'being too narrow', i.e. the syllogism is inconclusive because the scope of the middle term is too narrow.
A Śābdika against a Vaiśeṣika: "Sound is permanent because it is audible".

---

1. (Śabdotpattivāda and Śabdābhivyaktivāda are two schools of Śābdika, the former held the view that sound is produced; whereas the latter, that it is not produced but manifested through the application of effort. The Śabdotpattivādins classified sound into three kinds, and 'soundness' was one of them.)

B7. <u>Sapakṣaikadeśavṛtti vipakṣavyāpī,</u> 同品一分轉異品遍轉 'similar-partial, dissimilar-whole', i.e. the syllogism is inconclusive because the property expressed by the middle term is present in some similar instances and in all dissimilar instances.

A Śabdotpattivādin against a Śabdābhivyaktivādin: "Sound is not a product of effort, because it is impermanent".

B8. <u>Vipakṣaikadeśavṛtti Sapakṣavyāpī,</u> 異品一分轉同品遍轉 'dissimilar-partial, similar-whole', i.e. the syllogism is inconclusive because the property expressed by the middle term is present in all similar instances and in some dissimilar instances.

A Śabdābhivyaktivādin against a Śabdotpattivādin: "Sound is a product of effort, because it is impermanent".

B9. <u>Ubhayapakṣaikadeśavṛtti,</u> 俱品一分轉 'both-partial', i.e. the syllogism is inconclusive because the property expressed in the middle term is present in some similar instances and in some dissimilar instances.

A Śābdika against a Vaiśeṣika: "Sound is permanent, because it is intangible".

B10. <u>Viruddhāvyabhicāri,</u> 相違決定 'being counterbalanced', i.e. two syllogisms yield mutually opposite conclusions. A Vaiśeṣika against a Śabdotpattivādin: "Sound is impermanent because it is a product". The Śabdotpattivādin replies: "Sound is permanent because it is <u>an</u> object of audition, like 'soundness' ".

<u>Viruddha:</u> 相違 'the contradictories'

B11. <u>Dharmasvarūpaviparītasādhana,</u> 法自相相違 'contradicting expressed-predicate'.

A Śabdotpattivādin says: "Sound is permanent because it is a product".

A Śabdābhivyaktivādin says: Sound is permanent because it is a product of effort".

B12. <u>Dharmaviśeṣaviparītasādhana,</u> 法差別相違 'contradicting implied-predicate'.

A Sāṁkhya against a Buddhist: "The eyes are serviceable to another one's needs, because they are composite substances, like a bed".

B13. Dharmisvarūpaviparītasādhana, 有法自相相違 'contradicting expressed-subject'.

Kaṇāda says to Pañcaśikha: "Being is neither substance, nor quality nor action; because it possesses substance, quality and action, like particularity".

B14. Dharmiviśeṣaviparītasādhana, 有法差別相違 'contradicting implied-subject'.

The illustrative case is the same as B13.

C. Sādharmyadṛṣṭāntābhāsa 似同法喩 'fallacious positive exemplification'.[1]

Asiddha: 不成 'the undemonstrated'.

C1. Sādhanadharmāsiddha, 能立法不成 'undemonstrated middle', i.e. failure in demonstrating the property expressed by the middle term.

A Śābdika against a Vaiśeṣika: "Sound is permanent because it is incorporeal. Whatever is incorporeal is permanent, like atoms". Neither party accepted that atoms are incorporeal.

C2. Sādhyadharmāsiddha, 所立法不成 'undemonstrated predicate', i.e. failure in demonstrating the property expressed by the predicate.

Same syllogism but a different example 'like intellect' was used. Neither party accepted that intellect was permanent.

C3. Ubhayāsiddha, 俱不成 'undemonstrated both', i.e. failure in demonstrating the properties expressed by both the middle term and the predicate.

Same syllogism but a different example 'like a pot' was used. It is obvious that a pot is neither incorporeal nor permanent. Another illustrative case was given. A Śābdika against a Sautrāntika: "Sound is permanent because it is incorporeal, like space". This syllogism is fallacious on account of

---

1. NPD. pp. 5-7. NPH. Taishō 1630. p. 12b

'undemonstrated both' because the very existence of 'space' was rejected by the opponent and consequently it failed to demonstrate any property at all. This type was called in the Nyāyapraveśa 'non-existential undemonstrated both' as distinguished from the previous illustrative case.

Two odd types which do not belong to 'asiddha':

C4. Ananvaya: 無合 'lacking connection', failure in establishing a universal connection between the middle term and the major term.

"Sound is impermanent because it is a product, like a pot which is both impermanent and a product" without expressing the universal connection between 'being impermanent' and 'being a product'.

C5. Viparītānvaya, 倒合 'inverted connection', i. e. the universal connection established by the exemplification between the middle term and the major term is inverted.

"Sound is impermanent because it is a product, whatever is impermanent is a product, like a pot".

D. Vaidharmyadṛṣṭāntābhāsa 似異法喩 'fallacious negative exemplification'.

Avyāvṛtta 不遣 'the unexcluded'.

D1. Sādyadharmāvyāvṛtta, 所立法不遣 'unexcluded predicate', i. e. failure of the negative exemplification in excluding the property expressed by the predicate.

"Sound is permanent because it is incorporeal. Whatever is not permanent is not incorporeal, such as atoms".

D2. Sādhanadharmāvyāvṛtta, 能立法不遣 'unexcluded middle', i. e. failure of the negative exemplification in excluding the property expressed by the middle term.

The same syllogism but a different example 'such as action' was used.

D3. Ubhayāvyāvṛtta, 俱不遣 'unexcluded both', i. e. failure of the negative example in excluding the properties expressed by both the middle term and the predicate.

A Śābdika against a Sarvāstivādin: "Sound is permanent because it is incorporeal. Whatever is not permanent is not incorporeal, such as space".

Two odd types which do not belong to 'avyāvṛtta'

D4. Avyātireka, 無離 'lacking exclusion'. This term seems to be ambiguous. It actually means that the negative exemplification fails to establish a negative universal connection between the negation of the property expressed by the major term and the negation of the property expressed by the middle term. "Sound is permanent because it is incorporeal. It is unlike a pot, which is neither permanent nor incorporeal" without expressing the universal connection between 'not being permanent' and 'not being incorporeal'.

D5. Viparītavyātireka, 倒離 'inverted exclusion', i.e. the negative universal connection established by the negative exemplification is inverted.

"Sound is permanent because it is incorporeal. Whatever is not incorporeal is not permanent, such as a pot".

The above illustrative cases are quoted from the text of the Nyāypraveśa, but the names of schools of the disputants are taken from the Great Commentary. As I have said before, the records of 'So-and-so against So-and-so' should not be taken too seriously. Only a part of this material is from historical records, and the rest is assumed for illustration only. Unfortunately the author did not point out which ascriptions are factual and which ones are assumed.

The reason why he should add 'So-and-so against So-and-so' is that the validity also depends on who the disputing parties are. A syllogism may be a valid one if it is used by A against B, but the same syllogism may be a fallacious one if it is used by C against D. The relativity of validity will be discussed later.

312. Some Queries on Śaṁkarasvāmin's List of Fallacies

A list of fallacies should be comprehensive and all individual fallacies should be independent and not reducible to one another. However, most lists made by western and eastern logicians, including Aristotle, have been so far unsatisfactory. They are defective through either incompleteness or overlapping.

In India the list of fallacies was not a theory but a kind of common code which was legislated and modified by a number of schools holding different views. Such a list can hardly be systematic.

Śaṁkarasvāmin's list is not an exception. However, his list is a fairly good one among the works in his time. In many other works on logic, there is a list of 'fallacious refutation' which is even more unsystematic and pointless. The entire abolition of the list of fallacious refutation in the Nyāyapraveśa should be regarded as an improvement.

3121. Queries on individual fallacies

31211. B3.

The illustrative case given in the fallacy B3 is, "There is fire because there is mist". In the commentary, it is suggested that there was some 'mist-like thing', which may be any one of the following: mist, dust, smoke or mosquitoes.[1] Since one could not decide which one it definitely was, the reason is considered as 'being doubtful'.

If one term or premiss is 'doubtful', then the number of fallacies would be doubled, because there are the fallacies for the 'wrong' ones and there are those for the 'doubtful' ones. Why is it confined to the middle term only?

If the reason is 'because there is mist', it will be a wrong one and not 'doubtful'.

If it is "because there is some 'mist-like thing'", which includes the possibility of smoke, the major premiss will be:

"Some mist-like thing (i.e. smoke) implies the existence of fire; (while some other mist-like thing does not)". This is inconclusive type B9 - 'both-partial'.

31212. B4.

In the list the fallacy A7 'unaccepted subject' was regarded as a fallacy of the reason.

It seems that there is some difference between the premisses "Hares have horns" and "unicorns have horns" and that when the probandum

1. NPGC. Taishō 1840. p.121 c.

(the first member of the syllogism) is already fallacious because the minor term represents a null class, the disputant still tries to prove it; then both the probandum and the proof are fallacious. It is nevertheless not justified to regard one fallacy as two separate ones. Should this be the case, (i. e. one part of the syllogism is considered as fallacious because of the fault of another part), then the total number of fallaices would be much more increased than the present form.

Then why did Śaṁkarasvāmin put this fallacy into two? One possible explanation is that he adopted the fallacy B4 from Dignāga. It was written in the Nyāyamukha: "... (nor is it a pakṣadharma) when the subject is not accepted; e. g. 'the ātman is all pervading, because it produces joy, etc.' Reasons of these kinds cannot be considered as a proof".[1]

Perhaps Śaṁkarasvāmin failed to realize that while Dignāga wrote the above mentioned passage, the four fallacies of the probandum including A7 were not mentioned by Dignāga, but were later added by Śaṁkarasvāmin himself.

As a result, when he compiled a list of fallacies, he included both what Dignāga had mentioned and what Dignāga had not; thus he repeated the same fallacy twice. Therefore either A7 or B4 is redundant.

31213. A8, B1, C3 and D3

Although an argument may be vitiated by two or more fallacies occurring together, every fallacy should be independent by itself and should not be compounded in the list of fallacies. In this respect, A8 is the combination of A6 and A7; B1 can be included in B2; C3 is the combination of C1 and C2; D3 is the combination of D1 and D2. All these are redundant.

31214. B7, B8 and B9

Fallacies B7, B8 and B9 are not parallel to B5. All of them belong to the category of 'being too broad'. Therefore, either B7, B8 and B9 should be included in B5; and the resultant fallacy be called 'being too broad'; or the fallacy B5 should be given a new name parallel to the other three, namely
'ubhayapakṣavyāpi', 俱品遍轉 'both-whole', defined by "the syllogism is inconclusive because the property expressed in the middle term is present in all similar instances and in all dissimilar instances'.

1. NM. Taishō 1628. p. 1b.

31215. B12 and B14

Fallacies B12 and B14 concern not only the truth of the premisses but also the ambiguity of terms as well. If all the terms are precisely and uniquely defined, these two fallacies will be the same as B11 and B13 respectively.

On the other hand if the apparent meaning and the implied meaning of a term should be discriminated in the list of fallacies, the fault of ambiguity should be extended to other fallacies as well, why should they be confined to these two only?

31216. B13 and B14

According to the verbal meaning of the terms 'dharmisvarūpaviparītasādhana' and 'dharmiviśeṣaviparītasādhana', these two fallacies should be related to the minor premiss and can be interpreted in two possible ways, namely:

a. that the negation of the minor premiss is true, or
b. that the minor premiss can yield a conclusion which is contradictory to the probandum.

If the first interpretation is correct, these two fallacies should become a special case of the 'asiddha', but this is most unlikely the case.

In the second interpretation, if the contradictory middle is defined as 'a middle which can yield a conclusion which is contradictory to the probandum', then the fallacies B13 and B14 should not be called 'contradictory', because no conclusion can be derived at all; the following formulae, in both quantified and unquantified forms, are false:

$N(f \supset \sim g). N(g \supset h) \supset N(f \supset \sim h);$
$(p \supset \sim q). (q \supset r) \supset (p \supset \sim r).$

These two types are the most difficult ones in the list; they will be separately discussed in a later chapter.

31217. C4, C5, D4 and D5

One very puzzling item in the list of fallacies is the dṛṣṭāntābhāsa, the fallacies in exemplification. In the Nyāyapraveśa there are five fallacies for the positive exemplification and five for the negative. The first three pairs are very simple - failure either in demonstrating or in excluding the properties given in the reason.

The last two pairs are something quite different. C4 is 'lacking connection', i.e. the exemplification gives only a concrete example in which there is an 'accidental co-existence'[1] of two properties denoted by the middle and the major term, without giving a necessary connection between these two properties.

In the word of the Great Commentary,[2]

> "If one does not say 'whatever is a product is impermanent, like a pot', one cannot prove that the property of being a product necessarily implies the property of being impermanent. Because of lacking connection, the truth of sound being a product cannot prove the truth of its being impermanent. Therefore 'lacking connection' is a fallacy of the exemplification."

Is this fallacy a factual one, or merely a formal one - lacking an additional clause "whatever is g is h"? Strangely enough, the explanation in the Great Commentary is unusually brief.

Dharmakirti said of this case: "necessary concomitance is either absent or not rightly expressed", that is to say, this can either be formal incompleteness or involve material errors.

He gave an illustrative case on C4 when a material mistake was committed:[3]

> "This man is subject to passions,
> Because he speaks.
> Whoever speaks is subject to passions, like our Mr. So-and-so".

The above illustrative case was interpreted in different ways by Dharmottara and Vidyabhusana:

The former says:

> "What is really proved by this example is merely the fact of a coexistence in Mr. So-and-so of the faculty of speech together with his passions. But the necessary logical subordination (of the first attribute to the second) is not proved. Therefore the example is deficient in regard of (the universality and necessity) of the concomitance."[4]

---

1. Stcherbatsky 12, p.238.
2. NPGC. Taishō 1840. p.135 c.
3. Nyāyabindu. p.116.
4. Stcherbatsky 12, p.238. NBT. p.62.

The latter says:

The person in the street (i. e. Mr. So-and-so) cannot serve as an example, as it is questionable whether he is passionate, that is, it involves doubt as to the validity of the major term."[1]

Up to now we have four different ways of interpretation of the fallacy C4, namely:

1. that the fallacy is merely formal incompleteness, as is maintained in the Great Commentary;

2. that it is questionable whether the example can illustrate the property given by the major term, as Vidyabhusana says in his interpretation;

3. that the example fails to illustrate a universal concomitance, as Dharmakīrti and Dharmottara hold[2];

4. that the major premiss itself is not a universal concomitance, as suggested in the last alternative of interpretation.

The four possible interpretations are considered one by one as follows:

1. In many surviving texts on logic, the major premiss "whatever is g is h" is very frequently suppressed in three-membered syllogisms. Should such very common suppression be considered as fallacious because of 'lacking connection'?

2. The case in which it is questionable whether the example can illustrate the property given by the major term should be a special case of C2 - 'undemonstrated predicate', in which the example fails to demonstrate the property expressed by the major term, not because it is certain that it does not possess the property but because it is doubtful whether it possesses the property or not.

---

1. Vidyabhusana 21, p. 314.
2. To put all cases in the third interpretation in symbols, we have:

C4: the positive example illustrates only $(Ex)(gx.hx)$ but fails to illustrate $(x)(gx \supset hx)$;
C5: the positive example illustrates $(x)(hx \supset gx)$ instead of $(x)(gx \supset hx)$;
D4: the negative example illustrates only $(Ex)(\sim gx. \sim hx)$ but fails to illustrates $(x)(\sim hx \supset \sim gx)$;
D5: the negative example illustrates $(x)(\sim gx \supset \sim hx)$ instead of $(x)(\sim hx \supset \sim gx)$.

3. It is hard to believe that the universal concomitance $(x)(gx \supset hx)$ can be abstracted from the exemplification $(Ex)(gx.hx)$. If it is not enough for the exemplification to give just an 'accidental co-existence', what else can an example give?

Both Dharmakīrti and Dharmottara condemned the exemplification of 'like Mr. So-and-so' as fallacious, but neither of them had given a correct one conforming to their standard. I am doubtful whether there is such a thing at all.

4. Suppose the fallacies C4 and C5 concern the defects of the major premiss, then such mistakes should not be listed in the fallacies of exemplification because they have already been included in the fallacies of the reason.

The fallacy C4 'lacking connection' will then become equivalent to B7 'similar-partial and dissimilar-whole' (the Hetucakra 1. 6. 7) and B9 'both-partial' (the Hetucakra 1. 6. 9).

The fallacy C5 'inverted connection' will become equivalent to B5 'being too broad' (the Hetucakra 1. 4. 7) and B8 'dissimilar-partial, similar-whole' (the Hetucakra 1. 4. 9).

Similarly the fallacies D4 and D5 are also superfluous.

Dharmakīrti held the view that exemplification is included in a process called 'pointing out the three aspects of the reason' (trairūpya), also known as 'substantiation of the reason' (hetusamarathana). It is used for non-experts only while experts can follow the inference as soon as the reason is stated without requiring any exemplification.

The above statement shows that the exemplification is not the major premiss but a concrete example. When the hetu is 'substantiated', it will at once become a particular event and not a range of events. I do not know how it can possibly point out all three aspects of the reason.

It was mentioned by W. V. Quine: "beginners commonly make the mistake of concluding that I must become '$(Ex)(Fx \supset Gx)$'".[1] If such a mistake is commonly made by beginners of logic today, it is reasonable to assume that a similar mistake could have very naturally been made by our ancient predecessors.

---

1. Quine: Methods of Logic, p. 87

I presume that ancient logicians could have made the following discrimination:

valid exemplification: $(Ex)(gx.(gx \supset hx))$;
fallacy C4: $(Ex)(gx.hx)$;
fallacy C5: $(Ex)(hx.(hx \supset gx))$.

They failed to realize that the expression $(Ex)(gx \supset hx)$ is equivalent to $(Ex)(\sim(gx. \sim hx))$, i. e. there is at least one object which is not both g and non-h.

$$(Ex)(gx. \sim(gx. \sim hx)) \equiv (Ex)(gx.hx) \equiv (Ex)(hx. \sim(hx. \sim gx)); \text{ or,}$$
$$(Ex)(gx.(gx \supset hx)) \equiv (Ex)(gx.hx) \equiv (Ex)(hx.(hx \supset gx)).$$

Therefore the discrimination between their 'valid exemplification' and the two 'fallacious ones' is not justified.

People might object that although Śaṁkarasvāmin might fail to realize the identity of the above three expressions, it is most unlikely that Dharmakīrti could fail to do so.

I should like to say that their failure is not only possible but also quite likely. We think that the identity is very obvious just because we possess much better tools; without which the handling of expressions like 'being impermanent', 'not being impermanent', 'being produced by effort' and 'not being produced by effort' is not quite an easy job.

The development of thought is like a living organism in which the views of earlier thinkers, both correct and erroneous, are contained, preserved and absorbed, both consciously and unconsciously, by latter ones, including both followers and opponents of the earlier ones. The conception of argument from analogy of Vātsyāyana has deeply influenced, whether consciously or unconsciously, the minds of later Indian logicians. Such an influence can be revealed only by reading between the lines.

Both Vātsyāyana and Dignāga used exemplification in syllogism, yet they used it very differently in sense. As I have mentioned in Chapter 226, the premiss $(Ex)(gx.hx)$ can never prove the truth of $(x)(gx \supset hx)$, but is good enough to prove the falsehood of $(x)(gx \supset \sim hx)$. In other words, it can help us to avoid the four 'paradoxical types', which yield a conclusion of $(x)(fx \supset hx).(x)(fx \supset \sim hx)$. It has nothing to do with the 'universal connection' or 'universal concomitance'.

However, in the compilation of the lists of fallacies, the ghost of Vātsyāyana appeared again in the unconscious mind of the compilers, and Dignāga's correct interpretation of the true function of exemplification was hidden. This is my explanation of why the four fallacies C4, C5, D4 and D5 were put in the list at all.

3122. Queries in general - Ambiguity of terminology

In Chapter 125 I have remarked on the ambiguity of the term *anumeya*, which led to the misinterpretation of the *Trairūpya*. The same situation happens in the list of fallacies. It is extraordinary that all the three terms, namely *pakṣābhāsa*, *hetvābhāsa* and *dṛṣṭāntābhāsa*, are ambiguous.

Does the term '*pakṣa*' mean the *probandum*, or the minor term, or the major term? Does the term '*hetu*' mean the middle term, or the minor premiss, or the major premiss? Does the term *dṛṣṭanta* mean the concrete example, or the major premiss?

One single word can answer all the above questions, i.e. "yes". Let us consider them separately as follows:

Among the nine types of *pakṣābhāsa*, A1, A2, A3, A4, A5 and A9 are related to the *probandum*; A6 is related to the major term; A7 is related to the minor term; A8 is related to both terms.

Among the fourteen types of *hetvābhāsa*, B1, B2, B3 and B4, i.e. 'the unproved', are related to the minor premiss; B5, B6, B7, B8, B9, B10, B11 and B12, i.e. the whole of 'the uncertains' and one part of 'the contradictories', are related to the major premiss; B13 and B14 are probably related to the minor premiss.

Among the ten types of *dṛṣṭāntābhāsa*, C1, C2, C3, D1, D2 and D3 are related to the concrete examples; C4, C5, D4 and D5 are related to the major premiss.

Because of lack of system, the overlapping of fallacies in the list is unavoidable.

Chinese commentators interpreted the fallacies of exemplification as follows:

The fallacies C1, C2, C3, D1, D2 and D3 are concerning the 'yü-i' (喻依), i.e. 'the concrete example which illustrates (the universal concomitance)'. The positive and negative concrete examples can be symbolized as

$ge.he \supset (Ex)(gx.hx)$
$-ge'.-he' \supset (Ex)(-gx.-hx).$

The fallacies D4, D5, C4 and C5 are concerning the 'yü-t'i' (喻體), i.e. 'the universal concomitance which is the abstract of exemplification'. The positive and negative concomitance can be symbolized as

$(x)(gx \supset hx)$
$(x)(-hx \supset -gx).$

In A6, the term 'viśeṣaṇa' (the qualifier) is used; in A7, 'viśeṣya' (the qualificand) is used. In B4, 'āśraya' (that which the hetu is based on) is used. In C1 and D2, 'sādhana' (that which proves) is used; in C2 and D1, 'sādhya' (that which is to be proved) is used.

In fact, the terms 'viśeṣya', 'āśraya' and 'sādhya' all mean the minor term here. (They might mean something else in other occasions). The term 'viśeṣaṇa' means the major term; the term 'sādhana' means the middle term.

The diversity in use of terms may be explained by the fact that the relation between a minor term and a major term is that between the qualificand and the qualifier, and the relation between a minor term and a middle term is that between 'that which is to be proved' and 'that which proves'. It is still not justified to use a variety of terms in the same list.

Here I should like to mention again the controversy caused by the layman Lü Ts'ai. All the surviving documents were written in ornamental style which conveys not much practical sense, yet two sentences quoted by Ming Hsüan attracted my attention:[1]

宗依宗體留依去體以爲宗
喻體喻依去體留依以爲喻

There is obviously some mistake either in the manuscript or in the printing. The following, in which both sentences can make sense, is my own conjecture; without positive proof I do not wish to assert that it is the correct text:

宗依宗體去依留體以爲宗
喻體喻依去體留依以爲喻

1. Taisho 2053, p. 265

The Chinese, strictly following the Indian tradition, called three different things, namely: the probandum, the major term and the minor term, the same name 'tsung'. Therefore in many commentaries, when we see the term 'tsung', we have to find out ourselves what this term means from its particular context.

Similarly the Chinese called two different things, namely: the concrete example and the condition of a universal concomitance (vyāpti), which can be expressed by a major premiss, the same name 'yü'.

Sometimes, but not always, they did distinguish the usage of these terms. They called the probandum 'tsung-t'i' and the major and minor terms 'tsung-i'; they called the concrete example 'yü-i' and the condition of concomitance 'yü-t'i'.

I translate Lü Ts'ai's words, according to my conjecture, as following:

> "Of the two interpretations of the word 'tsung', namely (1) 'tsung' in the sense of the probandum and (2) 'tsung' in the sense of terms, the first interpretation but not the second should be retained.
>
> "Of the two interpretations of the word 'yü', namely (1) 'yü' in the sense of the condition of concomitance and (2) 'yü' in the sense of the concrete example, the second interpretation but not the first should be retained."

This is to say, the major and the minor terms should never be called 'tsung', and the condition of concomitance should never be called 'yü' in the first place, and the confusion in terminology is purely artificial without any reason. If my emendation is correct, then Lü Ts'ai's objection is justified.

31222. Lack of System

At the first glance it seems that the list of fallacies in the Nyāyapraveśa, with the exception of A6, A7, A8 and A9, follows strictly Dignāga's Pramāṇasamuccaya and Nyāyamukha. In fact Dignāga's own exposition is quite different from that of the Nyāyapraveśa. Let us compare the passages concerning the hetu from the Nyāyamukha and the Nyāyapraveśa: Dignāga first explained the Hetucakra and then by applying the last two clauses of the Trairūpya he sorted out which types should be rejected. He did not say: "there are six inconclusive types, namely..... ;

there are four contradictory types, namely.....", as the author of the Nyāyapraveśa did. This difference is in fact a crucial one. In other words, the author of the Nyāyapraveśa merely fossilized Dignāga's words without really understanding what Dignāga meant to say.

It seems to be too strong to say, although it might be the hard fact, that the Nyāyapraveśa was written by a man who did not really understand Dignāga's logic; yet it is almost safe to say that this book was not a premature draft of the Nyāyamukha by Dignāga himself, but a poor interpretation of the Nyāyamukha by somebody else.

Distinguished scholars who maintained the view that this book was written by Dignāga wrote a lot of scholarly articles full of names, titles, dates and quotations, but not much about the theory itself. It is like authenticating a painting simply by referring to documentation without a glance at the painting itself. Moreover, from the point of view of common sense, a wrong attribution of a painting to a well-known master is a most usual practice, but a wrong attribution of a great master's work to a very unfamiliar name is highly improbable.

The appearance of B7, B8 and B9 in the list of fallacies must have bewildered many beginners, and logic seems to be more sophisticated and less easily approachable than it should be. Who would have thought that they are defective in the first place! It is not always the case that the difficulty of a system is due to its profundity; sometimes it may be due to its misleading character.

The fact that the Nyāyapraveśa had been very popular in both India and China is easily understandable. It is quite a desirable thing for most people to take a short-cut by acquiring a set of formulae in order to practise the technique of debate immediately without having to take the trouble of understanding its theory. Therefore its popularity does not prove its true value.

The trend of sheer scholasticism existed in both Buddhist and non-Buddhist schools during their later stages of development. Kumārila's six types and Bhāsarvajña's eight types of contradictories are nothing but further senseless elaboration.

313. The Hetucakra, the Trairūpya and the List of Fallacies

The three items are closely related and a list showing their interrelations is essential for the understanding of Dignāga's system as a whole. The following list is mainly based on the opinion of the Great Commentary:

validity		the Hetucakra	the Trairūpya
valid		1. 4. 8 or 1. 6. 8	no violation
Fallacy	B1	2 +	violating I
"	B2	2 +	" I
"	B3	2 or 3 +	" I
"	B4	2 +	" I
"	B5	1. 4. 7	" III
"	B6	1. 5. 8	" II
"	B7	1. 6. 7	" III
"	B8	1. 4. 9	" III
"	B9	1. 6. 9	" III
"	B10		
"	B11	1. 5. 7 or 1. 5. 9	" II & III
"	B12	1. 5. 7	" II & III
"	B13	1. 5. 7 *	" II & III *
"	B14	1. 5. 7 *	" II & III *
"	C4	1. 6. 7 or 1. 6. 9 ++	" III ++
"	C5	1. 4. 7 or 1. 4. 9 ++	" III ++
"	D4	1. 6. 7 or 1. 6. 9 ++	" III ++
"	D5	1. 4. 7 or 1. 4. 9 ++	" III ++

* These are put in according to the opinion of the Great Commentary. The author holds the view that the illustrative cases of B13 and B14 have gone beyond the scope of 1. 5. 7 and should not be put in this list.

+ These are put in by the author. The types 2 and 3 have been defined in Chapter 1133.

++ These are also put in by the author with the understanding that these four fallacies are interpreted as committing material mistakes in the major premiss. They should be deleted from the list if they are otherwise interpreted.

314. K'uei Chi's Treatment of the List of Fallacies

From the treatment of the list of fallacies we understand that K'uei Chi was not unaware of its lack of system. However, unlike Dharmakīrti, who modified the earlier list by altering the original framework, K'uei Chi was very modest and reserved in his attitude. Instead of criticizing the text, he defended it in his answers to questions by his contemporaries.

K'uei Chi's attempt was to improve the system without altering its original framework. His solution was to put new factors in all the fallacies in the list, and to give a detailed analysis of every fallacy. For instance, in the fallacy A2 'contradicting inference', when the factor of 'which party' is introduced, the question 'whose inference is contradicted?' will be involved. If the inference of the disputant or both parties is contradicted, the syllogism is fallacious. But if the inference of the opponent alone is contradicted, the syllogism is not fallacious.

He introduced quite a number of such new factors, but he actually analysed the fallacies according to a few important factors only, and did not bother about the unimportant ones. Then he gave illustrative cases for the fallacies analysed. As a result such analysis and illustrative cases occupy about one half of his book.

The first few fallacies were analysed by him in detail. Illustrative cases were given for most of the possible combinations. The latter ones were in much less detail. The work on analysis of fallacies was a very tedious task, which could bore anybody who laid a hand on it, including the author himself.

His method and attention shifted in the course of elucidation. For instance, in the beginning he paid more attention to the factors 'wholly', 'partially', 'the disputant', 'the opponent', etc.; but near the end he shifted to other factors; in the beginning he listed all possible cases, whether valid or fallacious, but near the end he listed the fallacious cases only.

If we compare K'uei Chi's treatment of fallacies with Dharmakīrti's with respect to their background, we see that the former was in a very unfavourable situation. It was easy for Dharmakīrti to study a great number of texts by authors of many generations and various schools of

Buddhism, Nyāya and Vaiśeṣika; he could remain critical without much difficulty.

The situation of K'uei Chi was entirely different. The <u>Nyāyapraveśa</u> was one among the very rare texts on logic in China, was brought from India by his teacher Hsüan Tsang at the risk of his life and was therefore regarded as a sacred book. Consequently K'uei Chi could not be very critical in writing his commentary. From his <u>Great Commentary</u> we can easily judge that he was a gifted logician. It is rather a pity that he did not have a chance to read some post-Dignāgean great works on logic. Had he done so his <u>Great Commentary</u> would be quite a different work.

K'uei Chi's treatment of the list of fallacies is very lengthy and it will not be very meaningful to quote all his words and illustrative cases. Instead of doing so I shall treat it as follows:

a. I shall list all the new factors introduced by him, both the important and unimportant ones and represent them by symbols (3141);

b. I shall formulate all fallacies according to the important factors stressed by him (3142);

c. I shall modify the above-mentioned formulae in case they are not systematic enough (3143);

d. I shall translate a part of his illustrative cases in order to give a rough idea of his treatment (3144).

3141. New Factors introduced by K'uei Chi

The new factors are symbolized as follows:

1. W = Wholly
   P = partially

2. E = expressed (i. e. in the sense as its names represents)
   I = implied

3. Q = being doubtful
   Z = unfounded

4. X = existential
   Y = non-existential

5. D = disputant
   O = opponent
   B = both the disputant and the opponent
   N = neither the disputant nor the opponent

Most of the above factors are actually adopted from Śamkarasvāmin's list of fallacies. W and P are from B7 and B9; E and I are from B11 to B14; Q and Z are from B3 and B4; D, O, B and N are from B1 and B2.

K'uei Chi just gave a broader interpretation of these terms. Only X and Y are not from Śaṁkarasvāmin's list.

What do the new factors mean? It is convenient not to explain them at the present stage, but to make a list of all fallacies first.

Fallacies	New Factors											
A1	W	P							D	O	B	N
A2	W	P	E	I					D	O	B	N
A3	W	P							D	O	B	N
A4	W	P							D	O	B	N
A5	W	P			Q				D	O	B	N
A6	W	P	E	I	Q				D	O	B	N
A7	W	P	E	I	Q				D	O	B	N
A8	W	P	E	I	Q				D	O	B	N
A9	W	P										
B1	W	P					X	Y				
B2	W	P					X	Y	D	O		
B3	W	P							D	O	B	
B4	W	P					X	Y	D	O	B	
B5									D	O	B	
B6									D	O	B	
B7									D	O	B	
B8									D	O	B	
B9									D	O	B	
B10			E	I					D	O	B	
B11									D	O	B	
B12									D	O	B	
B13									D	O	B	
B14									D	O	B	
C1	W	P			Q	Z	X	Y	D	O	B	
C2	W	P			Q	Z	X	Y	D	O	B	
C3	W	P			Q	Z	X	Y	D	O	B	
C4												
C5												
D1	W	P			Q	Z			D	O	B	
D2	W	P			Q	Z			D	O	B	
D3	W	P			Q	Z			D	O	B	
D4												
D5												

The way of reading of the above list shows what the new factors mean For instance,

A1 reads: "The probandum contradicts, wholly or partially, the perception of the disputant, or of the opponent, or of both, or of neither".

A2 reads: "The probandum contradicts, wholly or partially, the inference of the disputant, or of the opponent, or of both, or of neither, in its expressed meaning or in its implied meaning".

B1 reads: "The truth of the minor premiss is rejected, wholly or partially, being existential or non-existential, by both parties".

B2 reads: "The truth of the minor premiss is rejected, wholly or partially, being existential or non-existential, by either the disputant or the opponent".

3142. A Detailed Study of the Fallacies by Considering the New Factors

In this chapter only the important factors are considered. For the sake of convenience, we have to use a new set of symbols which are different from those used in Chapter 3141. A few of them are used all through; whereas a few others vary their meanings from one fallacy to another. The common symbols are as follows:

i = invalid
v = valid
W = wholly
P = partially
iv = invalid not because of committing the fallacy in question but because of committing some other fallacy.

A1. 'Contradicting Perception'

The symbols used specially in this fallacy are:

per = perception
\+ = not contradicting
\- = contradicting

These two symbols are put in the order 'disputant-opponent'; i. e.

++ = contradicting neither
+- = contradicting the opponent only
-+ = contradicting the disputant only
-- = contradicting both

W -+ per $U(f \supset h)$	i
W +- per $U(f \supset h)$	v
W -- per $U(f \supset h)$	i
W ++ per $U(f \supset h)$	v
P -+ per $U(f \supset h)$	i
P +- per $U(f \supset h)$	v
P -- per $U(f \supset h)$	i
P ++ per $U(f \supset h)$	v

For example, the first formula reads: "That every f is h contradicts, wholly, the perception of the disputant but not that of the opponent" - this is invalid.

A2. 'Contradicting Inference'
A3. 'Contradicting Testimony'
A4. 'Contradicting Convention'
A5. 'Contradicting Oneself'

These four are similar; therefore let us use the same symbol 'inf' for all of them, and use the symbols + and - as before:

W -+ inf $U(f \supset h)$ i
W +- inf $U(f \supset h)$ v
W -- inf $U(f \supset h)$ i
W ++ inf $U(f \supset h)$ iv
P -+ inf $U(f \supset h)$ i
P +- inf $U(f \supset h)$ v
P -- inf $U(f \supset h)$ i
P ++ inf $U(f \supset h)$ iv

K'uei Chi discriminated the fallacy A4 'contradicting convention' into two kinds, namely 'contradicting the learned convention' which is related to scholars and 'contradicting the unlearned convention' which is related to any 'men in the street'.[1]

The list for the 'learned convention' is the same as that of A2, but that for the 'unlearned convention' is simpler; where both the disputant and the opponent are excluded because neither of them are 'unlearned'. Then only two possibilities are left, namely:
contradicting common people's convention is invalid; not contradicting is valid. The list is modified as follows:

A4'. 'Contradicting the Unlearned Convention'

con = convention

W - con $U(f \supset h)$ i
W + con $U(f \supset h)$ v
P - con $U(f \supset h)$ i
P + con $U(f \supset h)$ v

1. NPGC. Taishō 1840. p. 116 c.

A6. 'Unaccepted Predicate'

+ = accepted by
- = rejected by

W -+ Eh i
W +- Eh i
W -- Eh i
W ++ Eh v
P -+ Eh i
P +- Eh i
P -- Eh i
P ++ Eh v

A7. 'Unaccepted Subject'

+ = accepted by
- = rejected by

W -+ Ef i
W +- Ef i
W -- Ef i
W ++ Ef v
P -+ Ef i
P +- Ef i
P -- Ef i
P ++ Ef v

A8. 'Unaccepted Both'

+ = accepted
- = rejected

1. (-+Eh). (+-Ef) i
2. (+-Eh). (-+Ef) i
3. (--Eh). (-+Ef) i
4. (--Eh). (+-Ef) i
5. (-+Eh). (--Ef) i
6. (+-Eh). (--Ef) i
7. (--Eh). (--Ef) i
8. (--Eh). (++Ef) = A6
9. (-+Ef). (+-Eh) = 2
10. (+-Ef). (-+Eh) = 1
11. (--Ef). (-+Eh) = 5
12. (--Ef). (+-Eh) = 6
13. (-+Ef). (--Eh) = 3
14. (+-Ef). (--Eh) = 4
15. (--Ef). (--Eh) = 7
16. (--Ef). (++Eh) = A7
17. (-+Ef). (-+Eh) i
18. (+-Ef). (+-Eh) i
19. (--Ef). (--Eh) = 7
20. (++Ef). (++Eh) v

By adding the factors W and P, the above twenty types are multiplied by four and become eighty. For instance, the first type can be

1a. W(-+Eh). W(+-Ef)
1b. P(-+Eh). W(+-Ef)
1c. W(-+Eh). P(+-Ef)
1d. P(-+Eh). P(+-Ef)

A9. 'Being Pre-established'

\+ = agreed by
\- = disagreed by

W -+ U(f ⊃ h)	i
W +- U(f ⊃ h)	v
W -- U(f ⊃ h)	i
W ++ U(f ⊃ h)	i
P -+ U(f ⊃ h)	i
P +- U(f ⊃ h)	i
P -- U(f ⊃ h)	i
P ++ U(f ⊃ h)	i

B1. 'Both Untrue'

\+ = agreed by
\- = disagreed by

W Eg. --U(f ⊃ g)	i
W - Eg. --U(f ⊃ g)	i
P Eg. --U(f ⊃ g)	i
P - Eg. --U(f ⊃ g)	i

In this fallacy and several others following, the problem of whether the middle term represents a null or a non-null class enters in. Therefore in the formulae there is the factor Eg.

B2. 'Either Untrue'

\+ = agreed by
\- = disagreed by

W Eg. +-U(f ⊃ g)	i
W Eg. -+U(f ⊃ g)	i
W - Eg. +-U(f ⊃ g)	i
W - Eg. -+U(f ⊃ g)	i
P Eg. +-U(f ⊃ g)	i
P Eg. -+U(f ⊃ g)	i
P - Eg. +-U(f ⊃ g)	i
P - Eg. -+U(f ⊃ g)	i

B3. 'Being Doubtful'

\+ = not questioned by
\- = questioned by

W --U(f ⊃ g)	i
W +-U(f ⊃ g)	i
W -+U(f ⊃ g)	i
P --U(f ⊃ g)	i
P +-U(f ⊃ g)	i
P -+U(f ⊃ g)	i

B4. 'Being Unfounded'

+ = agreed by
- = disagreed by

W	$Eg. --(Ef.\ U(f \supset g))$	i
W	$Eg. +-(Ef.\ U(f \supset g))$	i
W	$Eg. -+(Ef.\ U(f \supset g))$	i
W	$-Eg. --(Ef.\ U(f \supset g))$	i
W	$-Eg. +-(Ef.\ U(f \supset g))$	i
W	$-Eg. -+(Ef.\ U(f \supset g))$	i
P	$Eg. --(Ef.\ U(f \supset g))$	i
P	$Eg. +-(Ef.\ U(f \supset g))$	i
P	$Eg. -+(Ef.\ U(f \supset g))$	i

B5. 'Being too Broad'

+ = agreed by
- = disagreed by

$+-\ U(g)$	i
$-+\ U(g)$	i
$--\ U(g)$	i

B6. 'Being too Narrow'

+ = agreed by
- = disagreed by

$+-\ U(-g)$	i
$-+\ U(-g)$	i
$--\ U(-g)$	i

B7. 'Similar-partial, Dissimilar-whole'

+ = agreed by
- = disagreed by

$+-\ U(g\ V\ h)$	i
$-+\ U(g\ V\ h)$	i
$--\ U(g\ V\ h)$	i

B8. 'Dissimilar-partial, Similar-whole'

+ = agreed by
- = disagreed by

$+-\ U(g \subset h)$	i
$-+\ U(g \subset h)$	i
$--\ U(g \subset h)$	i

B9. 'Both Partial'

+ = agreed by
- = disagreed by

$+-\ U(g\ T\ h)$	i
$-+\ U(g\ T\ h)$	i
$--\ U(g\ T\ h)$	i

B10. 'Being Counter-balanced'

+ = agreed by
- = disagreed by

+- $(U(f \supset g). U(g \supset h) \supset U(f \supset h)). (U(f \supset g'). U(g' \supset -h) \supset U(f \supset -h))$
-+ "
-- "

B11. 'Contradicting Expressed Predicate'
B12. 'Contradicting Implied Predicate'

+ = not contradicting
- = contradicting

+- $U(f \supset g). U(g / h) \supset U(f \supset -h)$ i
-+ $U(f \supset g). U(g / h) \supset U(f \supset -h)$ i
-- $U(f \supset g). U(g / h) \supset U(f \supset -h)$ i

or

+- $U(f \supset g). U(g \underline{v} h)$ $U(f \supset -h)$ i
-+ $U(f \supset g). U(g \bar{v} h)$ $U(f \supset -h)$ i
-- $U(f \supset g). U(g \underline{\bar{v}} h)$ $U(f \supset -h)$ i

C1. 'Undemonstrated Middle'

+ = agreed by
- = disagreed by

(the meaning of these two symbols will be the same from here onwards)

+- ge i
-+ ge i
-- ge i

C2. 'Undemonstrated Predicate'

+- he i
-+ he i
-- he i

C3. 'Undemonstrated Both'

(+- ge). (+- he) i and other possible combinations.

C4. 'Lacking Connection'
C5. 'Inverted Connection'

No detailed analysis in these two fallacies.

D1. 'Unexcluded Predicate'

+- (-he') i
-+ (-he') i
-- (-he') i

D2. 'Unexcluded Middle'

+- (-ge') i
-+ (-ge') i
-- (-ge') i

D3. 'Unexcluded Both'

(+-(-ge'). +-(-he')) i and other possible combinations.

D4. 'Lacking Exclusion'

D5. 'Inverted Exclusion'

No detailed analysis in these two fallacies.

3143. Re-arrangement of K'uei Chi's Formulation of Fallacies with Respect to New Factors

In the previous chapter there is a general lack of system in K'uei Chi's formulation. It is most unlikely that he did not know his job well, it is perhaps because he did it with a rush and he did not have time to put his formulation in order.

This is quite understandable. In his comparatively short time of life, this great genius on philosophy and logic had done an incredibly large amount of work: writing one hundred authoritative commentaries including the monumental work of the Commentary on the Vijñaptimātratāsiddhi, and working as the chief assistant of Hsüan Tsang in the translation of 1,335 fasciculi of Sanskrit texts into Chinese. Most of his work was done between his ordination by the Imperial Order in 654 and the death of Hsüan Tsang in 664. It is reasonable to assume that his Great Commentary was written in a very short period of time.

The following re-arrangement is not much more than putting his formulation in a logical order.

In the formulation the following symbols are used:

v = valid

i = invalid

iv = invalid not because of committing the fallacy in question but because of committing some other fallacy.

* = combinations which are practically impossible; for instance, 'not contradicting, partially' is meaningless.

A1.

W	++	per $U(f \supset h)$	v
P	++	per $U(f \supset h)$	*
W	+-	per $U(f \supset h)$	i
P	+-	per $U(f \supset h)$	i
W	-+	per $U(f \supset h)$	i
P	-+	per $U(f \supset h)$	i
W	--	per $U(f \supset h)$	i
P	--	per $U(f \supset h)$	i

A2, A3, A4, A5.

W	++	inf $U(f \supset h)$	iv
P	++	inf $U(f \supset h)$	*
W	+-	inf $U(f \supset h)$	v
P	+-	inf $U(f \supset h)$	v
W	-+	inf $U(f \supset h)$	i
P	-+	inf $U(f \supset h)$	i
W	--	inf $U(f \supset h)$	i
P	--	inf $U(f \supset h)$	i

A4'.

W	+	con $U(f \supset h)$	v
P	+	con $U(f \supset h)$	*
W	-	con $U(f \supset h)$	i
P	-	con $U(f \supset h)$	i

A6, A7, A8

(++Ef). (++Eh)		v
(++Ef). (+-Eh)	A6	i
(++Ef). (-+Eh)	A6	i
(++Ef). (--Eh)	A6	i
(+-Ef). (++Eh)	A7	i
(+-Ef). (+-Eh)	A8-18	i
(+-Ef). (-+Eh)	A8- 2	i
(+-Ef). (--Eh)	A8- 6	i
(-+Ef). (++Eh)	A7	i
(-+Ef). (+-Eh)	A8- 1	i
(-+Ef). (-+Eh)	A8-17	i
(-+Ef). (--Eh)	A8- 5	i
(--Ef). (++Eh)	A7	i
(--Ef). (+-Eh)	A8- 4	i
(--Ef). (-+Eh)	A8- 3	i
(--Ef). (--Eh)	A8- 7	i

A9

W ++ U(f ⊃ h)	i
P ++ U(f ⊃ h)	*
W +- U(f ⊃ h)	v
P +- U(f ⊃ h)	i
W -+ U(f ⊃ h)	i
P -+ U(f ⊃ h)	i
W -- U(f ⊃ h)	i
P -- U(f ⊃ h)	i

B1, B2

W Eg. ++ U(f ⊃ g)	v
P Eg. ++ U(f ⊃ g)	*
W Eg. +- U(f ⊃ g)	i
P Eg. +- U(f ⊃ g)	i
W Eg. -+ U(f ⊃ g)	i
P Eg. -+ U(f ⊃ g)	i
W Eg. -- U(f ⊃ g)	i
P Eg. -- U(f ⊃ g)	i
W -Eg. ++ U(f ⊃ g)	i
P -Eg. ++ U(f ⊃ g)	*
W -Eg. +- U(f ⊃ g)	i
P -Eg. +- U(f ⊃ g)	i
W -Eg. -+ U(f ⊃ g)	i
P -Eg. -+ U(f ⊃ g)	i
W -Eg. -- U(f ⊃ g)	i
P -Eg. -- U(f ⊃ g)	i

B3.

W ++ U(f ⊃ g)	v
P ++ U(f ⊃ g)	*
W +- U(f ⊃ g)	i
P +- U(f ⊃ g)	i
W -+ U(f ⊃ g)	i
P -+ U(f ⊃ g)	i
W -- U(f ⊃ g)	i
P -- U(f ⊃ g)	i

B4.

W Eg. ++ U(f ⊃ g)	v
P Eg. ++ U(f ⊃ g)	*
W Eg. +- U(f ⊃ g)	i
P Eg. +- U(f ⊃ g)	i
W Eg. -+ U(f ⊃ g)	i
P Eg. -+ U(f ⊃ g)	i
W Eg. -- U(f ⊃ g)	i
P Eg. -- U(f ⊃ g)	i
W - Eg. ++ U(f ⊃ g)	i
P - Eg. ++ U(f ⊃ g)	*
W - Eg. +- U(f ⊃ g)	i
P - Eg. +- U(f ⊃ g)	*
W - Eg. -+ U(f ⊃ g)	i
P - Eg. -+ U(f ⊃ g)	*
W - Eg. -- U(f ⊃ g)	i
P - Eg. -- U(f ⊃ g)	*

B5.

++ U(g)	i
+- U(g)	i
-+ U(g)	i
-- U(g)	v

B6.

++ U(~g)	i
+- U(~g)	i
-+ U(~g)	i
-- U(~g)	v

B7.

++ U(g V h)	i
+- U(g V h)	i
-+ U(g V h)	i
-- U(g V h)	v

B8.

++ U(g ⊂ h)	i
+- U(g ⊂ h)	i
-+ U(g ⊂ h)	i
-- U(g ⊂ h)	v

B9.

++ U(g T h)	i
+- U(g T h)	i
-+ U(g T h)	i
-- U(g T h)	v

or B5, B7, B8, B9.

++ E(g. ~h)	i
+- E(g. ~h)	i
-+ E(g. ~h)	i
-- E(g. ~h)	v

or B6.

++ - E(g. h)	i
+- - E(g. h)	i
-+ - E(g. h)	i
-- - E(g. h)	v

C1.

++ ge	v
+- ge	i
-+ ge	i
-- ge	i

C2.

++ he	v
+- he	i
-+ he	i
-- he	i

C3.

C3 is just combinations of C1 and C2.

C4.

++ U(g V h) or ++ U(g T h)	i
+- U(g V h) or +- U(g T h)	i
-+ U(g V h) or -+ u(g T h)	i
-- U(g V h) or -- U(g T h)	v

C5.

++ $U(g \subset h)$ or ++ $U(g)$	i
+- $U(g \subset h)$ or +- $U(g)$	i
-+ $U(g \subset h)$ or -+ $U(g)$	i
-- $U(g \subset h)$ or -- $U(g)$	v

D1.

++ ($\sim$he')	v
+- ($\sim$he')	i
-+ ($\sim$he')	i
-- ($\sim$he')	i

D2.

++ ($\sim$ge')	v
+- ($\sim$ge')	i
-+ ($\sim$ge')	i
-- ($\sim$ge')	i

D3.

D3 is just combinations of D1 and D2.

D4.

D4 is the same as C4, because $U(\sim h \supset \sim g) \equiv U(g \supset h)$.

D5.

D5 is the same as C5, because $U(\sim g \supset \sim h) \equiv U(h \supset g)$.

3144. A Specimen of K'uei Chi's Illustrative Cases

A few examples will be enough to illustrate K'uei Chi's treatment of the list of fallacies:[1]

In the fallacy A2 'contradicting inference', he says:

"(The probandum) may contradict the inference either wholly or partially and there are four possible cases each, namely:

1. Contradicting, wholly, the disputant but not the opponent. A Vaiśeṣika says: "Inherence (samavāya) is not an existence". This school admitted the existence of inherence through inference.

2. Contradicting, wholly, the opponent but not the disputant. A Hīnayāna Buddhist against a Mahāyāna Buddhist: "Manas, i.e. the seventh consciousness, is not an existence". The Mahāyāna Buddhists accepted the existence of manas through the inference that the manovijñāna (the sixth consciousness) must be based on something, which is manas, because all the five sensuous consciousnesses are based on five sense-organs.

3. Contradicting, wholly, both the disputant and the opponent. "A pot is permanent', as illustrated in the text.

4. Contradicting, wholly, neither the disputant nor the opponent. This is not fallacious because of 'contradicting inference', but is fallacious because of 'being pre-established', because an argument should always involve a disagreement with the opponent.

5. Contradicting, partially, the disputant but not the opponent. A Vaiśeṣika against a Buddhist: "None of our six categories are existent". Among the Vaiśeṣika's six categories, five can be known through perception and the last one, inherence, can be known through inference.

6. Contradicting, partially, the opponent but not the disputant. A Mahāyāna Buddhist against a Sarvāstivādin: "All the ten sensuous āyatanas (five sense data and five sense organs) are unreal". The latter considered that all human beings, except the Buddha, can know the existence of the five sense organs through inference only.

7. Contradicting, partially, both the disputant and the opponent. A Mīmāṁsā against a Buddhist: "All kinds of sound are permanent". The disputant accepted the permanence of the sound of the Vedas only but not other kinds.

8. Contradicting, partially, neither the disputant nor the opponent. There is no illustrative case because it is easy".

The above is a rough translation of one passage from the Great Commentary as a specimen of K'uei Chi's treatment of the list of fallacies. Among the eight cases, he considered (2) and (6) as valid, (4) and (8) as fallacious not because of A2 but because of A9. Actually the case (8) is virtually impossible.

1. NPGC Taishō 1840. p. 114 c.

He brought in two more factors, namely, 'contradicting inference in the expressed sense of the terms' and 'contradicting inference in the implied sense of the terms'. The eight cases mentioned above involve the 'expressed sense' only. If the 'implied sense' of the subject, or of the predicate, or of both, is involved, there will be many more combinations. K'uei Chi did not carry out his programme fully in this respect.

3145. Compounding of Fallacies

A defective argument may be defective in various ways, therefore fallacies may be compounded. Besides analysis of fallacies, K'uei Chi also discussed in detail the compounding of fallacies, and gave numerical figures showing how many combinations there can be.

From the numerical figures it seems that he knew the formula $nCr = n! / r!(n-r)!$, where nCr means the number of combinations of n things taken r things at a time.

His work in compounding is reasonably accurate. For instance, he did not compound the fallacies B5 to B9, in which if one commits one, one will not commit another.

However, since the numerical figures were calculated by K'uei Chi according to his own personal opinion so that the system might not be 'too simple or too much in detail', the result will naturally be arbitrary and indefinite. Therefore, the idea of 'total number of possible combinations of fallacies' is fundamentally impracticable.

The work on analysis is quite meaningful, because the new factors are relevant to the validity of the syllogism. The work on compounding is not really so meaningful; the figures of thousands of varieties of compounded fallacies convey not very much valuable information to us, like those which had usually worked out by Uddyotakara. It is therefore not discussed in this work.

As a matter of fact, Śaṁkarasvāmin's original list itself is already superfluous because of unnecessary compounding, for instance, A8 is the combination of A6 and A7; C3 is the combination of C1 and C2, etc., as I have mentioned in 31213.

32. Dharmakīrti's Modification of the List of Fallacies

Dharmakīrti reduced the numbers of fallacies of probandum and of reason, but enlarged the numbers of fallacies of the positive and negative exemplification.

A. Fallacies of the Probandum: [1]

'The Contradictories'

- **A1' 'Contradicting Perception'**
- **A2' 'Contradicting Inference'**
- **A3' 'Contradicting Convention'**
- **A4' 'Contradicting Oneself'**

B. Fallacies of the Reason: [2]

'The Unproved'

- **B1' 'Both Untrue'**
- **B2' 'Either Untrue'**
- **B3' 'Being Doubtful'**
- **B4' 'Being Unfounded'**

'The Uncertains'

- **B5' 'Being too Broad'**
- **B6' 'Being too Narrow'**

'The Contradictory'

- **B7' 'Being Contradictory'**

C. Fallacies of the Positive Exemplification: [3]

'The Undemonstrated'

- **C1' 'Undemonstrated Predicate'**
- **C2' 'Undemonstrated Middle'**
- **C3' 'Undemonstrated Both'**

'The Doubtful'

- **C4' 'Doubtful Demonstration of the Predicate'**
- **C5' 'Doubtful Demonstration of the Middle'**
- **C6' 'Doubtful Demonstration of Both'**

'Unsound Concomitance'

- **C7' 'Lacking Concomitance'**
- **C8' 'Concomitance Unshown'**
- **C9' 'Inverted Concomitance'**

D. Fallacies of the Negative Exemplification: [4]

'The Unexcluded'

- **D1' 'Unexcluded Predicate'**
- **D2' 'Unexcluded Middle'**
- **D3' 'Unexcluded Both'**

---

1. NB. p.111. 2. NB. p.111-4.
3. NB. p.116-7. 4. NB. p.117-8.

'The Doubtful'

D4' 'Doubtful Exclusion of the Predicate'
D5' 'Doubtful Exclusion of the Middle'
D6' 'Doubtful Exclusion of Both'

'Unsound Concomitance'

D7' 'Lacking Negative Concomitance'
D8' 'Negative Concomitance Unshown'
D9' 'Inverted Negative Concomitance'

Since the names of the above fallacies are almost self-explanatory and Dharkīrti's logic is beyond the scope of the present work, I shall not go into details. The reason why I have mentioned his list is that it can help us to understand Śaṁkarasvāmin's list better. I should like to make only the following points:

1. He combined B5, B7, B8 and B9 into one, namely B5'. All the four infringe the same rule, namely the third clause of the Trairūpya, by the existence of a counter-example. The difference existing among them is entirely irrelevant to their being fallacious: killing a man by the right hand and doing so by the left hand are equally condemned as committing a murder. In the list of fallacies, it is the rule of the Trairūpya, and not that of the Hetucakra, that matters. Therefore there is no reason why they should be put in different types and Dharmakīrti's modification is undoubtedly an improvement.

2. He reduced the fallacies of the contradictory to one. His B7' is equivalent to Śaṁkarasvāmin's B11.

Vidyabhusana's interpretation of the fallacy B7' is utterly incomprehensible. He says:[1]

"(7) Sound is eternal, because it is a product.
(Here 'product' is not homogeneous with 'eternal', that is, the middle term is opposed to the major term).
(8) Sound is eternal, because it is a product.
(Here 'product' is not heterogeneous from 'non-eternal')."

This is one of the many occasions in which readers may be discouraged by the thought that they are not intelligent enough to grasp the meaning of profound scriptures. In this case, however, I am very much in doubt whether the great Pandit himself could understand what he was writing.

1. Vidyabhusana 21, p. 313.

According to the Nyāyabindu:[1]

"When the reverse of two aspects of the reason is true, the fallacy is 'contradictory'. What are the two aspects? Its presence in similar and absence in dissimilar instances, e.g. the property of being a product, or that of being produced by effort, becomes a contradictory reason, if the permanence of sound is to be deduced from it".

Vidyabhusana's formulation should be written as follows:

"(7) Sound is eternal, because it is a product.
(Here the property of being a product is absent from the property of being eternal, but it is wholly present in the property of being non-eternal).

(8) Sound is eternal, because it is a product of effort.
(Here the property of being a product of effort is absent from the property of being eternal, but it is partially present in the property of bening non-eternal)."

Furthermore, I do not think that Vidyabhusana's (7) and (8) were regarded by Dharmakīrti as two different kinds of fallacies, in spite of the fact that he continued in the Nyāyabindu as follows:

"Is there a third variety of a contradictory argument? Why is it not mentioned here? Because it is implied in the two other ones."

Since Dharmakīrti had combined B5, B7, B8 and B9 into one, it is hard to believe that he should differentiate Śaṁkarasvāmin's B11 into two. The reason why B11 should not be differentiated into two, is precisely the same as the reason why B5, B7, B8 and B9 should be combined into one. The reason why he said, "Is there a third variety..." is that the two varieties are sub-types only. To add sub-types to main types will certainly cause confusion.

3. Fallacy B12 'contradicting implied predicate' was deleted by Dharmakīrti because "there is no material difference between an expressed and an intended predicate".[2]

4. Fallacy 10 'being counter-balanced' was deleted by Dharmakīrti because "when the argument is founded on the observation of facts, there is no room for contradiction".[3]

5. Fallacy B6' differs slightly from the B6 of Śaṁkarasvāmin in dealing with two clauses of the Trairūpya jointly, namely E(~ f.g.h) and ~E(g. ~h).

1. NB. p.113; BL. Vol.2, p.201.
2. NB. p.114; BL. Vol.2, p.205.
3. NB. p.115; BL. Vol.2, p.224-5.

The fallacy B6 is said to occur when either (1) one of the two clauses is not satisfied and the other one is questionable, or (2) both clauses are questionable. There should be three possibilities altogether, namely:

i. E(~f. g. h) is not satisfied, i. e. ~E(~f. g. h);
~E(g. ~h) is questionable.

ii. ~E(g. ~h) is not satisfied, i. e. E(g. ~h);
E(~f. g. h) is questionable.

iii. both E(~f. g. h) and ~E(g. ~h) are questionable.

He gave two illustrative cases as follows:

ii. "A certain man is omniscient; because he is a speaker".[1]

In this case the existence of a counter-example - a speaker who is not omniscient, can be affirmed; while the existence of a similar example, a speaker who is omniscient, is questionable.

iii. "The living body has a soul, because it possesses vital functions".[2]

In this case only two classes of things which possess vital functions can possibly exist, namely those who have a soul and those who have not. These two embrace between them all and there is no third alternative. Neither the existence of a thing with vital functions and with a soul, nor the existence of a thing with vital functions but without a soul can be affirmed or be denied. This case is therefore uncertain.

6. The fallacies B13 and B14 'contradicting subject' are the most difficult ones in the Chinese text; both Chinese and Japanese logicians took very great pains in interpreting them. A number of books were devoted to the study of "Contradictories' only.

Dharmakīrti's treatment gave a short cut to the solution of the problem, namely deleting them altogether from the list of fallacies.

These two should not have been put in the list in the first place. A more detailed discussion of their illustrative cases will be made in a later chapter.

7. Dharmakīrti's C1' to C6' are equivalent to Saṁkarasvāmin's C1 to C3, with the addition of a new factor, whether the example fails to possess the property in question or it is uncertain that the example possesses that property. Therefore the number of fallacies is doubled.

---

1. NB. p. 114; BL. Vol. 2, p. 206.
2. NB. p. 114; BL. Vol. 2, p. 208.

8. Dharmakīrti's C7' and C8' are equivalent to Śaṁkarasvāmin's C4, with the addition of a new factor, whether the lacking of concomitance is a material mistake or formal incompleteness.

9. Dharmakīrti's D1' to D6' are equivalent to Śaṁkarasvāmin's D1 to D3; the former's D7' and D8' are equivalent to the latter's D4. Their differences are similar to the above.

All illustrative cases are recorded in Buddhist Logic.

To sum up, in the Dharmakīrti's amended list, the four 'asiddha' B1' to B4' are related to the minor premiss, the two 'anaikāntika' B5' and B6' and the one 'viruddha' B7' are related to the major premiss. They are clearly divided and there is no overlapping.[1]

The 'Being Doubtful' ones appear in the minor premiss (B3'), the major premiss (B6'), the positive exemplification (C4' to C6') and the negative exemplification (D4' to D6'). Such an arrangement is reasonably systematic.

The 'contradictory' B7' appears in the major premiss but not in the minor premiss. This is justified because if the minor premiss is a negative proposition, it cannot derive a contradictory conclusion and therefore should not be called 'viruddha'.

All the above characteristics show that Dharmakīrti's list is much more systematic than Śaṁkarasvāmin's.

33. The Relativity of Validity

Let us turn back to Śaṁkarasvāmin's list. In spite of its lack of system, his list has some important consequences which should not be ignored. Several fallacies, A1, A2, A3, A4, A6, A7, A8, A9, B1 and B2, point to one important principle - that the validity of a syllogism is something relative.[2]

It depends not only on the syllogism itself, but also on the background of the debate and the standpoints of both disputing parties. Therefore, a syllogism made by disputant A against his opponent B at a time-and-place C may be valid, but the same syllogism made by disputant D made

1. Stcherbatsky 12, pp. 235-251.
2. The word 'validity' is used here in its narrower sense corresponding to the word 'fallacy' in its broader sense used in Chapter 311, because the factor of convention is involved. It is in that sense that it is relative.

against his opponent E at a time-and-place F may be invalid. Let us consider the two factors separately as follows.

331. The Background of a Debate

A probandum contradicting either an established convention (A4) or established knowledge from observation (A1) or from inference (A2) is faulty because of being absurd; whereas a probandum merely confirming the truth of established convention or knowledge without giving anything new (A9) is faulty because of being pointless.

What is to count as an established convention or knowledge is not absolute but varies with time and place. When new facts are observed or inferred, new conventions are established, the validity of a syllogism should be reconsidered in order to conform to new situations. Therefore the validity of a syllogism holds only at the time of the debate.

332. The Standpoints of Disputing Parties

3321. Fallacies Relating to Standpoints

A probandum contradicting the doctrine of the disputant is faulty not because his doctrine should be undisputed but because he had committed himself to that doctrine and contradicting it means self-contradicting. (A3)

If the truth of the minor premiss is not accepted by the disputant, it is naturally considered as null and void; if it is not accepted by the opponent, it will not be good enough to be a reason for convincing him, therefore the syllogism is not valid either. (B1 and B2)

If any one of the terms in a syllogism belongs to an empty class, for instance, "A unicorn is wise", the proposition is neither true nor false, but yields no sense. A syllogism with such a probandum is invalid.

The problem of being empty or not is not always so obvious as the existence of a unicorn or a cat; in philosophical debates the existence of an entity is not infrequently questioned. When the existence of an entity expressed by a term in a syllogism is not agreed by two disputing parties, the controversy will be shifted from the probandum to the problem of existence of an entity, therefore the syllogism is considered as invalid. (A6, A7 and A8)

3322. An Extended Interpretation of the 'Empty Class'

A few terms in the Great Commentary, 有體, 極成 and 共許 are used almost interchangeably, but they suggest a progress in the interpretation of the 'empty class'.

First, the terms 有體 (representing an existent entity) and 無體 (not representing an existent entity) are used at the earliest stage. In our language they mean 'belonging to a non-empty class' and 'belonging to an empty class' respectively.

Then two terms with a more modest and accurate claim are used, namely, 極成 (being established as final) and 不極成 (not being established as final).

However, the above improvement is still not precise enough, because in a philosophical debate, the existence of an entity can hardly be unanimously agreed by all schools. Moreover, in a debate the main aim is to convince the opponent, therefore it is the opinion of the opponent and not that of the general public that matters. The third alternative is even more realistic, namely, 共許 (being accepted by both), 自許 (being accepted by the disputant only), 他許 (being accepted by the opponent only) and 俱不許 (being rejected by both parties).

The most important consequence of the introduction of the idea of 'acceptance' is that the notion of 'empty class' becomes something relative. We have the following relations:

Both-accepted = non-empty to both parties;
Opponent-accepted only= non-empty to the opponent but empty to the disputant;
Disputant-accepted only = non-empty to the disputant but empty to the opponent;
Both-rejected = empty to both parties.

Furthermore, the scope of 'empty class' becomes wider. In its ordinary sense, it means

1. classes of things which are factually non-existent, such as 'hare's horn' whose non-existence is universally known;

2. classes of things which are logically impossible, such as 'barren woman's son'.

Now two more meanings are added:

3. classes of things which are not accepted by a disputing party, such as 'God' to an atheist;

4. classes of things which are unfamiliar to a disputing party, such as technical terms to a non-specialist.

3323. Three Types of Syllogism.

With reference to the factor of 'acceptance' K'uei Chi classified syllogisms into three types, namely,

1. 'both-accepted'
2. 'opponent-accepted'
3. 'disputant-accepted'

The fourth combination 'neither-accepted' is excluded because it is fundamentally invalid.

The above names are actually in shortened form, they should read "syllogism whose terms are accepted by both parties as representing non-empty classes and whose minor premiss is accepted by both parties as true", etc.

K'uei Chi defined the three types of syllogism as follows:[1]

"In the 'disputant-accepted' syllogism, all members (the probandum, the reason and the exemplification) should be accepted by the disputant. Similarly for the 'opponent-accepted' and 'both-accepted'."

The effect of the syllogism in convincing the opponent differs in different types. Among the three, the 'both-accepted' is the strongest, it can both demonstrate one's own opinion and refute another's. The 'opponent-accepted' is weaker, it can refute another's opinion only. The 'disputant-accepted' is the weakest, it can demonstrate one's own opinion only.

3324. Qualifying Clauses.

A general principle given in the fallacies A6, A7 and A8 of the pakṣābhāsa by Śaṁkarasvāmin is that if either the major or the minor term is unaccepted by either one party or by both parties, the syllogism will be considered as invalid. In other words, both terms should be agreed by both parties as non-empty.

The above rule was neither advocated by Dignāga nor by Dharmakīrti, but it was greatly extended by K'uei Chi, of whose own system, the treatment of the empty classes is a characteristic feature.

1. NPGC. Taishō 1840. p. 116 a.

Suppose in a debate it happens that one term is not accepted by both parties or more terms are not accepted, is it still possible to carry on the debate? The text of the Nyāyapraveśa says nothing about this problem, but the Great Commentary discusses it in detail, and records many actual cases of debates in India.

The device is like the following: an unaccepted term may be artificially made to become accepted by adding qualifying clauses. The clause "what I call..." may be added to a term which is accepted by the disputant only, and the clause "what you call. . ." may be added to one which is accepted by the opponent only.

The factor of 'acceptance' concerns not only the existential condition of terms, but also the truth of premisses. For instance, fallacies B1 and B2 concern whether the truth of the minor premiss is accepted by disputing parties. Qualifying clauses are also required in premisses which are not 'both-accepted'. When only the disputant accepts the truth of the premiss, he should say, "I hold the opinion that..."; when only the opponent accepts it, the disputant should say, "It has been alleged that...".

A further point has to be considered. Even when a term is familiar to and accepted by both parties, it may mean one thing to one party and something different to another party, because it may be defined differently either in intension or in extension. In this case, a phrase, "according to an interpretation accepted by both parties..." should be added.

Moreover, one term may have different interpretations in different occasions even if it is used by the same man. Under such condition a qualifying phrase, such as, "in its conventional sense" or "in its absolute sense", should be added.

All these should be settled in every stage of the argument, then the point of controversy will be one and only one without being diverted to the problem of empty classes or difference in interpretation.

3325. Validity of the Three Types of Syllogism

K'uei Chi did not go very far concerning the three types of syllogism. Only recently a contemporary logician Chancellor Ch'en Ta Ch'i has made an extensive analysis in this respect. His treatment of the three types is very complicated and is beyond the scope of this work.[1] Only a few important points are mentioned as follows:

> In a syllogism, when all the terms are accepted by both parties as non-empty and all premisses and exemplification are accepted by both parties as true, the syllogism is 'both-accepted'.
>
> In a syllogism, when at least one term is accepted by the opponent only as non-empty, or at least one of the premisses or of the exemplification is accepted by the opponent only as true, and the remaining terms and premisses and exemplification are both accepted, the syllogism is 'opponent-accepted'.
>
> In a syllogism, when at least one term is accepted by the disputant only as non-empty, or at least one of the premisses or of the exemplification is accepted by the disputant only as true, and the remaining terms, premisses and exemplification are both accepted, the syllogism is 'disputant-accepted'.

The above three definitions exclude the case when some of the terms, premisses or exemplification are rejected by the disputant and some of them are rejected by the opponent in one and the same syllogism, the syllogism will be neither 'disputant-accepted' nor 'opponent-accepted' but invalid.

When a term, premiss or exemplification is rejected by both parties in a syllogism, the syllogism will be invalid, except in the case of 'opponent-accepted' type. For instance, the exemplification 'hare's horn' and 'barren woman's son', etc. are frequently used in debates.

Since the list of fallacies was mainly designed for the 'both-accepted' type, a new list must be prepared for three types. Chancellor Ch'en has made new lists for this purpose.[2]

3326. Reductio ad absurdum

In the Great Commentary, propositions are classified into four types as follows:[3]

> 1. The subject represents a non-empty class and the predicate is affirmative, as in "Sound is impermanent" $(x)(fx \supset hx).(Ex)(fx)$.

---

1. Ch'en 1. pp. 248-61.
   Ch'en 2. pp. 188-96.
2. Ch'en 1, pp. 281, 287, 312, 319, 327 and 356
3. Lü 1, pp. 9-10.

2. The subject represents a non-empty class and the predicate is negative, as in "Sound is not permanent"
$(x)(fx \supset -hx).(Ex)(fx)$.

3. The subject represents an empty class and the predicate is affirmative, as in "What you called 'soul' should be impermanent"
$(x)(fx \supset hx). -(Ex)(fx)$.

4. The subject represents an empty class and the predicate negates its existence, as in "Unicorn does no exist"
$-(Ex)(fx)$.

The third type is applied in the 'opponent-accepted' syllogism in refutation. The complete argument of the illustrative case is as follows:

"If what you called 'soul' has functions,
It would be impermanent, like a hand or foot.
You hold the view that it has functions,
Meanwhile you also hold the view that it is permanent.
Then it would be both permanent and impermanent and this is absurd".

Here the opponent can accept that the soul has functions but cannot accept that it is impermanent. The aim of this type is to press the opponent to fall into self-contradiction. Its structure is different from the other types. It is not only a syllogism, but a conjunction of a syllogism and another component, either a <u>modus tollens</u> when the opponent's conclusion is false, or a <u>reductio ad absurdum</u> when the conclusion contradicts the opinion of the opponent.

1. A syllogism and a <u>modus tollens</u>:

i. r
ii. $(p \supset q).(q \supset -r) \supset (p \supset -r)$
iii. $(p \supset q).(q \supset -r)$
iv. $(p \supset -r)$
v. $r.(p \supset -r) \supset -p$
vi. $-p$

2. A syllogism and a <u>reductio ad absurdum</u>:

i. $(p \supset r)$
ii. $(p \supset q).(q \supset -r) \supset (p \supset -r)$
iii. $(p \supset q).(q \supset -r)$
iv. $(p \supset -r)$
v. $(p \supset r).(p \supset -r) \supset -p$
vi. $-p$

This kind of argument is more impressive in the quantified form. At the end of Chapter 2244, I have introduced the formula:

$U(f \supset h).U(f \supset -h) \supset -E(f)$

By the above formula the Indians managed to prove the non-existence of a thing; the device is ingenious because it is much more difficult to prove the non-existence of a thing than to prove its existence. It has been widely applied by Buddhists in refutation, particularly by the Mādhyamika. When the school was split into the Prāsaṅgika and the Svātantrika, the difference on the application of logic was one of the main issues. The <u>reductio ad absurdum</u> argument was regarded by the Prāsaṅgika as the only means in acquiring valid knowledge through logic.

The above-mentioned formula means that the existence of a thing can be refuted by pointing out that should such a thing exist, it would possess two mutually contradictory properties. In order to achieve such a result, two different ways of approach were used.

The First Method

Let $U(f \supset h)$ be the view held by the opponent. It is most unlikely that he holds the view $U(f \supset -h)$ at the same time, because they are too obviously incompatible (on the assumption of existential import). Therefore the disputant must find a property g, which is acceptable to the opponent but which will imply the property $-h$; then a syllogism may be set up as usual:

i.	-+	$U(f \supset h)$
ii.	-+	$U(f \supset g)$
iii.	++	$U(g \supset -h)$
iv.		$U(f \supset g). U(g \supset -h) \supset U(f \supset -h)$
v.	from ii., iii., and iv.,	$U(f \supset -h)$
vi.		$U(f \supset h). U(f \supset -h) \supset -E(f)$
vii.	from i., v., and vi.,	$-E(f)$

The Second Method

In the previous type the opponent accepts that the subject possesses the property g which implies the negation of the property h. But in case the disputant fails to find such a property, i. e. the opponent does not accept that the subject possesses this property, another method is used.

An object usually possesses more than one property, say h and h'. Let $U(f \supset h)$ and $U(f \supset h')$ be the views held by the opponent. The disputant must find a property g, such that g implies the negation of h, and the negation of g implies the negation of h'. It is not necessary to have the acceptance of the opponent that the subject f possesses property g. Let us consider the possibilities as follows:

A. Considering $U(f \supset g)$:

i.		$U(f \supset g). U(g \supset -h) \supset U(f \supset -h)$
ii.	++	$U(g \supset -h)$
iii.	from i. and ii.,	$U(f \supset g) \supset U(f \supset -h)$
iv.	-+	$U(f \supset h)$
v.	from iii. and iv.,	$U(f \supset g) \supset U(f \supset h). U(f \supset -h)$
vi.		$U(f \supset g) \supset -E(f)$

B. Considering $U(f \supset -g)$:

i.		$U(f \supset -g). U(-g \supset -h') \supset U(f \supset -h')$
ii.	++	$U(-g \supset -h')$
iii.	from i. and ii.,	$U(f \supset -g) \supset U(f \supset -h')$
iv.	-+	$U(f \supset h')$
v.	from iii. and iv.,	$U(f \supset -g) \supset U(f \supset h'). U(f \supset -h')$
vi.		$U(f \supset -g) \supset -E(f)$

However, A and B are not exhaustive, as $U(f \supset g)$ is not equivalent to $-U(f \supset -g)$. $U(f \supset g)$ and $U(f \supset -g)$ may be both true or both false, therefore two more possibilities have to be considered:

C. Considering $U(f \supset g)$ and $U(f \supset -g)$ as both true:

i. $U(f \supset g). U(f \supset -g) \supset -E(f)$

D. Considering $U(f \supset g)$ and $U(f \supset -g)$ as both false:

i. $-U(f \supset g). -U(f \supset -g) \supset E(f. -g). E(f. g)$

The disputant must find reason to prove that the alternative D is impossible, otherwise the argument will be inconclusive.

333. The Four Logical Alternatives

The catuṣkoṭi, the set of four alternatives, i.e. affirmation, negation, both and neither appears everywhere in Buddhist texts. Its interpretations by many authors are either vague, or mystifying or mistaken.

For instance, Mrs. Rhys Davids and B. M. Barua interpreted it as a set of laws of thought, i.e. two of the alternatives are supposed by them to be equivalent to the law of contradiction and that of the excluded middle.[1] Such an interpretation is obviously wrong.

Only recently a very critical survey of this topic was made in K. N. Jayatilleke's 'Early Buddhist Theory of Knowledge'.[2] It covers references in the early period of Buddhism and makes valuable contributions to the solution of difficult problems.

---

1. Barua 2, p. 47.
2. Jayatilleke 1, pp333-351.

From the examples in Buddhist texts, we know that the catuṣkoṭi is not one single pattern of alternatives but includes a variety of patterns which differ greatly from one another. Therefore all patterns should be considered separately.

Among the various patterns, some belong to the restricted predicate logic and some belong to propositional logic; some involve contradictions, some involve contrarieties, some involve neither of them.

In the examples which follow let us denote the four alternatives by

+- affirmation
-+ negation
++ both affirmation and negation
-- neither affirmation nor negation

Ia. +- Some state of mind is dhyāna but not samādhi.
-+ Some state of mind is samādhi but not dhyāna.
++ Some state of mind is both dhyāna and samādhi.
-- Some state of mind is neither dhyāna nor samādhi.

This pattern involves neither contradiction nor contrariety and seems to be irrelevant to the usual puzzle of the catuṣkoṭi. However, this is the fundamentl pattern of the four alternatives from the point of view of logical priority. The next example will go one step further:

b. +- Some people torment themselves.
-+ Some people torment others.
++ Some people torment both themselves and others.
-- Some people torment neither themselves nor others.

In this example there is contradiction between 'self' and 'other' but no contradiction between 'self-torment' and 'other-torment'. Therefore they can be rephrased as, "There are self-tormentors", etc. and can be expressed as follows:

+- $(Ex)(fx. \sim gx)$
-+ $(Ex)(\sim fx. gx)$
++ $(Ex)(fx. gx)$
-- $(Ex)(\sim fx. \sim gx)$

IIa. +- The goal can be attained by knowledge.
-+ The goal can be attained by conduct.
++ The goal can be attained by both knowledge and conduct.
-- The goal can be attained by neither knowledge nor conduct.

b. +- The soul is happy.
-+ The soul is unhappy.
++ The soul is both happy and unhappy.
-- The soul is neither happy nor unhappy.

There is neither contradiction nor contrariety in IIa., but there is contrariety in IIb. 'Being happy' and 'being unhappy' are two extremes, therefore they are not exhaustive. The third alternative is made factually possible by interpreting it as 'mixed feelings'. The type II can be expressed as follows:

+- p
-+ q
++ p. q
-- ~p. ~q

IIIa. +- All Greeks are brave.
-+ All Greeks are not brave. (In normal English: 'No Greek is brave'.)
++ All Greeks are brave and all Greeks are not brave.
-- Not all Greeks are brave and not all Greeks are not brave.

b. +- All unicorns are brave.
-+ All unicorns are not brave.
++ All unicorns are brave and all unicorns are not brave.
-- Not all unicorns are brave and not all unicorns are not brave.

Although the two predicates 'being brave' and 'not being brave' are contradictory, the two propositions "all Greeks are brave" (A form) and "all Greeks are not brave" (E form) are not contradictory but contrary. Therefore they are not exhaustive. This type can be expressed either in universal or in existential form as follows:

+- $(x)(fx \supset gx)$
-+ $(x)(fx \supset \sim gx)$
++ $(x)(fx \supset gx). (x)(fx \supset \sim gx)$
-- $\sim(x)(fx \supset gx). \sim(x)(fx \supset \sim gx)$

+- $\sim(Ex)(fx. \sim gx)$
-+ $\sim(Ex)(fx. gx)$
++ $\sim(Ex)(fx. \sim gx). \sim(Ex)(fx. gx)$
-- $(Ex)(fx. \sim gx). (Ex)(fx. gx)$

When we take account of the existence or non-existence of the subject, the third alternative of IIIa becomes

$$(Ex)fx. \sim(Ex)(fx. \sim gx). \sim(Ex)(fx. gx) = (Ex)fx. \sim(Ex)fx$$

which is inconsistent; the fourth alternative of IIIb. is also unsatisfactory since it asserts the existence of what is known not to exist:

$$\sim(Ex)fx. (Ex)(fx. \sim gx). (Ex)(fx. gx) = \sim(Ex)fx. (Ex)fx$$

IV. +- The soul is identical with the body.
-+ The soul is different from the body.
++ The soul is both identical with and different from the body.
-- The soul is neither identical with nor different from the body.

This example is quoted from the avyākṛta, in which only the first two alternatives appear. According to T. R. V. Murti: "One does not however see why the last question too could not be logically formulated in the fourfold way like the others."[1]

In this type 'being identical' and 'being different' are truly mutually contradictory. Let us express the first two propositions by q and $\sim q$. Since the existence of the 'soul' is not universally accepted, these propositions should be preceded by an implied antecedent p "soul exists" or "it is accepted that soul exists".

I shall use $(p \supset q)$ to represent "p implies q" and

$-(p \supset q)$ to represent "p does not imply q".

I do not use $\sim(p \supset q)$ because it is equivalent to $(p.\sim q)$ and gives a quite different meaning. The difference between $-(p \supset q)$ and $\sim(p \supset q)$ is that the former can be any one of the eight functions in Group A and Group C mentioned in Chapter 2244, i. e.

$$-(p \supset q) = (p\ T\ q) \vee (p \vee q) \vee (p \subset q) \vee (p) \vee (p / q) \vee (p \underline{\vee} q) \vee (\sim\bar{q}) \vee (p.\sim q) \quad \text{Df.}$$

whereas the latter can only be one particular function of the eight, i. e.

$$\sim(p \supset q) = (p.\sim q)$$

Then this type may be formulated as follows:

+-	$(p \supset q)$		$(p \supset q).-(p \supset \sim q)$
-+	$(p \supset \sim q)$		$-(p \supset q).\ (p \supset \sim q)$
++	$(p \supset q).(p \supset \sim q)$	or	$(p \supset q).\ (p \supset \sim q)$
--	$-(p \supset q).-(p \supset \sim q)$		$-(p \supset q).-(p \supset \sim q)$

This type is equivalent to the theorems on propositional logic analogous to the hetucakra mentioned in Part I of this work.

V. In the beginning of Nāgārjuna's Mūlamadhyamakakārikā the following lines give four alternatives:[2]

"Things are not originated by themselves;
Nor are they originated by others;
Neither by both; nor without cause;
Therefore there is no origination".

It seems that by rejecting all four possible ways of origination, namely, by one's self, by others, by both and by neither, one can reject origination. But in fact there is an implied antecedent, i. e. things are self-subsistent or independent of conditions. Only when one

1. Murti 1, p. 38.
2. Taishō 1564. p. 2 b.

admitted that things are isolated and independent of conditions, one will fall into the difficulty mentioned above. Therefore by rejecting all four possibilities of origination, one can reject the origination of all things which are independent of conditions. The aim of the argument is to negate the existence of things with such a characteristic.

'One's self' and 'others' seem to be contradictory, but 'originated by oneself' and 'originated by others' are not. Therefore 'originated by oneself' and 'originated by others' are not mutually exclusive.

Now we have to start with 'origination with a cause' and 'origination without a cause'. 'Origination with a cause' can be further discriminated into three, namely, 'origination by oneself', 'origination by others' and 'origination by both'.

Let us formulate this case as follows:

p = The existence of beings is intrinsic or self-subsistent (svabhāva).

q = It involves inevitably an origination.

r = Origination has a definite cause.

s = Origination has no definite cause.

r_1 = The cause is the result itself.

r_2 = The cause is other than the result.

Step I

i.	$p \supset q$	
ii.	$q \supset (r \underline{v} s)$	
iii.	$\sim r$	(This will be proved in Step II)
iv.	$\sim s$	
v.	$\sim r . \sim s$	(From iii. and iv.)
vi.	$(\sim r . \sim s) \supset \sim (r \underline{v} s)$	(This is a modified form of de Morgan's law, the reverse is not true)
vii.	$\sim (r \underline{v} s)$	(From v. and vi.)
viii.	$\sim (r \underline{v} s) \supset \sim q$	(The contraposition of ii.)
ix.	$\sim q$	(From vii. and viii.)
x.	$\sim q \supset \sim p$	(The contraposition of i.)
xi.	$\sim p$	(From ix. and x.)

Step II

i.	$r \supset (r_1 \vee r_2)$	
ii.	$-r_1$	
iii.	$-r_2$	
iv.	$-r_1 . -r_2$	(From ii. and iii.)
v.	$(-r_1 . -r_2) \equiv -(r_1 \vee r_2)$	(De Morgan's law)
vi.	$-(r_1 \vee r_2)$	(From iv. and v.)
vii.	$-(r_1 \vee r_2) \supset -r$	(The contraposition of i.)
viii.	$-r$	(From vi. and vii.)

In the above formulation, I used $(r \underline{v} s)$ for the exclusive disjunction and $(r_1 \vee r_2)$ for inclusive disjunction. The former is equivalent to $-(r \equiv s)$; the latter is implied by $-(r_1 \equiv r_2)$:

$$-(r \equiv s) \equiv (r \underline{v} s); \qquad -(r_1 \equiv r_2) \supset (r_1 \vee r_2).$$

The reason why I use $(r \underline{v} s)$ and $(r_1 \vee r_2)$ instead of $(r \underline{v} -r)$ and $(r_1 \vee -r_1)$ is that the two latter are tautologies and therefore they are independent of the antecedent q. With such an interpretation the entire procedure would become impossible.

VI. The last one is the really puzzling and controversal one. It involves straightforward contradiction and no evasion is possible.

a. +- The world is finite.
   -+ The world is infinite.
   ++ The world is both finite and infinite.
   -- The world is neither finite nor infinite.

b. +- The Tathāgata exists after death.
   -+ The Tathāgata does not exist after death.
   ++ The Tathāgata both exists and does not exist after death.
   -- The Tathāgata neither exists nor does not exist after death.

Whether true or false, are these propositions possible and independent from one another?

The first interpretation is that they can be all possible and independent if they are referring to different levels of truth or observed from different points of view. But suppose it is understood that they are all referring to the same level of truth and observed from the same point of view, is there any solution? There are obviously the following problems:

1. By the law of non-contradiction, the third alternative $p . -p$ is always false.

2. By the law of excluded middle, the fourth alternative $-p. --p$ is always false.

3. By the law of double negation, the fourth alternative, $-p.--p \equiv -p.p \equiv p.-p$, is equivalent to the third alternative.

4. In the text none of the four alternatives is accepted. It seems that the negation of the first is equivalent to the affirmation of the second; the negation of the second is equivalent to the affirmation of the first; the negation of the first and the second is equivalent to the affirmation of the fourth. How is it possible to negate all four simultaneously? This is the reason why de la Vallée Poussin said, "We are helpless!"[1]

The second interpretation is that when a proposition is false its negation may not necessarily be true. For instance, if one refuses to accept "The rent believes in original sin" as a true proposition, one has to reject its negation also, "The rent does not believe in original sin".

One may say that the above example is nonsense. However, is it easy to draw a line between nonsense and impossibility?[2] Perhaps this is the reason why Buddha's answer to the four questions was not a rejection by negation, but a rejection by silence - a most extraordinary method of dialectic.

Jayatilleke says:

> "Until recently it was believed in the western world that Aristotelian logic was the only logic and that it reflected the structure of reality but, with the discovery of many-valued logics by Łukasiewicz and Lobachevsky, this view is no longer universally held... The Buddhist four-fold logic is in this respect no more true or false than the Aristotelian and its merits should be judged by its adequacy for the purpose for which it is used".[3]

The truth value 1/2 in Łukasiewicz's three-valued logic is undefined, there is no reason why it should not be interpreted as 'partially true', 'indeterminate' or 'paradoxical'.

However, I should rather like to mention another system - intuitionism. L. E. J. Brouwer rejected the laws of excluded middle and of double negation; A. Heyting designed a calculus to suit this

1. Poussin 9, p. 111.
2. W. & M. Kneale, The Development of Logic, p. 671.
3. Jayatilleke 1, p. 350.

purpose. Therefore the formulae $p \vee \neg p$ and $\neg\neg p \supset p$ are not theorems in their system.

Now we can formulate the four alternatives as:

$$p, \qquad \neg p, \qquad p \wedge \neg p, \qquad \neg p \wedge \neg\neg p.$$

34. A Study of a few Illustrative Cases

341. On Vaiśeşika's Categories

Let us start this lengthy and complicated story with a quotation from Prof. Randle's book:[1]

> "Sāmānya (generality) is neither substance, quality nor action; because it depends upon one substance and possesses quality and action.
>
> The statements here made contradict the definition of sāmānya as given by those who maintain that it is a separate category. The property of depending on one substance would prove the contradictory of what is maintained, for it would prove that sāmānya was either quality or action: and similarly the character of possessing quality or action would prove that it was substance. (The example is entirely artificial: it could have no existence except as an instance of an argument in a logic manual)".

His rendering of the text agrees with that in the History of Indian Logic[2] and both of them seem to be copied from Sugiura's book,[3] which is very unreliable.

Prof. Randle's own interpretation of the case is also incorrect. He considered that the hetu of the syllogism is a disjunction, instead of a conjunction, of three premisses. His interpretation is imcomprehensible and not to the point.

His remark in brackets deviates again from the fact. Juding from the existing literature, this syllogism was not specially coined as an example in a logic manual; on the contrary, it is of primary importance in early Vaiśeşika philosophy. The Great Commentary gives us a very detailed account of how this syllogism was used by Kaṇāda to convince his disciple Pañcaśikha (五頂) of his system of categories.

One can hardly not be astonished by the great wealth of literature concerning this fallacy and its illustrative case, written by the

1. Randle 2, p. 204-5.
2. Vidyabhusana 21, p. 295.
3. Sugiura 1, p. 66.

Japanese élite of logicians. We do not know how much there was during the T'ang Dynasty; the eight surviving works collected in the Taishō Tripitaka alone[1] are equivalent to a couple of volumes of the Encyclopaedia Britannica in size. These works are entitled 'Commentaries on the Four Viruddhas', yet only B13 and B14 are of major concern, because B11 and B12 are rather simple fallacies. Even if these people were wasting their time in writing these huge books, their work has at least some significance from the historical point of view.

In the text of Nyāyapraveśa,[2] the subject of the probandum is not sāmānya, but bhāva (being), which was used here in the sense of 'sattā' (existence). This coincides with the text in the Vaiśeṣika sūtra. Let us consider several more renderings:

> "(It is) existent, in respect of substance, attribute and action. Existence is a different object from substance, attribute and action".[3]
>
> "Existence possesses (i.e. exists in) substances, attributes and actions; ... it is the cause of the general notion (with respect to the first three categories) that they are existent and an independent entity". (sic)[4]
>
> "Sattā (called 'bhāva' in the text) is not a dravya; ... it exists in a single dravya. Sattā (bhāva) is not a guṇa. For, it resides in a guṇa. Sattā (bhāva) is not a karma. For, it resides in a karma".[5]

In the above we can find expressions like, "Existence is existent in respect of...", "Existence possesses..." and "Existence exists in...". What exactly do they mean?

The logical structure of the proposition, "Human beings exist" is radically different from that of the proposition, "Human beings are mortal". In modern symbolism it can be formulated only by using an existential quantifier to bind a variable, as in the rendering $(Ex)hx$, and certainly not by writing anything of the pattern $(x)(hx \supset Ex)$.

---

1. See Bibliography.
2. Dhruva 1. Notes pp. 54-5, 69.
3. Sinha 1, p. 46.
4. Ui 1, p. 116.
5. Dhruva 1, p. 69.

In the proposition "Existence exists" the word 'exist' is used both as predicate and as subject. I wonder how this proposition can be expressed by a well-formed formula.

Despite its absurdity, let us force an interpretation as follows:

The thesis of the Vaiśeṣika:

> "Existence is neither substance, nor attribute, nor action; because it exists in substance, attribute and action".

The antithesis of the Buddhist:

> "If the so-called 'existence' exists in substance, attribute and action; it should be either substance, attribute or action".

The Buddhist's antithesis is a mere refutation and not affirmative, because the terms and the reason are unaccepted by them.

According to the Great Commentary, this syllogism was used by Kaṇāda to convert his own disciple. Suppose it were used for a 'Vaiśeṣika versus Buddhist' debate; it would also commit the fallacies of unaccepted major (A5), the unaccepted minor (A6) and the unproved middle (B2), in addition to B13 and B14.

What was the Vaiśeṣika driving at by saying, "Existence is neither substance, nor attribute nor action"? He had his 'implied meaning' and here the notion of 'sāmānya' entered in. He was trying to establish a system of logical categories of which 'existence' was considered as the highest universal (parasāmānya) or genus summum, in contrast with the species infima (antya viśeṣa). Let us put his implied meaning as follows:

The thesis of the Vaiśeṣika:

> "Existence, as the highest universal of all things, is an independent category other than substance, attribute and action; because it exists in substance, attribute and action".

The antithesis of the Buddhist:

> "If the so-called 'existence' exists in substance, attribute and action, it should not be an independent category other than substance, attribute and action".

Since Kaṇāda's system of categories was defective, it was modified again and again by his followers.[1] The system of ten categories of Hui Yüeh (Candramati or Maticandra ?) was a later improvement.[2]

1. Lü 2, pp. 156-9.
2. Ui 1.

The relation existing among the categories seems to be of a genus-species pattern. According to various sources, we can draw a number of different Tree-diagrams. Let us consider the one shown in Prof. S. Bhaduri's Studies in Nyāya-Vaiśeṣika Metaphysics:[1]

- Reality (vastu)
  - Being (bhāva)
    - Existential (sattāsamavāyin)
      - Substance (dravya)
      - Quality (guṇa)
      - Action (karman)
    - Other-than-existential (svātmasat)
      - Universal (Sāmānya)
      - Particularity (viśeṣa)
      - Inherence (samavāya)
  - Non-being (abhāva)

The above system is obviously an improved one, in which the three notions of 'being', 'existential' and 'universal' are in three different levels, and consequently one should not be the 'implied meaning' of another. Paradoxically enough, the category of 'universal' is under 'other-than-existential'.

342. On the Existence of Soul

The debate on the existence of 'soul' belongs to the 'opponent-accepted' type of syllogism, because the very existence of the subject is questioned.

In actual practice, the opponent-type is used to a much larger extent than the other two, not only by Prāsaṅgikas but also by other schools of Buddhism. The both-accepted type is rarely used because it is difficult to have every element (term or premiss) accepted by both parties. The disputant-accepted type is not much favoured by Buddhists, because Buddhism as a whole is thought to be of a negative nature.

For the sake of convenience, the qualifying clauses, "what I call", "what you call", "I hold the view that" and "you alleged that" will be omitted and replaced by quotation marks, "...", in the citation of arguments below.

The word 'soul' is merely temporarily borrowed and should not be confused with the word used in western theology, whether it incidentally means the same thing in the east and the west.

---

1. Bhaduri 1, p. 21.

I use the word in its widest sense for an agent, conscious of its own continuing identity as a self, personality or ego. It ranges from the most primitive ego-consciousness of a child to the most profound elaboration of philosophers and theologians.

I use A. i., A. ii., A. iii., etc. for the syllogisms set up by the parties which held the view that soul existed and B. i., B. ii., B. iii., etc. for those set up by Buddhists.

The illustrative cases are not quoted from the Great Commentary on the Nyāyapraveśa, but from K'uei Chi's two commentaries on the Vijñāptimātratāsiddhi. The problem was discussed from three different angles in the following chapters.

3421. Discussion on 'soul' with reference to its dimension

If 'soul' has dimensions, there will be three possibilities, namely, 1) that its size coincides and varies with that of the physical body; 2) that its size is infinitesimal, or it is a 'point' without dimension; 3) that it is infinitely large like space.

34211. Soul with indefinite size

If its size coincides with the body, it would be flexible "like a cowhide, whose size increases when soaked with water and decreases when exposed to sunlight".[1]

It sounds very odd and fantastic when the existence of 'soul' is considered with reference to its 'size', particularly when it is compared with a cowhide. Yet all these arguments were actually recorded in the book. The view that soul is like cowhide was held by a sect called 'Nirgrantha'.

K'uei Chi pointed out that the property of being flexible (in the sense that it varies in size when the physical body grows) and the property of being permanent (in the sense of being constant) are incompatible. He established two syllogisms as follows:

B. i. "Soul" would not be flexible,
If "it is permanent",
Like space.[2]

B. ii. "Soul" would not be permanent,
If "it is flexible",
Like the air in a bag.[3]

---

1. VSC. Taishō 1830. p. 245 a.
2. Op. cit. p. 246 b.
3. Op. cit. p. 246 b.

K'uei Chi pointed out that the belief that a human being can have one and only one soul which is indivisible is incompatible with the belief that soul is flexible in size. He established two more syllogisms as follows:

B. iii. "Soul" would be divisible,
If "it is flexible",
Like the air in a bag.[1]

B. iv. "Soul" would not be an indivisible unit,
If "it is flexible",
Like a cowhide.[2]

Reflection on the difficulty that the properties divisibility and flexibility contradict the fundamental belief that soul is an indivisible and permanent unit naturally leads to the second alternative that it is infinitesimal.

34212. Soul with infinitesimal size

According to K'uei Chi, the second view that the size of the soul is infinitesimal was held by a sect called 'Pāśupata', worshippers of Śiva.

K'uei Chi pointed out that if it is infinitesimally small, it would not be able to cause the movement of the physical body which is much bigger. In order to make a clear contrast, he mentioned the physical body may be as big as 16,000 yojanas (about 200,000 miles) in the case of the heavenly body of Akaniṣṭha.

B. v. "Soul" would not be able to cause a much bigger body
to move instantaneously;
If "it is infinitesimally small",
Like an atom.[3]

The opponent defended himself by saying that the movement is not instantaneous, but a very fast one taking place at a short interval of time.

A. i. The movement of "soul" and body is not simultaneous
but needs a short time interval;
Because the movement is fast,
Like a circling torch.[4]

K'uei Chi said that the property of having movement is incompatible with the property of being permanent and the property of being 'one'.

---

1. Op. cit. p. 246 b.
2. Op. cit. p. 246 b.
3. Op. cit. p. 246 c.
4. Op. cit. p. 246 c.

B. vi. "Soul" would not be permanent,
Because "it has movement",
Like a circling torch.[1]

B. vii. "Soul" would not be 'one',
Because "it has movement",
Like a circling torch.[2]

34213. Soul with infinite size

The third alternative is that 'soul' is infinitely big like space. This view was held by Sāṁkhyas and Vaiśeṣikas, with the difference that the former regarded the soul as a 'doer', i. e. the agent which is responsible for all actions; while the latter regarded the soul as both a 'doer' and a 'receiver', i. e. that agent which is responsible for all actions and at the same time can feel all stimuli such as pleasure and pain.

The conception of soul common to both sects possesses three characteristics, namely,

1. that it is permanent, without beginning or end, came from the past, continues at present and goes to the future;
2. that it exists in all kinds of beings, i. e. it pervades all beings;
3. that it exists everywhere, i. e. it pervades all places.

There are two syllogisms in the text. The first one is to refute the view of the Sāṁkhyas:

B. viii. "Soul" would not unite with the physical body to feel;
Because "it is permanent and pervades all places",
Like space.[3]

The second one is to refute the view of the Vaiśeṣikas. This is a successive syllogism: $U(f \supset g). U(f \supset h). U(h \supset i) \supset U(f \supset i)$.

B. ix. "Soul" would not be able to unite with the physical body to act,
Because it has no movement,
Because "it is permanent and pervades all places",
Like space.[4]

In the text K'uei Chi did not mention who the debaters were.

It seems unlikely that the philosophers would start an argument about the 'size' of soul. Those who accepted its existence would

1. ibid.
2. ibid.
3. VSC. Taishō 1830. p. 245.
4. ibid.

naturally say, "Soul is not a material object, how can it have any size at all!"

Perhaps the Buddhist may start with this question: "If you say that there is a soul, can you tell me where it is?" Then the possible answers will be: "It exists all over the physical body", or "It does not occupy any space, i.e. it exists at a point only", or "It exists everywhere in the universe". Then all the three fall into the trap of the Buddhist. This is merely my speculation, but I am sure that the question 'where?' is much more probable than the question 'how big?'

3422. Discussion on Soul with reference to Individuality

It was further considered in the text whether the 'soul' was one thing commonly possessed by all human beings or each individual soul was possessed by one individual being.

First, assume that all beings possess a common soul:

B. x. Yajñadatta would act accordingly while Devadatta acts,
Because Yajñadatta possesses the same "soul" as that of Devadatta,
Like Devadatta.[1]

Secondly, assume that each individual being possesses its own soul:

B. xi. The "souls" of all beings and that of Devadatta would be merged in one single body,
Because "the souls are constantly pervading all places",
Like the soul of Devadatta.[2]

3423. Discussion on Soul with reference to Skandhas

"Skandhas" means physical-mental aggregates, which consist of rūpa (matter), vedanā (sensation), saṁjñā (concept formation), saṁskāra (volition) and vijñāna (consciousness).

The question is whether the soul is identical with the physical-mental continuum, or it is different from it. The first possibility was refuted as follows:

B. xii. "Soul" would not be permanent,
Because "it is identical with skandhas",
Like skandhas.[3]

B. xiii. "Soul" would not be one single unit,
Because "it is identical with skandhas",
Like skandhas.[4]

---

1. ibid.
2. ibid.
3. VSC. Taishō 1830. p. 247.
4. ibid.

B. xiv. Mental faculties are not the "soul",
Because they are not continuous and they depend on conditions,
Like sound.[1]

Sāṁkhyas considered that "soul" was different from skandhas. This view was refuted as follows:

B. xv. The "soul" would not be able to act and to feel,
Because "it is not included in the skandhas",
Like space.[2]

The Vātsīputrīya heresy of a quasi-permanent soul, which is neither identical with nor independent of the five skandhas, fits the third alternative. This view was refuted as follows:

B. svi. The "soul" would not be the real self,
Because "it depends on skandhas",
Like a pot.[3]

The above are only a few illustrative cases and I am not going to quote them all as the discussion is lengthy. These cases selected well illustrate the technique used in reducing the opponent's position to absurdity on principles and consequences which the opponent himself would accept.

In the case of debate on the existence of soul, the properties of being permanent and being a single unit are incompatible with the property of having functions, but the opponent has to accept them all.

These illustrative cases also show the function of exemplification. Logically speaking, the existence of a positive example proves nothing more than the fact that the class $\hat{z}(gz)$ is non-empty. There is no need to mention explicitly that the class $\hat{z}(gz.\,hz)$ is non-empty, because it is implied by the non-emptiness of the class $\hat{z}(gz)$ and the emptiness of the class $\hat{z}(gz.\,-hz)$ asserted by the third clause.

But from a psychological point of view, to present a pot to illustrate the fact that there exist things which are produced and at the same time are easily broken is more effective than to illustrate the fact that there exist things which are produced only.

From the illustrative cases in the debates, we can see that certain examples are ingeniously chosen, such as B. x. 'Devadatta', B. xi.

---

1. ibid.
2. ibid.
3. ibid.

'the soul of Devadatta', B.xii. 'skandhas', so that they can produce the maximum effect in "enlightening the opponent".

It is interesting to see that these examples are related to some degree to the minor term, the major term or the middle term. They are chosen by experts, because amateurs may either fail to find an example at all, or find a much weaker one. It is usually the case that when an ordinary man is asked to give an example, he will be exhausted in finding anything but the thing in question. This is analogous to the story when a man is asked to count the number of people in his group, he counts everybody except himself.

It is mentioned in the Pramāṇavārtika by Dharmakīrti that exemplification is only for amateurs and not for experts because the latter follow the inference as soon as the hetu is stated. I am very doubtful about this view. It is under the assumption that a positive example exists that it is unnecessary. Suppose the disputant fails to produce a positive example when it is demanded even by experts, then the syllogism will be faulty on account of lack of a positive example. Is the exemplification still unnecessary then?

343. The 'Smoke-Fire' Cases

The famous 'smoke-fire' case belongs to a new category. It says:

(1) The Probandum: The hill has fire (or the hill is fiery).
(2) The Reason: Because it has smoke (or it is smoky).
(3) The Exemplification: Whatever has smoke has fire, like the kitchen.
(4) The Application: The hill has smoke.
(5) The Conclusion: Therefore the hill has fire.

This simple syllogism is tricky because the word 'hill' serves as a grammatical subject. The probandum 'the hill is fiery' should be distinguished from 'Sound is impermanent', because 'being fiery' is not an inherent property of the hill. In fact, the word 'hill' means nothing else but a place, which is neither near enough to let the observer perceive both smoke and fire, nor far enough to hinder the observer from perceiving the smoke. It means 'there' where only smoke is perceivable but not fire.

It will be clearer if it is written as follows:

(1) To prove that: Fire occurs on the hill now.
(2) Whenever and wherever smoke occurs, then and there fire also occurs.
(3) If smoke occurs at a given time, now, and a given place, the hill; then fire must also occur then and there.
(4) Smoke occurs on the hill now.
(5) Therefore fire must occur there now.

Let t = time, N = now, S = smoke, F = fire,
p = place, H = hill, O = occurs

(1) To prove that: $O(F, N, H)$
(2) Proof: $(t)(p)(O(S, t, p) \supset O(F, t, p))$ (the major premiss)
(3) $O(S, N, H) \supset O(F, N, H)$ (by substitution)
(4) $O(S, N, H)$ (the minor premiss)
(5) $O(F, N, H)$ (by modus ponens)

The above confirms the five-membered syllogism, except that the steps (2) and (3) are reversed.

It is not necessary that the predicates of the antecedent and the consequent should be the same. The same proposition may be written: "Fire burns on the hill now, because smoke appears on it now".

$A(S, N, H)$ $B(F, N, H)$

Let us formulate this case in a general form:

S = subject of the antecedent
P = predicate of the antecedent
S' = subject of the consequent
P' = predicate of the consequent
b = space-time factor, called by Carnap 'basic particular' as a variable
B = space-time factor, as a constant

(1) To prove that $P'(S', B)$.
(2) $(b)(P(S, b) \supset P'(S', b))$.
(3) $P(S, B) \supset P'(S', B)$.
(4) $P(S, B)$.
(5) $P'(S', B)$. q. e. d.

If we ignore the internal complexity of 'basic particular', then the quantifier (b) can be dropped, and the process becomes a simple modus ponens:

(1) To prove that q.
(2) $p \supset q$,
(3) p.
(4) q. q. e. d.

Positive and negative examples were used as follows:

a. kitchen - where both smoke and fire exist;
b. lake - where neither smoke nor fire exists;
c. hot iron bar - where fire exists but smoke does not;
d. the fourth alternative, a place where smoke exists but fire does not, does not exist.

The three examples were actually used in a somewhat similar way to that in which variables are used in modern times and this approach was the earliest attempt in the formation of a 'truth matrix' in order to define material implication.

smoke	fire	combination	
yes	yes	yes	(such as the smoke and fire in a kitchen)
yes	no	no	(no such occasion at all)
no	yes	yes	(such as the fire in a hot iron bar)
no	no	yes	(such as absence of both on a lake)

The above coincides with the truth matrix 'TFTT' for material implication.

4. CONCLUSION

41. Ancient Symbolic Logic

The fact that the introduction of the sixteen dyadic functions in western logic was extremely late can probably be explained by the reason that such a theory requires a well-developed symbolic system and Venn's diagrams as the preliminary stage, without which it is difficult to jump to the notion of the dyadic functions.

Though the ancient Indians had neither invented Venn's diagrams nor a symbolic system like that we use today, they had nevertheless found out something similar, namely, the use of concrete illustrative cases, which include objects such as 'pot' and 'space', and properties such as 'being a product' and 'being impermanent'.

The application of concrete objects by Dignāga shows that he had undoubtedly visualized a diagram like Venn's in his mind. For instance:

1.4.7	space	pot	-	-
1.4.8	pot	-	-	space
1.4.9	pot	lightning	-	space

The complete list of functions by Dignāga and Uddyotakara is shown in Chapter 221.

Dignāga then used particular properties such as 'being a product', to represent classes in general, in his symbolism. The relations of two such properties constitute the dyadic functions as follows:

	Symbolism used by Dignāga & Uddyotakara	Our symbolism
1.4.7	relation between 'knowability' and 'permanence'	N(h + g)
1.4.8	relation between 'product' and 'impermanence'	N(g ≡ h)
1.4.9	relation between 'impermanence' and 'effort'	N(g ⊂ h)
1.5.7	relation between 'product' and 'permanence'	N(g $\underline{\vee}$ h)
1.5.8	relation between 'audibility' and 'permanence'	N(h $\overline{-}$ g)
1.5.9	relation between 'effort' and 'permanence'	N(g / h)
1.6.7	relation between 'impermanence' and 'non-effort'	N(g v h)
1.6.8	relation between 'effort' and 'impermanence'	N(g ⊃ h)
1.6.9	relation between 'incorporeality' and 'permanence'	N(g T h)
1.4.11	relation between 'product' and 'impermanence'	N(g x h) *
1.5.11	relation between 'audibility' and 'impermanence'	N(g ɑ h) *
1.6.11	relation between 'sensibility' and 'impermanence'	N(g + h) *
1.10.7	relation between 'product' and 'permanence'	N(g ⊅ h) *
1.10.8	relation between 'non-vitality' and 'soullessness'	N(g ↓ h) **
1.10.9	relation between 'sensibility' and 'permanence'	N(g - h) *
1.10.11	relation between 'knowability' and 'nameability'	N(g C h) ***

We can imagine how difficult it was to describe various kinds of relationship between two classes in abstract language in the time of Dignāga. He solved his problem by using particular cases to represent general formulae. For instance, whenever a class relationship of 'product-impermanence' is mentioned, one can at once translate it into the notion of a general function, which is equivalent to our function of narrow implication, or N(g ⊃ h).

The application of symbolism is not merely useful because of its brevity as a time-saving device; it is essential to represent the notions which are difficult to express in abstract language. In this respect the Indian method of borrowing particular things to represent something general, and our symbolic system of borrowing particular ideograms to represent something general, are actually similar devices to serve the same purpose. Therefore both Indian and our system can be called 'symbolic logic' in its broader sense.

---

* In types 1.4.11, 1.5.11, 1.6.11, 1.10.7 and 1.10.9, it is assumed that everything is impermanent.

** The illustrative cases used by Uddyotakara in types 1.10.8 and 1.10.11 are wrong ones; they are left as they were without being corrected.

*** The type 1.10.11 is practically impossible to be represented by any illustrative case at all. Borrowing Wittgenstein's words, I should say, "This type is without sense; it is part of the symbolism only, in the same way that 'O' is part of the symbolism of arithmetic".

42. Application of Indian Theories in Modern Logic

In the Appendix B of the History of Indian Logic, Professor Vidyabhusana devoted one chapter, titled Influence of Artistotle on the Development of the Syllogism in Indian Logic,[1] to ascertaining whether there is any genetical connection between Indian and Greek logic systems. Two kinds of syllogism were compared side by side in the section named 'The Syllogism in Indian Logic Conforms to the Logical Rules of Aristotle' The works Prior and Posterior Analytics and De Interpretatione were mentioned in another section called 'Migration of the Logical Theories of Aristotle from Alexandria into India.'

Perhaps he might have considered that the conformity of one theory to another was either an accident or the result of migration, and that since the first possibility was most unlikely, the second must be true. There is, however, a third possibility. The universality of logical reasoning results neither from accident nor from migration. Logic is applied everyday, by logicians as well as non-logicians. Logicians, whether Greek or Indian, were not the ones who created logic, but those who formulated it.

Moreover, it is very obvious that neither the five-membered nor the three-membered syllogism in India is perfectly identical with the Aristotelian syllogism. Consequently the genetical relationship between the two systems remains to be a problem.

It seems that these two systems were not only originated independently, but also developed in isolation. Each of them preserved and absorbed theories of its own founders, tackled its own problems, which are of course not necessarily common to both systems; naturally the rates of progress on various topics differ greatly in two systems. Therefore we should not judge Indian logic as a whole, but should judge each individual theory according to its own merit.

Generally speaking, Aristotelian logic is infinitely more primitive than modern logic, and Indian logic is even more primitive than Aristotelian. Consequently there is no comparison between Indian and modern logic. If we judge the topics individually, however, there is the possibility that we may chance to discover a topic with some novelty.

---

1. Vidyabhusana 21, pp. 497-513.

In modern books of logic, there are dyadic connectives in propositional calculus, such as '.', 'V', '⊃', etc. and those in the logic of classes, such as '∩', '∪', '⊂', etc. We are very familiar with them but we have not been told in the Prinicipia Mathematica how many such connectives there should be, nor have we been told whether there exists a system of such connectives or they appear at random.

It was in 1921 that we began to learn from L. Wittgenstein and E. L. Post that the total number of dyadic connectives in propositional calculus should be sixteen, i.e. $_2 2^n$ when n = 2, and that the connectives are interrelated.[1] In their works, however, nothing about the sixteen dyadic connectives in the logic of classes has been mentioned.

It seems that Gergonne's system of five class connectives was a natural consequence of the invention of Euler's diagrams. Similarly the system of sixteen dyadic connectives should appear long ago as a natural consequence of the invention of Venn's diagrams.

It is certainly true that only a few of the sixteen connectives are primary, whereas the majority of connectives can be derived from them. The secondary ones have neither practical value nor intuitive interpretation. An overall knowledge of the system is, nevertheless, not really trivial. We can see that there exists a correspondence among connectives of various systems of logic: propositional calculus, the logic of classes, the logic of relations, restricted predicate logic, etc.

Apart from connectives, there are theorems, such as the commutative law, the distributive law, the associative law, etc. common to a number of systems. Therefore it is probable to find out new theorems in one system analogous to some known theorems in another system. One example of a general nature is the extension of E. L. Post's theory of propositions to some other systems such as the logic of classes, in which the formula $_2 2^n$ is also applicable.

---

1. L. Wittgenstein, Tractatus Logico-Philosophicus, Eng. tr. London 1921. E. L. Post, Introduction to a General Theory of Elementary Propositions, American Journal of Mathematics 43, 1921, pp. 163-185. R. Carnap, The Formalization of Logic, Cambridge, Mass. 1943.

Let us use De Morgan's law as an example to illustrate particular theorems in various systems:

1. propositional logic: $-(q \vee r) \equiv (-q \,.\, -r)$
2. restricted predicate logic: $-U(g \vee h) \equiv E(-g \,.\, -h)$
3. logic of classes: (a) $-u(b \vee c) \equiv (\bar{b}\bar{c} \neq o)$

   (b) $\overline{(b \vee c)} \equiv (\bar{b} \,.\, \bar{c})$

The derivation of theorems in Chapter 244 does not represent a systematic approach, which is beyond the scope of the present work. The theorems there are derived from a few simple special cases arbitrarily chosen to serve the purpose of a specimen only. Arbitrarily chosen as they are, they nevertheless can cover quite a number of theorems, both known and unknown.

Like many other disciplines, logic is in constant progress and perhaps will never be 'perfect'. Shortly after Kant declared, "Formal logic was not able to advance a single step (after Artistotle) and is thus to all appearance a closed and complete body of doctrine",[1] J.D. Gergonne remarked that Aristotelian logic had fallen into general discredit during the eighteenth century, "though still taught in some Gothic academies".[2]

When the two mutually isolated systems of India and the West confront each other for the first time in the great 'clearing house' of modern world, it is not unlikely that there are important theories to be uncovered. In the rapid development of logic in our time, certainly we cannot expect too much from the study of an ancient system. Our modest result, which is not entirely disappointing, is that to the gigantic system of today's logic, we still have something to add, from an archaic system which is even more primitive than Aristotle.

---

1. Kritik der reinen Vernunft, English translation by N. Kemp Smith. 2nd ed. p. viii.

2. 'Essai de dialectique rationelle', Annales de Mathématiques, vii (1816-7), English translation by W. and M. Kneale, The Development of Logic, Oxford, 1962. p. 350.

ABBREVIATIONS
(for the bibliography)

ABORI	Annals of the Bhandarkar Oriental Research Institute (Poona)
Acta. Or	Acta Orientalia (Leiden)
AJP	American Journal of Philology
AM	Asia Major (Leipzig)
AMG	Annales du Musée Guimet
AQR	Asiatic Quarterly Review
Arch. Or.	Archiv Orientální. (Journal of the Czechoslovak Oriental Institute, Praha)
Athen.	The Athenaeum (London)
BB	Bibliotheca Buddhica (St. Pétersbourg & Leningrad)
BEFEO	Bulletin de l'Ecole Française d'Extrême-Orient (Hanoi)
BEHE (SPH)	Bibliotheque de l'Eçole des Hautes-Etudes (Sciences Philologiques et Historiques)
BI	Buddhist India (London)
Bibl. B.	Bibliographie Bouddhique
Bibl. I.	Bibliotheca Indica (Calcutta)
BIAP	Bull. Intern. de l'Acad. Polonaise de Sc. et de Lett. (Cracow)
BR	Buddhist Review (London)
BSOAS, BSOS	Bulletin of the School of Oriental (and African) Studies (London)
BSS	Bombay Sanskrit Series
CR	Calcutta Review
DLZ	Deutsche Literaturzeitung (Berlin & Leipzig)
ERE	Hasting's Encyclopaedia of Religion and Ethics (Edinburgh)
GOS	Gaekwad's Oriental Series (Baroda)
HOS	Havard Oriental Series
HTFH	Hsien Tai Fo Ḥsüeh (Peking)
IA	Indian Antiquary (Bombay & London)
IBK	Indogaku Bukkyōgaku Kenkyū (Tokyo)
IHQ	Indian Historical Quarterly

ILJ	**Indo Iranian Journal (The Hague)**
IT	**Indian Thought (Allahabad)**
JA	**Journal Asiatique (Paris)**
JAOS	**Journal of the American Oriental Society (Boston, New York & New Haven)**
JASB	**Journal of the (Royal) Asiatic Society of Bengal (Calcutta)**
JBBRAS	**Journal of the Bombay Branch of the (Royal) Asiatic Society (Bombay & London)**
JBRS	**The Journal of the Burma Research Society (Rangoon)**
JBTSI	**Journal of the Buddhist Text (and Anthopological) Society of India (Calcutta)**
JGJRI	**The Journal of Gaṅgānātha Jhā Research Institute**
JIH	**Journal of Indian History**
JORM	**Journal of Oriental Research, Madras**
JRAS	**The Journal of the Royal Asiatic Society of Great Britain (and Ireland) (London)**
JSL	**Journal of Symbolic Logic**
JTU	**Journal of the Taishō University (Tokyo)**
MB	**The Maha-Bodhi (and the United Buddhist World) (Calcutta)**
MCB	**Mélanges Chinois et Bouddhiques (Bruxelles)**
MO	**Mond Oriental (Upsala)**
NH	**Nei Hsüeh (Nanking)**
OLZ	**Orientalistische Literaturzeitung (Berlin & Leipzig)**
PAU, SCP	**Polska Akademia Umiejetności, Sprawozdanie z czynności i posiedzeń (Cracow)**
PEW	**Philosophy, East and West (Honolulu)**
PT	**Philosophical Transactions**
PTSTS	**Pāli Text Society Translation Series (London)**
RC	**Revue Critique d'Histoire et de Litterature (Paris)**
RO	**Rocznik Orientalistyczny (Kraków, Lwów, Warszawa)**
RPL	**Revue Philosophique de Louvain**
SBB	**Sacred Books of the Buddhists**
SBE	**Sacred Books of the East (Oxford)**
SBH	**Sacred Books of the Hindus**
ST	**The Supplementary Tripiṭaka (Kyoto)**

Taishō	The Taishō Tripiṭaka (Tokyo)
Tōhoku	The Tōhoku Tripiṭaka (Sendai)
TOS	Trübner's Oriental Series (London)
TP	T'oung Pao (Leiden)
WZKM	Wiener Zeitschrift für die Kunde des Morgenlandes (Wien)
ZB	Zeitschrift für Buddhismus und Verwandte Gebiete (Leipzig & Munchen)

BIBLIOGRAPHY A

Ācārāṅgasūtra, Agamodaya Samiti, Surat

Ālambanaparīkṣā of Dignāga:

a. Tōhoku 4205

b. Taishō 1619, 1624

Ālambanaparīkṣāvṛtti of Dignāga:

a. Tōhoku 4206

b. Taishō 1619, 1624

Ālambanaparīkṣāṭīkā of Vinītadeva, Tōhoku 4241

Antarvyāpti of Ratnākaraśānti, Tōhoku 4260

Anuyogadvāra of Āryarakṣita, Agamodaya

Anyāpohavicārakārikā of Kalyāṇagupta, Tōhoku 4246

Apohanāmaprakaraṇa of Dharmottara, Tōhoku 4250

Apohasiddhi of Śaṅkarānanda, Tōhoku 4256

Aṣṭasāhasrī of Vidyānanda, Nirnayasagar

Aṣṭaśatī of Akalaṅka, Nirnayasagar

Bāhyārthasiddhikārikā of Kalyāṇagupta Tōhoku 4244

Bālāvatāratarka of Dgra-las rgyal-ba Tōhoku 4263

Bhāṣāpariccheda of Visvanātha Nyāyapancānana Bhaṭṭa:

a. ed. by V. Tarkālaṁkara, Calcutta. 1821

b. ed. and part English tr. by E. Röer in the Bibl.I. Calcutta, 1850 as 'Divisions of the Categories of the Nyāya Philosophy'.

c. German tr. by O. Strauss, Leipzig. 1922.

d. English tr. by Swāmi Mādhavānanda. Calcutta. 1940.

Bṛhatī of Prabhākara   Madras University

Carakasaṁhitā. Edited by Jīvānanda Vidyāsāgara. Calcutta, 1877

Chen Wei Shih Liang Lueh chieh 眞唯識量略解
智旭 Chih hsü (Ming)   ST 731

Daśavaikālikaniryukti of Bhadraubāhu   Agamodaya

Dharmadharmiviniścaya of Jaitāri   Tōhoku 4262

Gādādhari, Chowkhambā Sanskrit Series 1913-27.

Hetubindu of Dharmakīrti   Tōhoku 4213

Hetubinduṭīkā of Vinītadeva   Tōhoku 4234

Hetubinduvivaraṇa of Acata   Tōhoku 4235

Hetucakraḍamaru of Dignāga:

(1) Tōhoku 4209

(2) ed. and tr. by Durgacharan Chatterji. IHQ. Vol. IX, 1933. pp. 266-72, 511-4.

Hetutattvopadeśa of Jaitāri   Tōhoku 4261

Īśvarabhaṅgakārikā of Kalyāṇagupta   Tōhoku 4247

Jñānabindu of Yaśovijaya Singhi Series, Calcutta

Kandalī of Śrīdhara Vizianagaram Series, Benaras

Kārikāvalī of Viśvanātha Nyāyapañcānana Bhaṭṭa:

a. ed. by G. Shastri Bākre, Bombay. 1903.
b. English tr. by E. Röer. 'Divisions of the Categories of the Nyāya Philosophy'. Bibl. I. Calcutta. 1850.
c. German tr. by O. Strass. Leipzig. 1922.

Kāryakāraṇabhāvasiddhi of Jñānaśrīmitra Tōhoku 4258

Kathāvatthu

a. ed. by A. C. Taylor, PTS. 1894-7
b. English tr. by S. Z. Aung and Mrs. Rhys Davids. 'Points of Controversy'. PTSTS. London. 1915.

Kāvyālaṅkāra of Bhāmaha Chowkhamba

Khaṇḍanakhaṇḍakhādya. Chowkh. Sanscr. Series, Benares.

Khaṇḍanoddhāra of Vācaspati Miśtra, ed. by Vindhyeśvariprasāda Dvivedin V. P. Dube, The Pandit 1903-08.

Kiraṇāvalī Bhāskara of Padmanābha Miśra, ed. by Gopi Nath Kaviraj Benares 1920.

Kṣaṇabhaṅgasiddhi of Dharmottara Tōhoku 4253

Kṣaṇabhaṅgasiddhivivaraṇa of Muktākumbha Tōhoku 4254

Kusumāñjali of Udayana. Edited and translated by E. B. Cowell and Maheśa Candra Nyāyaratna, Calcutta, 1864.
Edited by Candrakānta Tarkālaṁkara, Bibl. I. Calcutta, 1890-95.

Laghiyastrayī of Akalaṅka Singhi Series

Māṭharavṛtti of Māṭhara Chowkhamba

Milindapañha:

a. English tr. by T. W. Rhys Davids, Oxford. 1890, 1894.
b. German tr. by F. O. Schrader, Berlin, 1905.
c. German tr. by Nyāyatiloka, Munich. 1919.
d. French tr. by L. Finot, Paris. 1923.

Mīmāṃsāsūtra Kāshī Sanscr. Series, 42, Benares 1910.
Comm. thereon by Śabarasvāmin.

Muktāvalī of Viśavātha Nirnayasagar

Nadīyā-kāhinī, by Kumuda-Nāth Mallik, Calcutta, 1912.

Navadvīpa-mahimā, by Kāntichandra Rāṛhī, Hooghly, 1891.

Nyāyabindu of Dharmakīrti:

a. Tōhoku 4212
b. Kāshī S. S. XX. 1924.
c. English tr. by H. Bhattacharya, MB XXXI - XXXIII, 1923-5.
d. English tr. by Th. Stcherbatsky. Buddhist Logic II. Leningrad 1930.
e. Bibl. I. ed. by P. Peterson, Calcutta, 1889.

Nyāyabinduṭīkā of Dharmottara:

a. Tōhoku 4231
b. English tr. by H. Bhattacharya, MB XXXI - XXXIII, 1923-5.
c. English tr. by Th. Stcherbatsky. Buddhist Logic II. 1930.
d. Bibl. I. ed. by P. Peterson, Calcutta, 1889.

Nyāyabinduṭīkā of Vinītadeva: Tōhoku 4230

Nyāyabindupūrvapakṣasaṁkṣipta of Kamalaśīla: Tōhoku 4232

Nyāyabindupiṇḍārtha of Jinamitra: Tōhoku 4233

Nyāyakoṣa or Dictionary of Technical Terms of Indian Philosophy, by Bhīmācārya Jhalakīkar. Bhandarkar Oriental Research Institute Poona, third ed., 1928.

Nyāyakusumañjali of Udayana Chowkhamba

Nyāyamañjarī by Jayanta, Viz. Scr. Series VIII. 1895.

Nyāyamukha: of Dignāga

a. Chinese Text. tr. by Hsüan Tsang. Taishō 1628.
b. Chinese Text. tr. by I Tsing. Taishō 1629.
c. English translation by G. Tucci. Heidelberg, 1930.

Nyāyamukha: Chinese Commentary 因明正理門論述記 神泰 by Shen t'ai ST 717, Taishō 1839.

Nyāyapradīpa commentary by Viśvakarman on the Tarkabhāṣā.

Nyāyapraveśa:

a. Sanskrit Text ed. by N. D. Mironov. In T'oung Pao, 1931

b. With Haribhadra's Commentary. N. D. Mironov. In Festgabe F. R. Garbe, Erlangen 1927, 37-46.

c. Sanskrit Text with three commentaries, ed. by A. B. Dhruva. Baroda, 1930.

d. Tibetan Text, ed. by V. Bhattacharya. Baroda 1927.

e. Chinese Text. tr. by Hsüan Tsang. Taishō 1630.

f. Tibetan Text. Tōhoku 4208

Nyāyapraveśa: Chinese Commentaries

(1)	因明入正理論疏	文軌 by Wen kuei	ST 718,
(2)	疏	文軌 by Wen kuei	Nanking, 1934 (restored)
(3)	疏	窺基 by K'uei Chi	ST 719, Taishō 1840
(4)	義斷	慧沼 by Hui chao	ST 720, Taishō 1841
(5)	義斷纂要	慧沼 by Hui chao	ST 721, Taishō 1842
(6)	續疏	慧沼 by Hui chao	ST 722
(7)	前記	智周 by Chih chou	ST 723
(8)	後記	智周 by Chih chou	ST 724
(9)	疏抄略記	智周 by Chih chou	ST 725
(10)	解	眞界 by Chen chieh	ST 726
(11)	直解	王肯堂 by Wang K'en T'ang	ST 727
(12)	直疏	明昱 by Ming yü	ST 728
(13)	直解	智旭 by Chih Hsü	ST 729

Nyāyapraveśa: Japanese Commentaries

(1)	因明論疏	明燈抄	善珠	Taishō 2270
(2)		抄	藏俊	Taishō 2271
(3)		融貫抄	基辨	Taishō 2272
(4)		導	明詮	Taishō 2273
(5)		裏書	明詮	Taishō 2274
(6)		瑞源記	鳳潭	Shanghai, 1928

Nyāyapravesa: Japanese Commentaries on Four 'viruddha'

(1) 因明四相違 私記 觀理 Taishō 2275

(2) 略註釋 源信 Taishō 2276

(3) 略私記 眞興 Taishō 2277

(4) 義斷略記 眞興 Taishō 2278

(5) 纂要略記 眞興 Taishō 2279

(6) 抄 珍海 Taishō 2280

(7) 明本抄 貞慶 Taishō 2281

(8) 明要抄 貞慶 Taishō 2282

Nyāyaratnākara of Pārthasārathi Miśra, a commentary on the Ślokavārtik Chowkhamba Sanskrit Series, Benares, 1898.

Nyāyasāra of Bhāsarvajña:

a. ed. by S. C. Vidyabhusana, Bibl. I. Calcutta, 1910.

b. ed. by V. P. Vaidya, Bombay, 1910.

c. ed. by S. S. Sastri, Madras, 1961.

Nyāyasiddhāntamañjarī, by Janakī Nāth Bhattāchārya, in: The Pandit 1907-14.

Nyāyasiddhyāloka of Candragomin Tōhoku 4242

Nyāyasūcīnibandha of Vācaspati Miśra, printed as an appendix to the 1907 edition of the Nyāyavartika, and as preface to the 1920 edition of the Nyāyabhāṣya.

Nyāyasūtra of Gautama:

a. ed. & English tr. by S. C. Vidyabhusana, Sacred Books of the Hindus, Allahabad, 1911-3.

b. English tr. by Ballantyne, Allahabad, 1850-4.

c. ed. & German tr. by W. Ruben, Leipzig, 1929.

Nyāyasūtra of Gautama, edited or translated together with the following commentaries:

(1) Nyāyabhāṣya of Vātsyāyana:

a. ed. by J. Tarkapañcānana, Bibl. I. Calcutta, 1865.

b. ed. by G. S. Tailaṅga, Benares, 1896.

c. ed. by L. & R. Śāstrī, Benares, 1920.

d. ed. by N. S. Josī, Poona, 1922.

e. ed. by G. Jhā, Chowkhamba, 1925.

f. English tr. by G. Jhā, IT. Allahabad, 1910-20

(2) Nyāyasūtravṛtti of Viśvanātha Nyāyapañcānana Bhaṭṭa:

a. ed. with Nyāyasūtra, Calcutta, 1828.
b. ed. with Bhāṣya, Benares, 1920.
c. ed. with Bhāṣya, Poona, 1922.

(3) Nyāyavārtika of Uddyotakara:

a. ed. by V. P. Dvivedin, Bibl. I., Calcutta, 1907.
b. ed. by V. P. Dube, and L. Ś. Drāviḍa, Benares, 1915.
c. English tr. by G. Jhā, IT. Allahabad, 1910-1920.

(4) Nyāyavārtikatātparyatikā of Vācaspati Miśra:

a. ed. G. Ś. Tailanga, Benares, 1898.
b. ed. S. Ś. Drāviḍa, Benares, 1925.

(5) Nyāyavārtikatātparyapariśuddhi of Udayana:
ed. Bibl. I. 1911. (incomplete)

Nyāyāvatāra of Siddhasena Divākara. Edited and translated by S. C. Vidyābhūṣaṇa, Indian Research Society, Calcutta, 1909.

Padārthadharmasaṁgraha of Praśastpāda:

(1) with the Nyāyakandalī of Śrīdhara Miśra, ed. by V. P. Dvivedin, Vizianagram S. S. Benares. 1895.
(2) with the Lakṣaṇāvalī of Udayana, ed. by V. P. Dvivedin, Benares, 1885-97.
(3) with Kiraṇāvalī and Kiraṇāvalībhāskara of Padmanābha Miśra. ed. by G. Kavirāja. Benares. 1920.

Padārthatattvanirūpana of Raghunātha Śiromaṇi

a. with commentaries, in The Pandit, 1903-5.
b. English tr. by K. H. Potter, Harvard, 1957.

Paralokasiddhi of Dharmottara Tōhoku 4251

Prakaraṇapañcikā of Śālikanātha Chowkhamba

Pramāṇamimāṃsā of Hemacandra Singhi Series

Pramāṇanayatattvāloka of Vādidevasūri Yashovijay Granthamala, Kashi

Pramāṇaparīkṣā of Dharmottara Tōhoku 4248, 4249

Pramāṇasamuccaya of Dignāga:

a. Tōhoku 4203

b. Mysore University

Pramāṇasamuccayavṛtti of Dignāga:

a. Tōhoku 4204

b. Chinese tr. by Lü Ch'eng, NH. IV. 1928. pp. 165-236.

Pramāṇasamuccayaṭīkā of Jinendrabuddhi:

a. Mysore University.

Pramāṇavārttikakārikā of Dharmakīrti Tōhoku 4210

Pramāṇavārttikavṛtti of Dharmakīrti Tōhoku 4216

Pramāṇavārttikaṭīkā of Devendramati Tōhoku 4217

Pramāṇavārttikaṭīkā of Śākyamati Tōhoku 4220

Pramāṇavārttikālaṁkāra of Prajñākaragupta Tōhoku 4221

Pramāṇavārttikālaṁkāraṭīkā of Jina Tōhoku 4222

Pramāṇavārttikaṭīkā of Śaṅkarānanda Tōhoku 4223

Pramāṇvārttikavṛtti of Sūryagupta Tōhoku 4224

Pramāṇavārttikaṭīkāyāṁ tṛtīyaparivarta of Sūryagupta Tōhoku 4225

Pramāṇavārttikalamkāraṭīkā of Jamāri Tōhoku 4226

Pramāṇaviniścaya of Dharmakīrti Tōhoku 4228

Pramāṇaviniścayaṭīkā of Jñānaśribhadra Tōhoku 4228

Pramāṇaviniścayaṭīkā of Dharmottara Tōhoku 4229

Prameyakamalamārtaṇḍa of Prabhācandra Nirnayasagar

Pratibandhasiddhi of Śaṅkarānanda Tōhoku 4257

Pustakapaṭhopāya of Dānaśīla Tōhoku 4252

Śabda kalpadruma. Vākyalaṅkāra etc. ṣad-darśana-matadi-saṃyukta-Saṃskrtabhidhānam. Compiled by Rādhākānta Deva, Calcutta, 1821-51.

Ṣaḍdarśanasamuccaya, ed. Suali, Calcutta, Bibl. I.

Sahāvalambanirṇaya of Prajñākaragupta Tōhoku 4255

Sambandhaparīkṣā of Dharmakīrti | Tōhoku 4214

Sambandhaparīkṣāvṛtti of Dharmakīrti | Tōhoku 4215

Sambandhaparīkṣāṭīkā of Vinītadeva | Tōhoku 4236

Sambandhaparīkṣānusāra of Śaṅkarānanda | Tōhoku 4237

Sāṁkhyakārikā of Īśvara Kṛṣṇa:

a. ed. with the Bhāṣya of Gauḍapāda by B. Tripāṭhī, Benares S. S. 1883.

b. Kārikā tr. by H. T. Colebrook. Bhāṣya tr. by H. H. Wilson. London, 1837.

c. tr. by J. Davies in Hindu Philosophy. Trübner Oriental Series. 1881.

d. tr. by N. L. Sinha. SBH. 1915.

e. ed. & tr. by S. S. S. Sastri. Madras. 1935.

Sāṁkhyasūtra, with Sāṁkhyapravacanabhāṣya of Vijñāna Bhikṣu:

a. Fitzedward Hall, Bibl. I. Calcutta. 1856.

b. ed. by R. Garbe. HOS II, Harvard, 1895.

c. English tr. by N. L. Sinha, SBH. Allahabad. 1915.

d. German tr. by R. Garbe, Leipzig. 1889.

Sāṁkhyatattvakaumudī of Vācaspati Miśra:

a. tr. by R. Garbe, Munich, 1891.

b. ed. and tr. by G. Jhā, Bombay, 1896.

Saṁtānāntarasiddhiṭīkā of Vinītadeva | Tōhoku 4238

San Chih Pi Liang I Ch'ao 三支比量義鈔

明昱 by Ming Yü (Ming) | ST 730

Sanmatitarkaprakaraṇa of Siddhasena Divākara | Gujrat Vidyapith

Sanmatitarkaṭīkā of Abhayadeva | Gujrat Vidyapith

Saptapadārthī of Śivāditya. Ed. and tr. by D. Gurumurti, Madras, 1932.

Sarvadarśanasaṁgraha of Mādhava:

a. ed. by I. Vidyāsāgara. Bibl. I. 1858.

b. ed. by V. S. Abhyankara. Poona. 1924.

c. English tr. by E. B. Cowell & A. E. Gough, in the Pandit, 1874-8.

d. same translation, TOS. 1882, 1894.

Sarvajñasiddhikārikā of Kalyāṇagupta Tōhoku 4243

Śāstradīpikā of Pārthasārathi Miśra (tarkapāda only) with the commentary Siddhāntacandrikā of Rāma Kṛṣṇa. Edited by Srī Dharmadattasūri, Niraṇayasāgara Press, Bombay, 1915.

Siddhāntabindu of Madhusūdana Sarasvatī Kumbhakonam

Siddhāntamuktāvalī of Viśvanātha Nyāyapañcānana together with Bhāṣapariccheda, Dinakarīya, and Ramarudrīya, Benares, 1905.

Slokavārtika of Kumārila Bhaṭṭa on the tarkapāda or logical section of Sabara's Bhāṣya. Edited with the Nyāyaratnākara of Pārthasārathi Miśra, by Rāma Sāstrī Tailaṅga. Chowkhamba Sanskrit Series, Benares, 1898-1899. Translated by Gaṅgānātha Jhā, Bibl. I. Calcutta, 1900-1908.

Śrutiparīkṣākārikā of Kalyāṇagupta Tōhoku 4245

Sthānāṅgasūtra Agamodaya

Suśrutasaṁhitā (Āyurvedaprakāśa)

a. Education Press, Calcutta, 1835-6, 1874.
b. Latin tr. by Hessler, 1844.
c. English tr. by A. Banerji, Calcutta, 1885.
d. English tr. by K. K. Bhishagratna, Calcutta, 1907-16.

Sūtrakṛtāṅgasūtra Agamodaya

Syādvādaratnākara of Vādidevasūri Arhat Mata Prabhakara, Poona.

Tantravārtika of Kumārila Chowkhamba

Tarkabhāṣā of Ghābrijakaragupta Tōhoku 4264

Tarkabhāṣā of Keśavamiśra:

a. Bodleian Library, Sanskrit MS. 170d. (Winternitz 1307)
b. with the commentary of Govardhana, Sh. M. Paranjape. Poona. 1894. 1909.
c. ed. in the Pandit, also as reprints. Benares. 1901.
d. English tr. by G. Jhā. IT. Allahabad. 1910.
e. tr. by Poul Tuxen. Copenhagen. 1914.
f. ed. by D. R. Bhandarkar. Bombay. 1937.

Tarkakaumudī of Laugākṣi Bhāskara:

a. ed. by M. N. Dvivedin. Bombay S. S. 1886.

b. tr. by E. Hultzsch, in Zeitschr. d. dt. morgenld. Ges 61, 763.

Tarkasaṁgraha of Annambhaṭṭa:

a. Ed. by Bodas and Athalye, Bombay S. S. 1897. 1918

b. A Primer of Indian Logic according to Annambhaṭṭa's Tarkasaṁgraha. by M. S. Kuppuswami Sastri. Madras. 1932.

c. tr. by E. Hultzsch. Abhdlg. d. kgl. Ges. d. Wiss. zu Göttingen, phil. -hist. Kl. Berlin. 1907.

d. Le Compendium des Topiques. by A. Foucher. Paris. 1949.

Tarkaśāstra of Vasubandhu ?

a. Taishō 1633

b. Retranslation into Sanskrit by G. Tucci, Pre-Diṅnāga Buddhist Texts on Logic from Chinese Sources, Baroda, 1929

Tarka Tāṇḍava of Śrī Vyāsatīrtha with the comm., Nyāyadīpa of Srī Rāghavendratīrtha. Ed. by D. Srinivasachar. V. V. Madhwachar, and V. A. Vyasachar, Mysore 1932.

Tārkikarakṣā of Varadarāja. Edited in the Pandit by Vindhyeśvari Prasāda Dvivedin. Reprint, Benares, 1903.

Tātparyaṭīkā of Vācaspati Chowkhamba

Tattvabindu by Vācaspatimiśra with Tattvavibhāvanā by Ṛṣiputra Parameśvara, ed. by V. A. Ramaswami Śastri. Annamalai Univ. Sanskrit Series 3 Chidambaram 1936.

Tattvacintāmaṇi of Gaṅgeśa:

a. ed. with various commentaries in the Bibl. I. Calcutta, 1884-1891.

b. ed. with the commentary of Mathurānātha, in the Bibl. I. 1892-1900.

Tattvasaṁgrahakārikā of Śāntirakṣita

a. Tōhoku 4266

b. GOS.

Tattvasaṁgrahapañjikā of Kamalaśīla

a. Tōhoku 4266

b. GOS

Tattvārthaślokavārtika of Vidyānanda — Gandhi Natharang, Bombay

Tattvārthasūtra of Umāsvāti — Arhat Mata Prabhakara

Tattvārthasūtrabhāṣya of Umāsvāti — Arhat Mata Prabhakara

Tattvavaiśāradī of Vācaspati — Chowkhamba

Tattvopaplavasiṃha of Jayarāśi — GOS, Baroda

Trikālaparīkṣā of Dignāga — Tōhoku 4207

Upāyahṛdaya of Nāgārjuna ?

a. Taishō 1632
b. Retranslation into Sanskrit by G. Tucci, Pre-Diṅnāga Buddhist Texts on Logic from Chinese Sources, Baroda, 1929

Uttarādhyayanasūtra — Agamodaya

Vādanyāya of Dharmakīrti

a. Tōhoku 4218
b. Mahabodhi Society, Benares.

Vādanyāyaṭīkā of Vinītadeva — Tōhoku 4240

Vādanyāyavṛttivipañcitārtha of Śāntarakṣita — Tōhoku 4239

Vaiśeṣikasūtra of Kaṇāda, with Vaiśeṣikasutropaskāra of Saṁkara Miśra.

a. ed. in Bibl. I. 1861.
b. ed. by Jīvānanda Vidyāsāgara. Calcullta. 1886.
c. ed. and tr. by A. E. Gough, Benares. 1873.
d. tr. by N. L. Sinha. Sacred Books of the Hindus. Allahabad. 1911.
e. Die Lehresprüche der Vaiśesika-Philosophie von Kaṇāda. German tr. by E. Röer, in Żeitschr d. dt. morgenländ. Ges. 21, 1867; 22, 1868.

Vāsacadattā of Subandhu, ed. Fitzedward Hall, Bibl. I. Calcutta, 1859.

Vigrahavyāvartanī of Nāgārjuna

a. Taishō 1631
b. Tibetan text and English translation by G. Tucci, Pre-Diṅnāga Buddhist Texts on Logic from Chinese Sources, Baroda, 1929.

Vijñaptimātratāsiddhi of Ratnākaraśānti Tōhoku 4259

Viśālāmalavatī nāma pramāṇasmuccayatīkā of Jinendramatipāda Tōhoku 4268

Viśeṣāvaśyakabhāṣya of Jinabhadra Kṣamāśramana, Yashovijay Granthamala

Vyāptipañcakarahasyam of Mathurā Nātha Tarkavāgīśa with super-commentary of Śivadatta Miśra. Kashi Sanskrit Series 64.

Yuktiprayoga of Ratnavajra Tōhoku 4265

BIBLIOGRAPHY B

Athalye, Y. V.

1. The Tarka-sangraha of Annambhaṭṭa, Bombay Sanskrit Series 55, 1897.

Attenhofer, A.

1. E. Wolff: Zur Lehre vom Bewusstsein (Vijñānavāda) bei den späteren Buddhisten. (ZB. Jg. IX, S. 286. 1931.)

Banerjea, K. M.

1. Dialogues on the Hindu Philosophy, comprising the Nyāya, the Sānkhya, and the Vedānta, Calcutta, 1861.

Barua, B. M. (V.)

1. Prolegomena to a History of Buddhist Philosophy, Calcutta, 1918.
2. A History of Pre-Buddhistic Indian Philosophy, Calcutta, 1921. 1925.

Bhanot, S. D.

1. Diṅnaga; Kundamālā. Ed. with a Sanskrit commentary by Jai Chandra Sastri, and tr. into English by Veda Vyasa and S. D. Bhanot.

Bhaduri, Sadananda

1. Studies in Nyāya-Vaiśeṣika Metaphysics, Poona, 1947.

Bhattacaryya, D.

1. Baṅgalir Sarasvat Avadān, pratham bhāg. Baṅge Navyanyāyacarccā. Calcutta, 1951.

Bhattacaryya, D. C.

1. "Vāsudeva Sārvabhauma", (IHQ, XVI, 1940, pp. 58-69).

Bhattacharyya, H.

1. Nyāyabindu with Dharmottara's Commentary. Tr. into English (MB, XXXI, 1923, pp. 197-200, 215-23, 262-71, 300-5, 356-60, 391-6, 420-6, 463-9; XXXII, 1924, pp. 27-31, 65-70, 105-11, 183-90, 227-34, 287-91, 330-5, 400-7, 455-61, 520-6, 573-9, 622-8; XXXIII, 1925, pp. 29-37.)

Bhattacharya, S.

1. Daniel H. H. Ingalls on Indian logic. (PEW, V, 1955-6, pp. 155-62.)

Bhattacharya, T. S.

1. The Five Provisional Definitions of Vyāpti. (JGJRI. III, 1945. pp. 67-88, 169-88.)

Bhattacharyya, V.

1. The Nyāyapraveśa of Diṅnāge. (IHQ, III, 1927. pp. 152-60.)

2. Nyāyapraveśa of Ācārya Diṅnāga. Pt. II (Pt. I. ed. by A. B. Dhruva, 1930): Tibetan Text. Ed. with comparative notes Baroda; 1927.

3. Mahāyānaviṁśaka of Nāgārjuna. (Visvabharati Qly., VIII, 1930-31, Pts. 1-2, pp. 107-50.)

Reviewed by IHQ. VII, 1931, p. 212.

4. The Catuḥśataka of Āryadeva. Sanskrit and Tibetan texts with extracts from the commentary of Candrakīrti, reconstructed and ed. Pt. II, xxiv, 308 pp. Calcutta, 1931.

Reviewd by N. Dutt. (IHQ. IX, 1933, p. 608)

5. H. R. R. Iyengar: Diṅnāga's Pramāṇasamuccaya. (IHQ, VIII, 1932, pp. 624-7). (Review).

Bhimāccārya Jhalakikar

1. Nyāyakośa or Dictionary of the technical terms of the Nyāya philosophy. Poona, 3rd ed. 1928.

Bocheński, I. M.

1. Notiones historiae logicae formalis. (Angelicum, XIII, 1936. pp. 109-23.)

2. L'état et les besoins de l'histoire de la logique formelle. (Proceedings of the Xth International Congress of Philosophy, 1949. pp. 1062-4. Amsterdam.)

3. D. H. H. Ingalls: Materials for the Study of Navya-Nyāya Logic. (JSL. XVII, 1952, pp. 117-9) (Review).

4. Formale Logik. Freiburg/Munchen. 1956. (Eng. tr.) I. Thomas: A History of Formal Logic. Notre Dame, 1961.

Bodas, R. M.

1. A Historical Study of Indian Logic. (JBBRAS, XIX 1897, pp. 306-347.)

Brough, J.

1. Theories of General Linguistics in the Sanskrit Grammarians. (Transactions of the Philological Society, 1951, pp. 27-46.)

2. Ingalls: Material for the Study of Navya-Nyāya Logic. (JRAS, 1953-4, pp. 87-8.) (Review)

Charpentier, J.

1. H. R. Iyengar: Diṅnāga's Pramāṇasamuccaya. (BSOS, VI, pp. 1033-4). (Review)

Chatterjee, D.

1. Mūlamadhyamakakārikā of Nāgārjuna. Calcutta. Part I, 1957. Part II, 1962.

Chatterjee, S. C.

1. The Nyāya theory of knowledge: Calcutta 1950.
2. The theory of Pakṣatā in Indian logic, (The philos. quart. XIV 1938, pp. 52-59.)

Chatterji, D.

1. A Note on the Pramāṇa-samuccays. (ABORI, XI, pp. 195-6.)
2. Two Quotations in Tattvasaṃgrahapañjikā. (ABORI, XI, pp. 196-9.)
3. Hetucakranirṇaya. (IHQ, IX, 1933, pp. 266-72.)
4. The Problem of Knowledge and the Four Schools of Later Buddhism. (ABORI, XII, 1930-31, pp. 205. 15.)
5. Buddhist Logic (An Introductory Survey). (ABORI, XIII, 1931-32, pp. 77-85.)

Ch'en, Tah Ch'i 陳大齊

1. Yin Ming Ta Shu Li Ts'e 因明大疏蠡測

   An Elementary Survey of the Great Commentary on the Nyāyapraveśa. Chungking, 1945.

2. Yin Tu Li Tse Hsüeh 印度理則學

   Indian Logic. Taipei, 1952.

Ching Chih 敬之

1. Chung Kuan Tsung Pu Hsü Tzu Hsü Ti Wen T'i

   中觀宗不許自續的問題

   Problems on Prāsaṅgika's Rejection of Self-affirmative Argument.
   (HTFH pp. 9-13.)

Chou, Shu Chia 周叔迦

1. Yin Ming Hsin Li 因明新例

   New Illustrative Cases on Indian Logic. Shanghai (1930?)

Chün Pi Chi Mei 君毗極美

1. Ch'en Na I Hou Chih Liang Lun 陳那以後之量論

   The Post-Dignāga Logic in India.
   (Essays on History of Chinese Buddhism, Vol. 3, pp. 731-774. Taipei. 1956.)

Colebrook, H. T.

1. On the Philosophy of the Hindus. In the Transactions of the R. A. S., 1824. Published separately, London, 1837.

Conze, E.

1. Buddhist Thought in India, London, 1962.

Das, S. C.

1. Mādhyamika Vṛtti. Containing the aphorisms of Nāgārjuna with its commentary of Chandra Kīrti. Ed. by Dās & Sarat Chandra Sastri. Calcutta: Buddh. Text Soc., 1897.

Dasgupta, S.

1. History of Indian Philosophy, Cambridge, 1922. ff.

Damiéville, P.

1. Historique du systeme Vijñaptimātra. Introduction a la traduction japonaise du Tch'eng wei che loun par D. Shimaj(i). (S. Levi: "Un systeme de philosophie bouddhique", Paris 1932, pp. 15-42.)

Dhruva, A. B.

1. The Nyāyapraveśa. Pt. I (Pt. II, ed. by V. Bhattacharya, 1927): Sanskrit Text with Commentaries. Baroda: 1930. (GOS, No. XXXVIII.)

   Reviewed by C. S. S. (JIH, Aug. 1931, pp. 196-200.)

   Reviewed by M. Winternitz. (Arch. Or., IV, 1932, p. 392.)

   Reviewed by G. Tucci. (JRAS, 1933, p. 228.)

Dutt, N.

1. The Tattvasaṃgraha of Śāntirakṣita, ed. by Embar Krishnamacharya. (IHQ, V, pp. 813-21.) (Review).

2. V. Bhattacharya: The Catuḥśataka of Āryadeva. (IHQ, IX, 1933, p. 608.) (Review).

Edgerton, F.

1. The Meaning of Sāṁkhya and Yoga. (American Journal of Philology, XLIV, 1924.)

Faddegon, B.

1. The Vaiceṣika-system, Amsterdam, 1918.

Foucher, A.

1. Le Compendium des Topiques (Tarka-Saṃgraha) d'Annambhaṭṭa Paris, 1949.

Frauwallner, E.

1. Bemerkungen zu den Fragmenten Dignāgas. (WZKM, XXXVI, S. 136-9, 1929.)
2. Dignāgas Ālambanaparīkṣā. Text, Ueb. und Erläuterungen. (WZKM, XXXVII, S. 174-94. 1930.)
3. Beiträge zur Apohalehre. I: Dharmakīrti. (WZKM, XXXIX, S. 247-85; XL, S. 51-94. 1932-3.)
4. Saṃbandhaparīkṣā (Dharmakīrti) (WZKM, XLI, 261-300, 1934.)
5. II. Dharmottara. (WZKM, XLIV, 233-87, 1937.)
6. Dignāga und Anderes. ("Festschrift Moriz Winternitz". Leipzig 1933, S. 237.)
7. Zu den Fragmenten buddhistischer Logiker im Nyāyavārttikam. (WZKM, XL, S. 281-304. 1933.)
8. H.R.R. Iyengar: Dinnaga's Pramāṇasamuccaya. (WZKM, XL, S. 316-8. 1933.) (Review).

Ganguli, H.K.

1. Philosophy of Logical Construction. Calcutta, 1963.

Gard, R.A.

1. On the Authenticity of the Pai-lun and Shih-erh-men-lun. (IBK II, p. 751)
2. On the Authenticity of the Chung-Lun. (IBK III, p. 376)

von Glasenapp, H.

1. St. Schayer: Ausgewählte Kapitel aus der Prasannapadā. (Jahrbuch der Schopenhauer G., 1932, S. 361.) (Review).

Goreh, N.N.S.

1. A Rational Refutation of the Hindu Philosophical Systems, translated from the Hindī by Fitzedward Hall, 1860.

Grierson, Sir George A.

1. The Test of a Man, being the Purusha Parīkshā of Vidyāpati Thakkura, Oriental Translation Fund, New Series, vol. XXXIII.

Gupta, S.N.

1. The nature of inference in Indian logic. (Mind VI, 1895, pp. 159-175.)

Hacker, P.

1. Jayantabhaṭṭa und Vācaspatimiśra, ihre Zeit und ihre Bedeutung für die Chronologie des Vedānta, (Beitr. z. ind. Philos. u. Altertumskunde, W. Schubring z. 70. Geburtst. dargebr., Hamburg 1951, 162 ff.)

Hall, F.

1. Index: A Contribution towards an Index to the Bibliography of the Indian Philosophical Systems. Calcutta 1959.

Hataya, A.

1. The Logic of Satya-bhava (IBK III, p. 121)

Hirano, T.

1. The Identity of Akutobhaya and Buddhapālita's Mūlamadhyamaka-Vṛitti. (IBK III, p. 236)

Hou, Wai Lu 侯外廬

1. Chung Kuo Ssŭ Hsiang T'ung Shih (A Comprehensive History of Chinese Thought). Vol. 4a, Peking, 1959.

   中國思想通史

Hsiung, Shih Li 熊十力

1. Yin Ming Ta Shu Shan Chu 因明大疏刪注

   The Great Commentary on the Nyāypraveśa, abridged and annotated. Shanghai, 1926.

Hui Yüan 慧圓

1. Yin Ming Ju Cheng Li Lun Chiang I 因明入正理論講義

   Lectures on the Nyāyapraveśa. Shanghai.

Ihara, S.

1. Dignāga's Theory on Speech. (IBK I, p. 414)
2. The Anupalabdhi in Pramāṇavārttika. (IBK III, p. 90)

Ingalls, D. H. H.

1. Materials for the Study of Navya-Nyāya Logic. HOS. Vol. 40. Cambridge, Mass. 1951.

   Reviewed by I. M. Bochenski, (JSL. XVII, 1952, pp. 117-9).

   Reviewed by J. Brough, (JRAS, 1953-4, pp. 87-8).

   Reviewed by J. Filliozat, (JA, 240, 1952, pp. 409-10).

   Reviewed by J. Gonda, (Tijdschift voor Philosophie, XIII, 1951, pp. 727-8).

   Reviewed by J. Jordens, (RPL, 50, 1952, pp. 143-4).

   Reviewed by K. H. Potter, (PEW, IV, 1955, pp. 271-3).

   Reviewed by J. F. Staal, (IIJ, IV, 1960, pp. 68-73).

   Reviewed by S. Bhattacharya, (PEW, V, 1955-6, pp. 155-62).

2. The Comparison of Indian and Western Philosophy. (JORM, XXII, 1952-3, Parts I-IV, Madras, 1954. pp. 1-11.)

3. A Reply to Bhattacharya. (PEW, V, 1955-6, pp. 163-6).

4. Śaṅkara on the Question: Whose is avidyā? (PEW, III, 1953, pp. 69-72).

Iyengar, H. R. R.

1. Kumārila and Diṅnāga. (IHQ. III, 1927, pp. 603-6).

2. Vasubandhu and the Vādavidhi. (IHQ, V, No. 1, pp. 81-6. 1929).

3. Pramāṇa Samuccaya. Tibetan text (romanised), ed. and restored into Sanskrit with Vṛtti, Ṭīkā, and Notes. (Mysore University Publication).

Reviewed by H. N. Randle. (JRAS, 1933, pp. 155-7).

Reviewed by K. A. N. (JIH, Dec. 1931, pp. 314-5).

Reviewed by J. Charpentier. (BSOS, VI, pp. 1033-4).

Reviewed by E. Frauwallner. (WZKM, XL, S. 316-8. 1933).

Reviewed by V. Bhattacharya. (IHQ, VIII, pp. 624-7. 1932).

Jacobi, H.

1. Die Indische Logik. Göttingen, (Nachrichten, phil. -hist., 1901, pp. 458-482.)

2. On the Dates of the Philosophical Sūtras. (JAOS, XXXI, 1911.)

Jayatilleke, K. N.

1. Early Buddhist Theory of Knowledge, London, 1963.

Jhā, G.

1. Nyāya Sūtra, with Bhāṣya, Vartika, Vṛtti. Translated. (IT. 1911 ff.)

2. Prābhākara School of Pūrva Mīmāṁsā. (IT.)

3. Sadho Lal Lectures on Nyāya. (IT.)

4. Ślokavārtika. Translated. Bibl. I. Calcutta, 1900-8.

5. Sāṁkhyatattvakaumudī. Translated. Bombay, 1896.

6. Tarkabhāṣā. Translated. (IT. 1910.)

7. The Padārthadharmasaṁgraha of Praśastapada. Benares, 1916.

Johnston, E. H.

1. Early Sāṁkhya, R. A. S. London, 1937.

Kajiyama, Y.

1. On the Relation Between the Vaidalyaprakaraṇa and the Nyāyasūtra. (IBK V, p. 192)

2. The Logic of Great Pandit Mokṣākaragupta. (IBK VI, p. 73)

Kavirāj, G.

1. Gleanings from the History and Bibliography of Nyāya-Vaiśeṣika Literature. (The Prince of Wales Saraswatī Bhavana Studies III, pp. 79-157; IV, pp. 59-70; V, pp. 129-162.)

Keith, A. B.

1. Indian Logic and Atomism. London, 1921.

2. Buddhist Philosophy in India and Ceylon. Oxford: 1923.

3. Th. Stcherbatsky: La theorie de la connaissance et la logique chez les bouddhistes tardifs. (BSOS, IV, pp. 627-8. 1927). (Review).

4. The Authorship of the Nyāyapraveśa. (IHQ, IV, No. 1, pp. 14-22. 1928).

5. Vasubandhu and the Vādavidhi. (IHQ, IV, No. 2, pp. 221-7. Jun. 1928).

6. H. N. Randle: Indian Logic in the Early Schools, (BSOS, VI, pp. 1041-7.) (Review).

Konow, S. (or Konoff)

1. St. Schayer: Ausgewählte Kapitel aus der Prasannapadā. (Acta Or., X, pp. 386-7. 1932.) (Review).

de Körös, A. C.

1. Notes on Mādhyamika Philosophy. (JBTSI, VI, Pt. 4, p. 22. 1898.)

Krishnamacharya, E.

1. Tattvasaṅgraha, by Śāntarakṣita, with the comm. of Kamalaśīla. Skt. text, ed. with an introd. Baroda, 1926. GOS, No. XXX.

   Reviewed by F. Edgerton. (JAOS, 1929, p. 66.)

   Reviewed by Nalinaksha Dutt. (IHQ, V, No. 4, 1929, pp. 813-21.)

Kunst. A.

1. Probleme der buddhistischen Logik in der Darstellung des Tattvasaṅgraha. Krakau, 1939.

Lévi, S.

1. Ed. Specht: Deux traductions chinoises du Milindapañho. (Transac. of the IX. Intern. Congr. of Or., 1893.)

2. Un nouveau document sur le Milinda-Pracna. (CR, Ser. IV, T. XXI, pp. 232-7. 1893.)

3. S. Sugiura: Hindu Logic as preserved in China and Japan, (RC, 1901, No. 51, pp. 482-4.) (Review).

4. Vijñaptimātratāsiddhi. Deux traites de Vasubandhu: Viṁśatikā (La Vingtaine) accompagnee d'une explication en prose et Triṁśikā (La Trentaine) avec le commentaire de Sthiramati. Pt. I: Texte. Paris: Champion, 1925. (BEHE, SPH, Fasc. 245.)

   Reviewed by O. Stein. (OLZ. Bd. XXXI, S. 623-4. 1928.)

Lü, Ch'eng 呂澂

1. Yin Ming Kang Yao, 因明綱要

   An Outline of Logic, Shanghai.

2. Ju Lun Shi Ssu Yin Kuo Chieh, 入論十四因過解

   An Explanation of the Fourteen Fallacies of the Reason. (NH. III. 1927. pp. 143-60.)

3. Kuan Suo Yuan Lun Shih Lun Hui I 觀所緣釋論會譯

   A Comparison of Translations of the Alambanaparīkṣā. (NH. IV. 1928. pp. 123-64.)

4. Chi Liang Lun Shih Lioh Ch'ao. 集量論釋略抄

   A Commentary on the Pramāṇasamuccaya, Abridged. (NH. IV. 1928, pp. 165-236.)

5. Yin Ming Cheng Li Men Lun Pen Cheng Wen. 因明正理門論本證文

   The Chinese Version of the Nyāyamukha (as compared with the Pramānasamccaya.) (NH. IV. 1928. pp. 237-264.)

6. Yin Lun Lun T'u Chieh 因輪論圖解

   Diagrams and Interpretations of the Hetucakrahamaru. (NH. IV. 1928. pp. 265-70.)

Makita, T.

1. Characteristics of the Logic of Dharmakīrti and Dharmottara in Nyāyabindu. (IBK I, p. 424)

2. On the Anumāna Theory of Kumārila Bhaṭṭa. (IBK II, p. 607)

Masson-Oursel, P.

1. G. Tucci: Pre-Diṅnāga Buddhist Text on Logic. (JA, Oct-Dec. 1930, p. 354.) (Review).

Matsuo, G.

1. The Theory of Knowledge in Sāṁkhya Philosophy. (IBK VI, p. 118)

Mironov, N. D.

1. Dignāga's Nyāyapraveśa and Haribhadra's Commentary on it. (Jaina Shasan, Extra (Divali) No., Benares, 1911.)
2. Nyāyapraveśa. I: Sanskrit Text. Ed. and reconstructed. (TP. 1931, 1-2, pp. 1-24.)

Miyamoto, S.

1. Ultimate Middle and Voidness. Tokyo, 1943 (J)

Miyasaka, Y.

1. Pratyakṣa Theory in the Pramāṇavārttika (Chapter III) by Dharmakīrti. (IBK III, p. 682)
2. The Logic of Pramāṇavārttika and Its Author's Position. (IBK V, p. 399)
3. Fragments from Vasubandhu and Diṅnāga. (IBK VI, p. 23)

Mukerji, J. N.

1. Sāṁkhya, or The Theory of Reality, Calcutta, 1924.

Müller, Max

1. Six Systems of Indian Philosophy. Oxford, 1899. Appendix on Indian Logic contributed to Archbishop Thomson's Laws of Thought.

Murti, T. R. V.

1. The Central Philosophy of Buddhism. London, 1955.

Naik, B. S.

1. The theory of predication in Vedānta, (The philos. quart. XIV, 1938. pp. 214-220.)

Nakada, J.

1. A Consideration of Pramāṇa in the Nyāya-sūtra. (IBK, IV, p. 456)

Nakamura, H.

1. Buddhist Logic Expounded by Means of Symbolic Logic. (IBK, III, pp. 223-31, 1954.) (In Japanese).
2. Buddhist Logic Expounded by Means of Symbolic Logic. (IBK, VII, pp. 375-95, 1958.) (In English).

Nariman, G. K.

1. H. P. Shastri: Six Buddhist Nyaya Tracts. (JBRS, II, Pt. 1, pp. 116-7, 1912.) (Review).

Needham, J.

1. Science and Civilisation in China. Cambridge.

Nozawa, J.

1. Bhāvaviveka's exegesis on the Seventh Kārikā of the Twenty-fourth Chapter of the Madhyamaka Kārikā. (IBK II, p. 319)

2. The Commentary to the Mūla-madhyamaka-kārikā by Devacarman and by Guṇamati, Quoted in the Prajña-pradīpa. (IBK II, p. 443)

Obermiller, E. E.

1. Indices verborum Sanscrit-Tibetan and Tibetan-Sanscrit to the Nyāyabindu of Dharmakīrti and the Nyāyabinduṭīkā of Dharmottara. Preface by Th. Stcherbatsky, Leningrad, 1927-8. (BB, XXIV-V.)

Pathak, K. B.

1. Bhartṛhari and Kumārila. (JBBRAS, XVIII, 1892)

2. Dharmakīrti and Śaṁkarāchārya. (JBBRAS, XVIII, No. 48, pp. 88-96. 1894.)

3. On the Authorship of the Nyāyabindu. (JBBRAS, XIX, pp. 47-57. 1895-7.)

4. Śāntarakṣita's Reference to Kumārila's Attacks on Samantabhadra and Akalaṅkadeva. (ABORI, XI, 2, pp. 155-64.)

5. Śāntarakṣita, Kamalśīla and Prabhācandra. (ABORI, XII, 1, pp. 80-3.)

6. Dharmakīrti's Trilakṣanahetu attacked by Pātrakeśari and defended by Śāntarakṣita. (ABORI, XII, 1. pp. 71-80.)

7. Kumārila's Verses attacking the Jain and Buddhist Notions of an Omnicient Being. (ABORI, XII, 2, pp. 123-31.)

Pelliot, P.

1. M. Wallaser: The Life of Nāgārjuna from Tibetan and Chinses Sources. (TP, 1923, pp. 370-2.) (Review).

2. L. de la Vallee Poussin: Vijñaptimātratāsiddhi. (TP, XXVIII, p. 178, 1931.) (Review)

3. G. Tucci: The Nyāyamukha of Diṅnāga. (TP, XXVIII, p. 223. 1931.) (Review)

4. G. Tucci: Pre-Diṅnāga Buddhist Texts on Logic from Chinese Sources. (TP, XXVIII, p. 224. 1931.) (Review)

5. G. Tucci: Some Aspects of the Doctrines of Maitreya(nātha) and Asaṅga. (TP, XXVIII, p. 224. 1931.) (Review)

6. G. Tucci: Bhāmaha and Diṅnāga. (TP, XXVIII, p. 225. 1931.) (Review).

Peri, N.

1. A propos de la date de Vasubandhu. (BEFEO, XI, 1911, pp. 339 ff.)

Peterson, P.

1. The Nyāyabinduṭīkā. Calcutta, 1889.

Poussin, L. de la Vallée

1. Tibetan Text of the Mādhyamika Philosophy (from the Bstan-ḥguyr). (JBTSI, VII, Pt. 1, pp. 1-3. 1900.)

2. L. de la Vallée Poussin & F. W. Thomas: Le Bouddhisme d'apres les sources brahmaniques. Note preliminaire. (Museon, N. S. II, pp. 52-73, 171-207; III, pp. 40-54, 391-412. 1901-2.)

   Reviewed by L. Finot. (BEFEO, II, p. 201. 1902.)

   Reviewed by Goblet d'Alviella. (Bull. Ac. Roy. de Belg., Class de. Lettres, 1903, pp. 171-5; 1904, pp. 374-82.)

3. Nanjio's 1185. Bhāvaviveka. ("Albun Kern", 1903, pp. 581-3; JRAS, 1903, p. 581.)

4. Mūlamadhyamakārikās (Mādhyamikasūtras) de Nāgārjuna, avec la Prasannapadā, commentaire de Candrakīrti. St. Pétersbourg: Ad. d. Sc., 1903-13. (BB, IV.)

5. Madhyamakāvatāra par Candrakīrti. Tr. tribetaine. St. Pétersbourg, 19(07) - 12.

6. Tibetan Translation of the Nyāyabindu of Dharmakīrti. With the comm. of Vinītadeva. Calcutta: As. Soc., 1908-13. (Bibl. I.)

7. Madhyamakāvatāra (Chap. 1-6). Introduction au traité au milieu de l'Ācārya Candrakīrti avec le comm. de l'auteur. (Muséon, VIII, pp. 249-317; XI, pp. 217-358; XII, pp. 236-328. 1907-1911.)

8. Madhyamaka, Mādhyamikas. (ERE, VIII, pp. 235-7. 1915.)

9. The way to Nirvāṇa. Six lectures on ancient Buddhism as a discipline of salvation. Cambridge, 1917.

   Reviewed by Maung Tin. (JBRS, VII, Part 2, pp. 192-4. 1917.)

10. Vijñaptimātratāsiddhi, la Siddhi de Hiuan-Tsang. Tr. et ann. 1928-9.

    Reviewed by P. Pelliot. (TP, XXVIII, p. 178.)

11. J. Masuda: Saptaśatikā Prajñāpāramitā. (MCB, I, 1932, p. 388.) (Review).

12. St. Schayer: Ausgewählte Kapitel aus der Prasannapadā. (MCB, 1, p. 389 f. 1932.) (Review)

13. S. Yamaguchi: Traité de Nāgārjuna. (MCB, I, 1932, p. 392) (Review).

14. G. Tucci: Some Aspects of the Doctrines of Maitreya and Asaṅga. (MCB. I, 1932, p. 401.) (Review)

15. Th. Stcherbatsky: Buddhist Logic, II. (MCB, I, 1932, pp. 413-5.) (Review).

Prasad, J.

1. Discussion of the Buddhist Doctrines of Momentariness and Subjective Idealism in the Nyāyasūtras. (JRAS, 1930. pp. 31-9).

Radhakrishnan, S.

1. Indian Philosophy. London, 1927.

Raju, P.T.

1. The principle of four-cornered negation in Indian Philosophy. (The Review of Metaphysics VII, 1953, pp. 114-125.)

Randle, H.N.

1. A Note on the Indian Syllogism, (Mind, XXXIII, 1924. pp. 398-414.)

2. Fragments from Diṅnāga. London, 1927. (RAS, Prize Publication Fund, Vol. IX.)

3. Indian Logic in the Early Schools. Oxford, 1930.

   Reviewed by A. B. Keith. (BSOS, VI, pp. 1041-7.)

   Reviewed by W. Stede. (JRAS, 1931, p. 906.)

   Reviewed by W. Ruben. (OLZ, 36, 1933, S. 119-21.)

4. G. Tucci: Pre-Diṅnāga Buddhist Texts on Logic from Chinese Sources. (JRAS, 1931, pp. 422-6.) (Review).

5. H.R.R. Iyengar: Diṅnāga's Pramāṇasamuccaya. (JRAS, 1933, pp. 155-7.) (Review).

Rhys Davids, Mrs. C.A.F.

1. Points of Controversy, tr. by S.Z. Aung & Mrs. Rhys Davids, London, 1915.

2. Logic (Buddhist). (ERE, VIII, 1915, pp. 132-3.)

3. Th. Stcherbatsky: The Soul Theory of the Buddhists. (JRAS, 1925, pp. 129-30.) (Review)

4. Th. Stcherbatsky: The Conception of Buddhist Nirvāṇa. (BSOS, IV, pp. 852-3.) (Review).

5. The Milindapañho, ed. by V. Trenchker, photogr. repr., London, 1928.

6. Sāṅkhya Logic. (JTU, VI-VII, in commemoration of the sixtieth birthday of Prof. Unrai Wogihara, Pt. II, Apr. 1930. pp. 35-42.)

Rhys-Davids, T.W.

1. The Question of King Milinda. Tr. from the Pali Oxford: 1890-04. (SBE, XXXV, XXXVI.)

Reviewed by H. Oldenberg. (DLZ, Jg. XI, 1890, S. 1799 f.)

Reviewed by J. Beames. (AQR, Ser. II, Vol. IX, Jan.-Apr. 1895, pp. 145-52, 403-13.)

Reviewed by Athen., Mar. 26, 1892, p. 402; Sept. 12, 1896, p. 351.

Robinson, R.H.

1. Some Logical Aspects of Nāgārjuna's System. (PEW. VI, No. 4, Jan. 1957. pp. 291-308.)

Ruben, W.

1. The Stcherbatsky: The Conception of Buddhist Nirvāṇa. (OLZ, Bd. XXXI, S. 617-23. 1928.) (Review).

2. G. Tucci: The Nyāyamukha of Dignāga. (OLZ, XXXV, 1932, S. 345-7.) (Review).

3. G. Tucci: Pre-Diṅnāga Buddhist Texts from Chinese Sources. (OLZ, XXXV, 1932, S. 347-9.) (Review).

4. Th. Stcherbatsky: Buddhist Logic, II. (OLZ, XXXVI, 1933, S. 50 f.) (Review).

5. H.N. Randle: Indian Logic in the Early Schools. (OLZ, XXXVI, 1933, S. 119-21.) (Review).

Saint-Hilaire, J.B.

1. Le Nyaya. (Authenticité du Nyaya. Analyse du Nyaya. Appréciation de la doctrine du Nyaya.) (Mém. de l'Acad. Roy. d. Sc. Morales, III. 86 pp. Paris, 1841.)

2. Traductions des Soutras du Nyaya composé par Gotama. (Mém. de l'Acad. Roy. d. Sc. Morales, III. 10 pp. Paris, 1841.)

Sakurabi, H.

1. On Frauwallner's Dating of Vasubandhu. (IBK I, p. 202)

Sanghvi, S.

1. Advanced Studies in Indian Logic and Metaphysics. Calcutta, 1961.

stri, H.

1. The Discovery of a Work by Āryadeva in Sanskrit. (JASB, 1898, pp. 175-84.)

2. History of Nyāya-śāstra from Japanese Sources. (JASB, N.S.I. pp. 177-80. 1905.)

3. An Examination of the Nyāya-sūtra. (JASB, N.S.I, pp. 245-50. 1905.)

4. Some Notes on the Dates of Subandhu and Diṅnāga. (JASB, N.S.I, pp. 253-5. 1905.)

5. Six Buddhist Nyāya Tracts of Ratnakīrti, Paṇḍita Aśoka, and Ratnākaraśānti. Calcutta: As. Soc., 1910. (Bibl.I. No. 185.)

6. Notes on the newly found Manuscript of the Catuḥśatikā by Āryadeva. (JASB, 1911, pp. 431-6.)

7. Catuḥśatikā by Ārya Deva. (Mem. of the ASB, III, No. 8, pp. 449-514. 1914.)

Sastri, N.A.

1. The Madhyamakāvatāra of Candrakīrti (Chap. VI.) (JORM, V, 1-2, 1931, Supplement, pp. 17-32; VI, 1, Supplement, pp. 41-8.) (Ed.)

2. Madhyamārthasaṃgraha of Bhāvaviveka. (JORM, V, 1, pp. 41-9, 1931.) (Ed. & tr.)

Sastri, S.S.S.

1. Buddhist Logic in the Maṇimēkalai. (JIH, IX, 3, pp. 330-6. 1930.)

Schaeffer, P.

1. Nāgārjuna, Yukti-Ṣaṣṭika. Die 60 Sätze des Negativismus. Heidelberg, 1923.

Schayer, S.

1. Feuer und Brennstoff. Ein Kapitel aus dem Mādhyamika-śāstra des Nāgārjuna mit der Vṛtti des Candrakīrti. (RO VII, pp. 26-52. Lwow, 1929.)

   Reviewed by Louis de la Vallée Poussin. (MCB, I, p. 389 f. 1932.)

   Reviewed by E.J. Thomas. (JRAS, p. 167. 1933.)

2. Das zehnte Kapitel der Prasannapadā. (RO VII. Lwow, 1930.)

3. Ausgewählte Kapitel aus der Prasannapadā (V, XII, XIII, XIV, XV, XVI). Einleitung, Übersetzung und Anmerkungen. Cracow, 1931.

4. Enquiries into Buddhist Logic. (PAU, SCP XXXVII, Nr. 6, pp. 32-3, 1932; XXXVIII, Nr. 2, pp. 19-22, 1933.)

5. Studien zur indischen Logik. I. Der indische und der aristotelische Syllogismus. (BIAP 1932, Nos. 4-6, pp. 98-102.)

6. Über die Methode der Nyāya-Forschung. (Festerschrift für Moriz Winternitz, S. 248-57. Leipzig, 1933.)

7. G. Tucci: Some Aspects of the Doctrines of Maitreya and Asaṅga. (OLZ, 36, S. 122-7. 1933.) (Review).

8. Kamalśīlas Kritik des Pudgalavāda. (RO, VIII, pp. 68-93. Lwow, 1932.)

9. Studien zur indischen Logik II; Altindische Antizipationen der Aussagen-logik, (BIAP 1933, Nos. 1-6, pp. 90-6).

10. Staroindyskie antycypacje logiki wspolczesnej (Altindische Antizipationen der modernen Logik), (Ruch filoz XIII, 1935, 4).

11. Das mahāyānistische Absolutum nach der Lehre der Mādhyamikas. (OLZ, XXXVIII, pp. 401-5. 1935.)

Sen, Saileswar

1. A Study on Mathurānātha's Tattva-Cintāmaṇi-Rahasya. Wageningen, 1924.

Shih, Yuang-ming

1. The Defects of Buddhist Logic (hetu-vidyā) and Its Effects. (IBK III, p. 522)

Sinha, N.

1. The Vaiśeṣika Sūtras of Kaṇāda, Allahabad, 1911.

Smith, V.A.

1. The Early History of India. Oxford, 4th edn., 1924.

Staal, J.F.

1. Means of Formalization in Indian and Western Logic. (Proceedings of the XIIth International Congress of Philosophy. Venice, 1958.)

2. The Construction of Formal Definitions of Subject and Predicate. (PT. 1960. pp. 89-103.)

3. D.H.H. Ingalls: Materials for the Study of Navya-Nyāya Logic. (IIJ. IV, No. 1, pp. 68-73 1960.) (Review).

4. Correlations Between Language and Logic in Indian Thought. (BSOAS, XXIII, No. 1, 1960. pp. 109-22.)

5. Formal Structure in Indian Logic. (Synthese, XII, No. 2-3, 1960, pp. 279-86. Dordrecht - Holland.)

6. The Theory of Definition in Indian Logic. (JAOS, 81, 1961, pp. 122-6.)

7. Contraposition in Indian Logic. In Logic, Methodology and Philosophy of Science, Proceedings of the 1960 International Congress, Stanford, 1962.

Stasiak, St.

1. Fallacies and their classification according to the early hindu logicians, (RO VI, 1929, pp. 191-198.)

Stcherbatsky, Th. I.

1. Teorija poznanija i logika po uceniju pozdnejsich buddhistov. Cast' I-II. St. Pétersbourg: Tip-Lit. Gerol'd. 1903-9.

2. (Tr.) Erkenntnistheorie und Logik, nach der Lehre der späteren Buddhisten. München-Neubiberg, 1924.

3. (Tr.) La théorie de la connaissance et la logique chez les bouddhistes tardifs. Paris, 1926. (AMG, Bibl. d'Etudes, T. XXXVI.)

Reviewed by A. B. Keith. (BSOS, IV, 1927. pp. 627-8.)

Reviewed by V. R. R. Dikshitar. (IA, 1928, pp. 132-3.)

Reviewed by J. Przyluski. (JA, Apr-Jun. 1928, pp. 376-9.)

Reviewed by W. Ruben. (OLZ, XXXI, 1928. S. 508-9.)

4. Nyāyabindu. Buddiiskii uchebnik logiki sochinenie Darmakirti i tolkovanie na nego Nyāyabindutīkā sochinenie Darmottary. Sanktpeterburg: 1904. (BB, VIII).

5. Nyāyabinduṭīkāṭippaṇī. Tokkovanie na sochinenie Darmottary Nyayabinduṭīkā. Sanktpeterburg, 1909. (BB, XI.)

6. Tibetskii perevod sochinenie Saṃtānāntarasiddhi Dharmakīrtī i Samtānāntarasid dhitīkā Vinītadeva. Petrograd, 1916. (BB, XIX.)

Reviewed by L. V. P. (BSOS, I, Pt. 2, pp. 130-2. 1918)

7. Nyāyabindu. Buddiiskii uchebnik logiki sochinenie Darmakīrti i tolkovanie na nego Nyāyabinduṭīkā sochinenie Darmottary. Petrograd, 1918. (BB, VII.)

8. The Soul of Theory of the Buddhists. Being the appendix to the Abhidharmakośa of Vasubandhu, tr. and notes. St. Petersbourg, 1919. (Tr.)

Reviewed by C. A. F. Rhys Davids. (JRAS, 1925, pp. 129-30.)

9. The Conception of Buddhist Nirvāṇa. Leningrad, 1927.
Reviewed by S. N. Das Gupta: Some Aspects of Buddhist Philosophy. (Modern R., XLIV, pp. 62-71. 1928.)
Reviewed by J. Przyluski. (JA, avr.-juin 1928, pp. 376-9)
Reviewed by L. Wallace, (ZB, VIII, 1928, S. 398-405.)
Reviewed by W. Ruben. (OLZ, 36, S. 617-23. 1928.)
Reviewed by C. A. F. Rhys Davids. (BSOS, Vol. IV, pp. 852-3. 1928.)
Reviewed by J. Charpentier. (MO, 1929, pp. 332-5.)

10. E. Obermiller: Indices Verborum Sanscrit-Tibetan and Tibetan-Sanscrit to the Nyāyabindu of Dharmakīrti and Nyāyabinduṭīkā of Dharmottara. Leningrad 1927-8.

11. Dignāga's Theory of Perception. (JTU VI - VII, Pt. 2, Apr. 1930. 42 pp.)

12. Buddhist Logic. Leningrad 1930-32. (BB, XXVI.)
Reviewed by P. Pelliot. (TP, 1932, 1-2, pp. 239-40.)
Reviewed by L. de la Vallée Poussin. (MCB, I, 1932, pp. 413-5.)
Reviewed by W. Ruben. (OLZ, 36, 1933, S. 50 f.)
Reviewed by E. H. Johnston. (IA, 1933, p. 173.)

Stein, O.

1. S. Lévi: Vijñaptimātratāsiddhi, Pt. I. (OLZ, XXXI, S. 623-4. 1928.) (Review).

Strauss, O.

1. Des Viśvanātha Pañcānana Bhaṭṭācārya Kārikāvalī mit des Verfassers einigem Kommentar Siddāntamuktāvalī. Leipzig, 1922. (Tr.)

2. Th. Stcherbatsky: Erkenntnistheorie und Logik, nach der Lehre der späteren Buddhisten. München-Neubiberg, 1924. (Tr.)

3. Indische Philosophie, Mit der Abbildung eines Altindischen Steinbildnisses. München, 1925. (Gesch. d. Philo. in Einzeldarstel-lungen, Abt. I, Bd. II.)
Reviewed by Die Brockensammlung, Z. f. Angewandten Buddhismus, 1, Doppelheft, 1925, S. 112.

4. St. Schayer: Ausgewählte Kapitel aus der Prasannapadā. (OLZ, 1933, S. 571.) (Review).

Suali, L.

1. Introduzione allo Studio della Filosofia Indiana. Pavia, 1913.

Sueki, T.

1. An Explanation of Indian Logic from the Standpoint of Symbolic Logic. (IBK, V, 1957, pp. 160-1.)

Sugiura, S.

1. Hindu logic as preserved in China and Japan. Philadelphia, 1900.

Suzuki, D.T.

1. Notes on the Mādhyamika Philosophy. (JBTSI, VI, Pt. 3, pp. 19-22. 1898.)
2. The Mādhyamika School in China. (JBTSI, VI, Pt. 4, pp. 23-30. 1898.)
3. Philosophy of the Yogācāra. The Mādhyamika and the Yogācāra. (Museon, N.S. V, pp. 370-86. 1904.)

Takakusu.

1. On Vasubandhu, in JRAS, 1905. Also in BEFEO, IV, pp. 59 ff.

Takemura, S.

1. Characteristics of Buddhist Logic. (IBK II, p. 226)
2. Critique of the Tibetan Text of Pramāṇa-samuccaya. (IBK V, p. 91)

Takeuchi, S.

1. Hetupariṇāma and Phālapariṇāma. (IBK III, p. 685)

Tanaka, J.

1. The Logics of Prajñā-intuition. (IBK II, p. 230)

Thomas, E.J.

1. V. Gokhale: Akṣa-catakam; G. Tucci: The Nyāyamukha of Diṅnāga; C.A.F. Rhys Davids: The Man and the Word; E. Wolff: Zur Lehre vom Bewusstsein (Vijñānavāda) bei den späteren Buddhisten. (JRAS, 1931, pp. 482-4.) (Review)
2. St. Schayer: Feuer und Brennstoff. (JRAS, 1933, p. 167.) (Review).
3. Die Nyāyasūtra's Text. Übersetzung, Erläuterung und Glossar von W. Ruben. Leipzig, 1928. (JRAS, 1929, pp. 619-20.) (Review).

Thomas, F.W.

1. Nāgārjuna and Çalivahana. (Ath., 1899. p. 658.)
2. F.W. Thomas & H. Ui: "The Hand Treatise", a Work of Aryadeva. (JRAS, 1918, pp. 267-310.)

Tubianski, M.

1. On the authorship of Nyāyapraveśa, (Bull. de l'Acad. d. Sciences de l'URSS 1926.)

Tucci, G.

1. Lo Çataçāstra. Tradotto dal Cinese e commentato. Confutazione della teoria dell'ātman. (Alle Fonti delle Religioni, Anno II, Num. 4, pp. 32-43; Anno II, Num. 1. Maggio, 1923-4.) (Tr.)

2. The Nyāyamukha of Dignāga. Heidelberg, 1930. (Materialien zur Kunde des Buddhismus, Bd. XV.)

   Reviewed by E.J. Thomas. (JRAS, 1931, p. 483.)

   Reviewed by JTU, VIII, Jul. 1930.

   Reviewed by P. Pelliot. (TP, XXVIII, 1931. p. 223.)

   Reviewed by W. Ruben. (OLZ, 35, 1932, S. 345-7.)

3. Is the Nyāyapraveśa by Diṅnāga? (JRAS, 1928. pp. 7-15.)

4. On the Fragments from Diṅnāga. (JRAS, 1928, pp. 377-90; 905-6.)

5. The Vādavidhi. (IHQ, IV, No. 4, pp. 630-6. 1928.)

6. Pre-Diṅnāga Buddhist Text on Logic from Chinese Sources. 1929. (GOS, No. XLIX.)

   Reviewed by H.N. Randle. (JRAS, 1931, pp. 442-6.)

   Reviewed by P. Pelliot. (TP, SSVIII, p. 224.)

   Reviewed by P. Masson-Oursel. (JA, Oct-Dec. 1930, p. 354)

   Reviewed by W. Ruben. (OLZ, 35, 1932, S. 347-9.)

   Reviewed by M. Winternitz. (Arch. Or., IV, 1932, p. 393.)

7. Buddhist Logic before Diṅnāga (Asaṅga, Vasubandhu, Tarkaśāstras). (JRAS, 1929, pp. 451-88; corrections: ib., 1929, pp. 870-1.)

8. On Some Aspects of the Doctrines of Maitreya(nātha) and Asaṅga. 81 pp. Calcutta, 1930.

   Reviewed by P. Pelliot. (TP, XXVIII, p. 224. 1931.)

   Reviewed by L. de la Vallée Poussin. (MCB, I, 1932, p. 401.)

   Reviewed by St. Schayer. (OLZ, 36, 1933, S. 122-7.)

9. Bhāmaha and Diṅnāga. (IA, Jul. 1930, pp. 142-7.)

   Reviewed by IHQ, VI, 3, p. 593.

   Reviewed by P. Pelliot. (TP, XXVIII, p. 225. 1931.)

10. Notes on the Nyāyapraveśa by Śaṅkarasvāmin. (JRAS, 1931, pp. 381-413.)

11. A.B. Dhruva: Nyāyapraveśa, Pt. 1. (JRAS, 1933, p. 228.) (Review).

Ueno, J.

1. The Logical Construction of Paṭiccasamuppāda in Āgamas. (IBK IV, p. 112)

Ui, H.

1. The Vaiśesika Philosophy, according to the Daśapadārtha-Śāstra. Chinese Text, with introd., tr. and notes. London: R.A.S., 1917.

   Reviewed by London & China Express, Aug. 7, 1918, p. 432.

2. F.W. Thomas & H. Ui: "The Hand Treatise", a Work of Aryadeva. (JRAS, 1918, pp. 267-310.)

3. Der Ursprung der Trairūpyalingatheorie in der indischen Logik. (Résumé) (Commemoration Volume in honour of Prof. M. Anesaki), Tokyo 1934, pp. 343-5.)

4. 世親の因明學 (The Logic of Vasubandhu) (JTU, 1930.)

5. 東洋の論理 (The Logic of the East) Tokyo, 1951.

6. 印度哲學研究 (A Study of Indian Philosophy) 6 Vol. Tokyo, 1924-1930.

7. 印度哲學史 (History of Indian Philosophy) Tokyo, 1932.

Uno, J.

1. Naya-vāda in Jaina Logic. (IBK II, p. 610)

Vaidya, P.L.

1. Etudes sur Āryadeva et son Catuḥśataka (Chapitress 8-16.) 175 pp. Paris: Geuthner, 1923.

Vidyabhusana, S.C.

1. The Mādhyamika School of Buddhist Philosophy. Together with a short sketch of the leading Indian schools of philosophy. (JBTSI, III, Pt. 2; Pt. 3. 1895.)

2. The Philosopher Dignāga, a Contemporary of the Poet Kālidāsa. (JBTSI, IV, Pt. 3, 4, pp. 16-20. 1896.)

3. The Mādhyamika Aphorisms. (JBTSI, IV, Pt. 1, pp. 13-9; Pts. 3-4, pp. 3-9; V, Pt. 1, pp. 23-6; Pt. 3, pp. 21-7; VI, Pt. 4, pp. 19-22. 1896-8.)

4. History of the Mādhyamika Philosophy of Nāgārjuna. (JBTSI, V, Pt. 4, pp. 7-20. 1897.)

5. The Influence of Buddhism on the Development of Nyāya Philosophy. (JBTSI, VI, Pt. 3, pp. 4-8. 1898).
6. The Influence of Bengali on the Nyāya Philosophy (1902). 'The Bengalee'.
7. Nāgārjuna. J. of Mahabodhi Society, 1902.
8. Madhyamika Sutra. Chapter XI-XII. (MB, 12, pp. 104-7. 1905.)
9. Dignāga and his Pramāna-Samucchaya. (JASB, N.S. I, pp. 217-27, 1905.)
10. The Buddhist Version of the Nyaya Philosophy. (JBTSI, VII, Pt. 4, pp. 6-16. Mar. 1906.)
11. Hetu-cakra-hamaru, or Diṅnāga's Wheel of Reason, recovered from Labrang in Sikkim. 1906. (JASB. N.S. II.)
12. Indian Logic as preserved in Tibet. (JASB, N.S. III, pp. 95-102, 241-55, 541-51. 1907.)
13. Nyāya-Praveśa, or the Earliest Work Extant on Buddhist Logic by Dignāga. (JASB, N.S. III, pp. 609-17. 1907.)
14. A Description List of Works on the Mādhyamika Philosophy, No. 1. (JASB, IV, pp. 367-79. 1908.)
15. The Nyāysūtras of Gotama, Sacred Books of the Hindus, Allahabad, 1909.
16. History of the Mediaeval School of Indian Logic. Calcutta. 1909.

    Reviewed by A Guérinot. (JA, XV, Sér. X, pp. 161-4.)

    Reviewed by Monist, 19, p. 637.

    Reviewed by F.J. Payne. (BR, 2, p. 233 f.)
17. Uddyotakara, Contemporary of Dharmakīrti. (JRAS, 1914, p. 601.)
18. Nyāya-Bindu Bilingual Index. Sanskrit and Tibetan. Calcutta, 1917. (Bibl. I.) (Ed.)
19. Influence of Aristotle on the Syllogism in Indian Logic. (JRAS, 1918, p. 469.)
20. The Tattva-Cintāmaṇi, a most advanced Work on Hindu Logic (Summarised in English) (JASB N.S. XIV, 1918)
21. A History of Indian Logic; Ancient, Mediaeval and Modern Schools. Calcutta, 1921.

Vyasa, V.

1. Diṅnāga; Kundamāla, ed. and tr. by Veda Vyasa and S.C. Bhanot, Lahore, 1932.

Waley, A.

1. The Real Tripitaka, London, 1952.

Walleser, M.

1. Die Mittlers Lehre, nach der tibetischen version. Heidelberg, 1911.
2. Die Mittlers Lehre des Nāgārjuna, Heidelberg, 1912.
3. Buddhapālita; Mūlamadhyamakavṛtti. Tibetische Übers. St. Petersburgh, 1913-4. (BB, XVI.)
4. Prajñā Pradīpaḥ. A comment. on the Madhyamaka Sutra, by Bhavaviveka. Calcutta, 1914. (BI).
5. Ga-las-ḥjigs-med, die tibetische Version von Nāgārjuna's Kommentar Akutobhayā zur Mādhyamakakārikā. Heidelberg, 1923. (Materialien zur Kunde des Buddhismus, Heft 2.)
6. The Life of Nāgārjuna from Tibetan and Chinese Sources (AM, Hirth Anniv. Vol., pp.421-55.)

   Reviewed by P. Pelliot. (TP, 1923, pp.370-2.)
7. Der buddhistische Negativismus. (ZB, V. 1923.)
8. Die Lebenzeit des Nāgārjuna. (ZB, VI, S. . 95. f.)
9. La data di Nāgārjuna. (Alle Fonti delle Religioni, Anno. II, Num. 2, pp.1-15. 1923.)

Wassiljew, W.

1. Biographies of Açvaghosha, Nāgārjuna, Aryadeva and Vasubandhu. Tr. by Miss E. Lyall. (IA, 1875, IV, p.141.)

Windisch, E.

1. Über das Nyāybhāsya. Leipzig, 1889.

Winternitz, M.

1. A.B. Dhruva: Nyāyapraveśa. (Arch. Or., IV, 1932, p. 392 f.) (Review)
2. G. Tucci: Pre-Diṅnāga Buddhist Texts on Logic. (Arch. Or., IV, 1932, p.393.) (Review).

Wolff, E.

1. Zur Lehre vom Bewusstsein (Vijnānavāda) bei den späteren Buddhisten, Unter besonderer Berücksichtigung des Laṅkāvatārasūtra. Heidelberg, 1930. (Materialien zur Kunde des Buddhismus, Heft 17.)

   Reviewed by E.J. Thomas, (JRAS, 1931, pp.482-4.)

   Reviewed by A. Attenhofer. (ZB, IX, 1931, S. 286.)

   Reviewed by L. de la Vallée Poussin. (MCB, I, 1932, p.412)

Yamaguchi, E.

1. The Formative Basis of the New Hetu-vidya Logic. (IBK I, p.495.)

Yamaguchi, S.

1. Buddhism and Culture, Kyoto, 1960.
2. Dignāga; Examen de l'objet de la connaissance (Ālambana-parīkṣā.) Textes tibétain et chinois et trad. des stances et du commentaire, éclaircissements et notes d'apres le commentaire tibétain de Vinītadeva en collaboration avec Henriette Meyer. (JA, Jan.-Mar. 1929, pp. 1-65)
3. Traité de Nāgārjuna. Pour écarter les vaines discussions (Vigraha-vyāvartanī). (JA, Jul.-Sept. 1929, pp. 1-86).

   Reviewed by V. Lesny. (Arch. O r., 1932, p. 143.)

   Reviewed by L. de la Vallée Poussin. (MCB, I, 1932, p. 392.)

Yamasaki, T.

1. The Conception of Abhāva in the Nyāya-sūtra. (IBK II, p. 605)
2. The Logic of Trayasvabhāva. (IBK III, p. 245)

Yasui, K.

1. On the Controversy between Madhyamaka and Yogācāra. (IBK II, p. 241)

Yasumoto, T.

1. Candrakīrti's Critique of Buddhist Logicians. (IBK I, p. 426)
2. Candrakīrti's Critique of Dignāga School. (IBK II, p. 222)
3. On Uddyotakara's Examination of Definition of Perception. (IBK IV, p. 400)
4. An Aspect of the Formation of Indian Logic - Characteristics of Liṅgaparāmarśa in Nyāyavārttika. (IBK VI, p. 469)

Yü, Yü 虞愚

Yin Tu Lo Chi 印度邏輯

Indian Logic. Shanghai, 1939.